DEVON AND CORNWALL RECORD SOCIETY

New Series, Volume 42

Issued to members of the society for the year 1999

DEVON AND CORNWALL RECORD SOCIETY

New Series, Volume 42

LIBERALISM IN WEST CORNWALL: THE 1868 ELECTION PAPERS OF A. PENDARVES VIVIAN, M.P.

Edited with an Introduction by

EDWIN JAGGARD

Exeter
2000

ISBN 0 901853 42 9

Typeset for the Society by
Colin Bakké Typesetting, Exeter
and printed and bound for the Society by
Short Run Press Ltd, Exeter, Devon

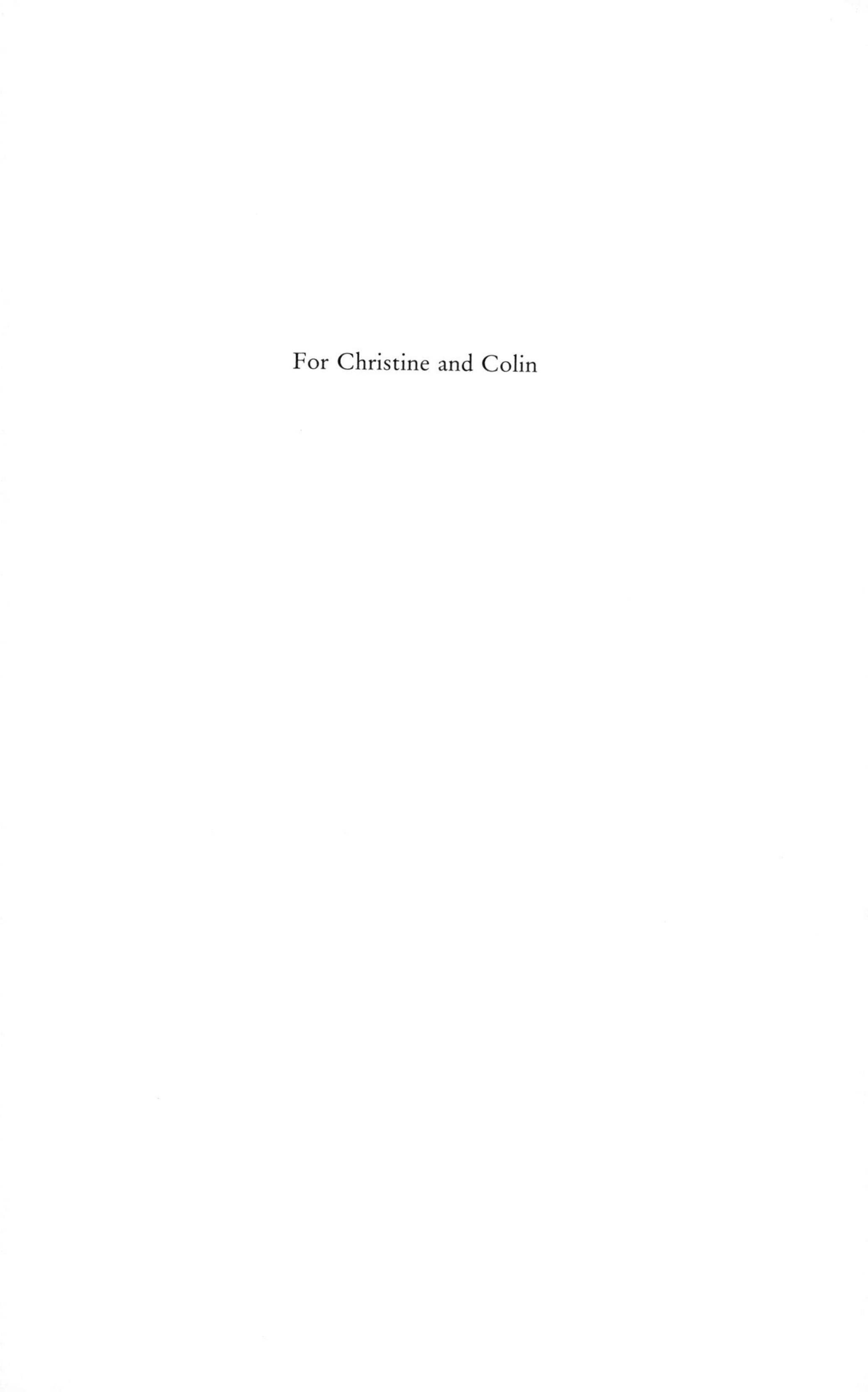

For Christine and Colin

CONTENTS

Acknowledgements ix

Note xi

Genealogical Table xii

Introduction xiii

THE 1869 ELECTION PAPERS OF
A. PENDARVES VIVIAN 1

Index 143

The Devon and Cornwall Record Society 151

ACKNOWLEDGEMENTS

The idea of publishing the Pendarves Vivian election correspondence arose during a conversation with Jonathan Barry while walking to the Devon and Exeter Institution one dull early March day in 1994. He believed that it would be appropriate to include a volume of 'modern' documents in this Series, a suggestion enthusiastically endorsed several weeks later by Christine North. I am grateful to both of them for encouraging me to pursue what until then had been no more than a whimsical idea. Confirmation that the proposal was worth pursuing came from Margery Rowe, who also motivated me to begin transcribing several letters, so that the Devon and Cornwall Record Society could appreciate the uniqueness of the correspondence. Thereafter her encouragement from distant Devon was always welcomed.

Notes from many of the 1868 letters were made as long ago as 1980 when I was involved in a very different project; detailed transcription occurred in November–December 1996, through the generosity of the former Faculty of Arts at Western Australia's Edith Cowan University. A small research grant was essential in order to translate an idea into something more tangible: it allowed me a period of uninterrupted time to work at the Cornwall Record Office in Truro, and, later, secretarial assistance. As always the Record Office staff provided a warm welcome and congenial working conditions: the County Archivist, Christine North, and Colin Edwards and David Thomas, patiently answered many questions about mid nineteenth-century Cornish and Welsh society. So, too, did Angela Broome at the Library of the Royal Institution of Cornwall.

Although he will claim no connection whatsoever with this volume, Les Douch unhesitatingly provided several useful suggestions for the Introduction, and at the end of long days his good friend Rex Hall happily diverted me into maritime history. Finally, although our meetings have been infrequent, John Rowe always inspires me with his deep knowledge of Cornish history, and his friendliness.

Living and working away from home results in an indebtedness different from that already acknowledged. Particular Cornwall Record Office staff have ensured that every visit to the county has been enjoyable, with wonderful hospitality, long walks along the South Coast Path and convivial discussion providing welcome interruptions to weekday introspection. During the course of several visits Canon Michael Geach has patiently broadened my understanding of Cornwall, its people, and religions. Equally generous with their hospitality and local knowledge have been Dave and June Cornall, one time neighbours Jean and Roy Lapham, John Treffry, and especially Pam and Paul Treseder of Truro's Marcorrie Hotel, where I have spent many comfortable nights. Although they are unaware of it, the staff of Bustopher Jones played their part too.

In Perth my debts are fewer, but equally deserving acknowledgement. As with the discipline of history as a whole, so modern British history is fighting for survival in a University system currently dominated by beliefs on 'relevance' and 'measurable employment outcomes'. Peter Bedford, Sherry Saggers, Peggy Brock, and Bill Leadbetter have never doubted History's future, constantly encouraging during numerous lunches to continue my research and writing. Iain Brash of the University of Western Australia's History Department happily clarified several points about mid-century electoral politics, and I found his *Papers on Scottish Electoral Politics 1832–1854* particularly useful as a guide to organizing the Pendarves Vivian correspondence. And, once again, I have been fortunate to enjoy the patience and help of my family, especially daughter Morwenna who compiled the index.

Lastly, I am grateful for the efforts of two people who, in different ways, brought the project to a successful conclusion. As she has done in the past, Christine Harvey typed several drafts of the correspondence, besides drawing my attention to numerous errors and inconsistencies in my transcribing and editing. Andrew Thorpe's very different role, via email, was to convince me to meet a deadline (almost!), and to complete the volume so that it conformed to the general standards of the series. The patience of each was more than I deserved.

Edwin Jaggard
School of International, Cultural and Community Studies
Edith Cowan University

NOTE

The 1868 electoral correspondence of Arthur Pendavres Vivian has been reproduced in its entirety. It should be noted that the letters were not catalogued by the Cornwall Record Office in date sequence, so they have been re-ordered to provide an easier presentation for readers. To avoid repetition and save space, closures of all letters have been omitted. The original capitalization and spelling have been retained; however, it has been necessary to standardize punctuation throughout. Any illegible words or names are indicated in the text by a question mark or a space. One of the drawbacks of being separated from Cornwall by two continents and several oceans is the inaccessibility of specialized biographical sources. Nevertheless, I hope I have identified all individuals who played a more than peripheral role in Pendarves Vivian's successful election for West Cornwall.

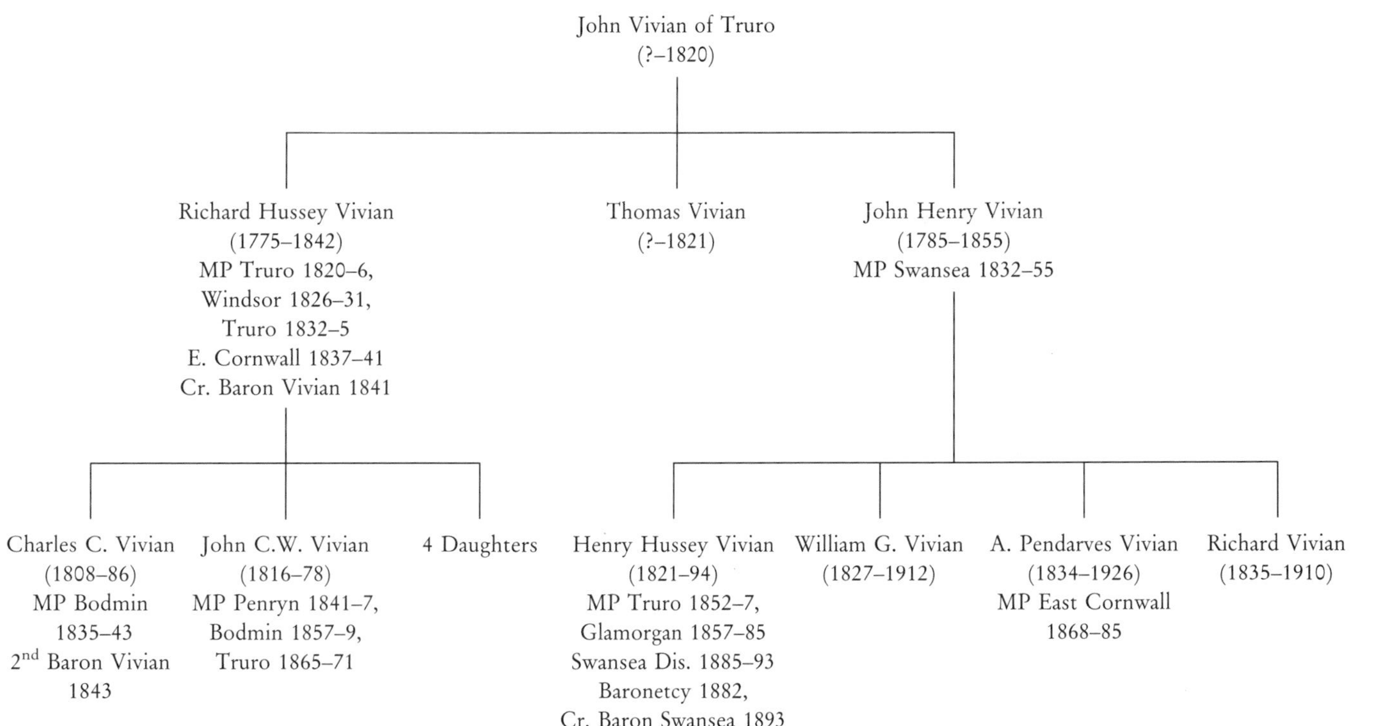
John Vivian of Truro
(?–1820)
Richard Hussey Vivian
(1775–1842)
MP Truro 1820–6,
Windsor 1826–31,
Truro 1832–5
E. Cornwall 1837–41
Cr. Baron Vivian 1841
Thomas Vivian
(?–1821)
John Henry Vivian
(1785–1855)
MP Swansea 1832–55
Charles C. Vivian
(1808–86)
MP Bodmin
1835–43
2nd Baron Vivian
1843
John C.W. Vivian
(1816–78)
MP Penryn 1841–7,
Bodmin 1857–9,
Truro 1865–71
4 Daughters
Henry Hussey Vivian
(1821–94)
MP Truro 1852–7,
Glamorgan 1857–85
Swansea Dis. 1885–93
Baronetcy 1882,
Cr. Baron Swansea 1893
William G. Vivian
(1827–1912)
A. Pendarves Vivian
(1834–1926)
MP East Cornwall
1868–85
Richard Vivian
(1835–1910)

Introduction

Arthur Pendarves Vivian (1834–1926), West Cornwall's Liberal MP from 1868 to 1885, is not mentioned in any of the many studies of mid Victorian politics. He represented a constituency among the most distant from Westminster, and one which, with its long history of Liberalism, was of relatively little concern to governments formed by Liberals or Conservatives. In some ways Vivian was a parliamentary nonentity, the quintessential backbencher working to promote the interests of his adopted county, diligently supporting his party's leaders, and only occasionally worrying the Whips by prolonged absences. He was elected unopposed in 1868, faced no opposition again in 1874 and 1880, and finally was defeated in 1885 when he was a candidate for the Camborne division, one of three carved out of West Cornwall earlier in the same year. It was, in many ways, an unexceptional career, only his defeat by the radical Charles Conybeare attracting national attention. Therefore what justification can there be for publishing his 1868 election papers?

The straightforward answer to this is that the correspondence, accounts, notes and reflections, provide a unique record of electioneering in an *uncontested* county division, immediately after the Second Reform Act. Owing to their apparent straightforwardness, in the past uncontested elections have attracted relatively little attention. Obviously important questions about why there may have been a change from one candidate and party to another, or any other outcome of a contest, cannot be asked. To modern day and uninformed observers one of West Cornwall's sitting Liberals, Richard Davey, decided to retire, a replacement was chosen, and thereafter political life went on much as it had done since 1832. However, the very smoothness of the transition disguises a host of questions: who was Arthur Pendarves Vivian, and why was *he* chosen to replace Davey; who were the people who considered him to be an appropriate Liberal candidate, even though he was an outsider living in Wales; did his election involve little more than selection, issuing an address, holding several meetings, and then going through the election day formalities? What Pendarves Vivian's correspondence reveals is complex commercial, industrial and political networks combining to produce what they regarded as a satisfactory result. This was an election fought for several months on the understanding there was every chance of a Conservative challenge. The changes to the county franchise embodied in the Second Reform Act meant there was the necessity to register the newly qualified voters in preparation for the contest. So the 1868 election in West Cornwall was not as unexceptional as it may seem.

Consisting predominantly of day to day correspondence *to* Vivian from prominent supporters and helpers, the papers expose the mechanics of electoral politics, from the machinations behind Vivian's eventual selection, to the organizing of a committee, along with the continuous gathering and analysis of electoral information. The papers contain little about the major policy issues dominating the election. Ideology of any kind is notably absent. Instead they expose the pragmatism of those involved, whose ultimate objective was to secure a majority of votes on polling day, or, if there was no likelihood of a contest, to lay the foundations for Vivian's longer term success.

It should also be emphasized that the papers are not merely a record of local happenings, containing little of relevance or interest beyond West Cornwall. Many questions are still being asked about the way in which the mid-Victorian electoral system actually functioned, not least, who controlled county politics at different times. Elsewhere I have written about the transference of the right to nominate county candidates 'from the hands of the various elites who enjoyed their powers in respect of their "property and character" into the hands of committees most of which were formally elected'.[1] The electoral politics of West Cornwall (and East Cornwall too), illustrate how this power was lost long before the 1880s. The contemporary meanings of the terms 'influence' and 'deference' have been exhaustively analysed in the past 30 years; one is prominent in the correspondence, the other completely absent. Occasionally there has been the tendency by historians to study constituencies in isolation; as the correspondence reveals, events in West Cornwall sometimes unfolded as a response to the developments elsewhere. Similarly, there was an important Welsh dimension to Cornwall politics, Vivian's candidacy personifying this. So anyone anticipating immersion in the localism of West Cornwall will find themselves swimming in a bigger pool than they may have contemplated.

I

Arthur Pendarves Vivian was the third son of John Henry and Sarah Vivian of Singleton near Swansea, while his grandfather, also John, was a Cornishman who lived in Truro. Pendarves Vivian was born on 4 June 1834 in London, was sent to Eton, then for three years studied civil engineering and metallurgy at Freiberg near Dresden in Germany before returning to England to enrol at Trinity College, Cambridge.[2] Soon afterwards, in 1855, his father died, leaving him the responsibility for managing the family's Hafod copper smelting and rolling works at Taibach, together with the Morfa colliery at Port Talbot and other industrial activities. For someone only 21 years of age this was a position of great responsibility, besides posing a formidable challenge. How much assistance Pendarves Vivian received from his brothers Henry Hussey [hereafter Hussey], William and Richard is unknown, but the business thrived under his management. He introduced several significant improvements in the smelting works, and invented an alloy of copper, zinc and steel to which he gave the name 'ferrobronze'. By 1885 the family business comprised several collieries, two large copper works, a foundry, nickel works, and the production of acid and manure, with many Cornishmen being employed because of the decline in the mining industry in their native county.[3]

In 1867 Pendarves Vivian married Lady Augusta Wyndham-Quin, second daughter of the third Earl of Dunraven, and they had four children, Henry Wyndham in February 1868, Gerald William (June 1869), Caroline Mabel (June 1873) and Clarise Gertrude (March 1875). Lady Augusta Vivian, whom her husband affectionately referred to in his diary as 'Darling', died in February 1877. Three years later, several weeks before the 1880 general election, Pendarves Vivian remarried, to Lady Jane Georgiana Dalrymple, daughter of the 10th Earl of Stair. They had two daughters, Edith Evelyn (December 1880) and Lilian Ursula (July 1888). Vivian never remarried after he became a widower for the second time in June 1914.

His parliamentary career commenced in 1868 with his successful election for West Cornwall. However it is interesting to note in George Clyma's letter to Hussey Vivian (PV 35/13), discussing Pendarves Vivian's likely candidacy, he remarked, 'this reminds me of his accompanying us for a short time when you was [sic] a Candidate for Truro', in 1852. So Pendarves Vivian was not a complete stranger to Cornish electoral politics, nor, no doubt, to those of Glamorgan which his eldest brother represented from 1857 until 1885. It appears the invitation for him to succeed the retiring Richard Davey as a West Cornwall Liberal MP came from John Michael Williams of Caerhays Castle in Cornwall, one of the county's wealthiest men and someone who has been described in another context as being 'as tough and hard nosed as any of his contemporaries' and 'a man who made enemies'.[4] Williams was one of the Liberal party's powerbrokers, although apart from a brief flirtation in 1858–9 he never sought to enter parliament for either party. The two men almost certainly knew each other through common business interests in South Wales, so the overture by Williams was understandable. And Vivian was a member of a family several of whose members had, or were currently, enjoying parliamentary careers as Liberals.

Nowhere in Vivian's 1868 papers, or in those covering his later career, are there summaries of his annual income; however, given his willingness to risk the expenses of a contested election for West Cornwall, it may be assumed that it was at least £5,000. In this sense then he was well qualified for the position of county member, just as his politics were 'on the right side'. Ideologically Vivian was loyal to Gladstone, willingly supporting Irish Church Disestablishment in 1868. In the 1880s he was described as 'A Liberal, in favour of the establishment of County Financial Boards, and of amendment in the Licensing Acts'.[5] By the end of his parliamentary career Pendarves Vivian's well known moderation was a drawback when he was opposed in the Camborne Division by the radical, Charles Conybeare, whose appeal to the working classes was based on supporting the abolition of the House of Lords, payment for MPs, female suffrage and repeal of the Game Laws, all of which Vivian opposed.[6]

During his parliamentary life Pendarves Vivian remained relatively inconspicuous, a county MP who was conscientious and tried to be well informed. In a notebook on Cornish matters he listed and often included details on such topics as the pilchard fisheries, fish tithes, the ownership of the pro-Liberal *West Briton* newspaper, mining (he and his wife visited Botallack mine near Cape Cornwall in 1871), extensions to the Newlyn and Mousehole harbours, and others. He was an indefatigable collector of useful information on the county and its economy.[7] Early in the 1880s he was prominent in the Cornwall Sunday Closing movement, unsuccessfully presenting at least two Bills to the House of Commons. Another cause which he ultimately had the satisfaction of seeing succeed was the laying of electric cables from offshore and remote lighthouses to coastguard and lifeboat stations. At each of the general elections Pendarves Vivian's published address was a comprehensive review of national and local issues. All the indications are that he was, within the limits of his time, a conscientious member who, because he was junior (in parliamentary terms) to John St Aubyn, often sought his opinions, and deferred to him on Cornish matters. Furthermore, he also relied heavily on the shrewd advice of another Cornishman, his agent Theophilus Downing.

From Pendarves Vivian's diaries the impression is gained of a wealthy businessman/landowner who, away from his commercial interests and parliament, particularly enjoyed hunting, shooting, and fishing. He caused some alarm to the West Cornwall Liberals in November 1871 when he and his wife travelled to Egypt where they embarked on a long, slow voyage up the Nile, finally returning to England in early April the following year. Unfortunately the latter half of the trip coincided with the opening months of the 1872 parliamentary session; in Cornwall, where there was still talk about him not being a resident of the county, concern was expressed about his prolonged absence. His agent, Downing, noted in February 1872:

> Attending Mr J.M. Williams at Pengreep thereon and fully discussing the best steps to be taken to protect your interest and Mr Williams thought I had better both write and telegram to you to hurry your return there being a feeling of dissatisfaction amongst your constituency at your continued absence and Col. Tremayne's name being mentioned v. freely.[8]

Reference will be made elsewhere to the ways in which the West Cornwall Conservatives (John Tremayne was their likely candidate), harassed the Liberals at every opportunity except at elections, when commonsense prevailed. On this occasion cables flashed back and forth between Cornwall and the British Consul at Cairo, as Vivian's political friends tried to keep the lid on an apparently volatile situation.

A second trip, soon after the death of his first wife, was undertaken in 1877–8, this time avoiding the parliamentary session. Pendarves Vivian travelled from England to Newfoundland, through Montreal and Quebec to Detroit, on to Chicago and then westwards, finally finishing in San Francisco. The journey, published in 1879 under the title *Wanderings In The Western Land*, seems to have been designed primarily to explore the hunting possibilities of the North American continent, with ducks, geese, bear, elk, buffalo—in short almost anything that had legs or wings—being hunted. The book reveals Vivian as a fascinated observer of the countryside and the peoples, as well as taking a deep interest in mining in all its various forms. Predictably he met many Cornish emigrants, although he failed to reflect on the reasons why they had left the county he represented in parliament. By the end of the journey he believed he returned home 'more English than I went out'.[9]

Aside from his parliamentary duties, business interests and travel, Pendarves Vivian undertook other community roles typical of someone with his wealth and status.[10] He joined the volunteer movement in 1859, became a Lieutenant Colonel in 1872, and thereafter commanded the 2nd Battalion of the Welsh Regiment until 1895. A year before-hand he was awarded a C.B. in recognition of his services, and in the year of his retirement (1902), received a knighthood. He was a magistrate and Deputy Lieutenant for Glamorgan, as well as being a magistrate for Cornwall. In 1889 the man who had previously been criticized as an outsider was appointed Sheriff of Cornwall, and by the beginning of the twentieth century he appears to have been living permanently at Bosahan on the Helford estuary, near Helston, the residence he purchased in 1883. Previously, in order to blunt criticism of his origins, he had lived at Place House in St Anthony-in-Roseland, and Glendorgal, on the northern coast at Newquay.[11]

Throughout his years in parliament and afterwards, Vivian took a personal interest in Cornish cultural life. Indeed, as the 1868 correspondence reveals, he was advised to do so by several of those who helped him in his first successful election campaign. At various times he was President of the Royal Cornwall Polytechnic Society, Royal Geological Society of Cornwall, Royal Institution of Cornwall, and the Miners' Association of Cornwall and Devon, all forums which helped him build political support within the county.

II

Nineteenth century electoral politics in Cornwall exhibited a fascinating combination of continuity and change. Before the First Reform Act of 1832, the era when the county was grossly over-represented in the House of Commons, Sir Lewis Namier and others regarded it as epitomizing the inadequacies of the unreformed system. Several of the small boroughs such as Bossiney, Mitchell and Tregony barely deserved the title village, all were controlled by patrons—members of the Cornish aristocracy or wealthy gentry, or outsiders—and in many bribery, treating and corruption were seen as part and parcel of a normal election. Grampound, the most infamous of all, was eventually disenfranchised in 1826; however, Penryn, Helston, Tregony and one or two others almost equalled its electoral depravity, their affairs repeatedly being scrutinized by the House of Commons.[12] One ironic consequence of these circumstances was the unwitting contribution the Cornish boroughs made in the 1820s to the stuttering parliamentary reform movement at Westminster, providing reformers with more than enough evidence to argue for change to the electoral system.

But this well known view of Cornish borough politics should not be accepted unquestioningly, because recently it has been found that in several of the larger towns such as Truro, Bodmin and Liskeard, many of the inhabitants took a more principled approach to politics.[13] In each there were clear signs, most apparent after 1800, that voters and non-voters alike chafed at the high-handed actions of the patrons, and sometimes openly agitated for their overthrow. Feelings ran high over important issues of the day, and, more importantly, numbers of townspeople revealed their willingness to follow a principled and consistent Whig or Tory line at and between general elections. There were unmistakable signs of what the late John Phillips has referred to as 'political modernization', with issues and principles being prominent in the development of partisanship—consistent support for a political party.[14]

County politics, too, did not necessarily fit the Namierite mould. In this instance the Cornwall electorate consisted of thousands rather than tens or hundreds. More than 3000 were entitled to vote at the contested 1790 county election, making methods of corruption or bribery far too expensive for candidates. What did exist was the influence exerted by landlords over tenants and others in the rural communities, although the effectiveness of this is very difficult to judge. Another difference from the boroughs was the openness of county elections: typically no single member of the aristocracy or wealthy gentry had the inclination, wealth or power, to dominate politics, although one or two attempted to do so. Logically this meant representation was confined to those whose social status was generally acknowledged, and who could afford a contest, as well as a London house during the parliamentary session. An unwritten rule of Cornish county politics was that members of the aristocracy and gentry who controlled boroughs, such as the Boscawen, Eliot, and Edgcumbe families, plus members of the gentry aspiring to this status such as Francis Basset, later Baron De Dunstanville, and Sir Christopher

Hawkins, should not interfere in county affairs. Decisions about representation were left to a clique of wealthy families, the Carews, St Aubyns and Molesworths among them.

This representation by arrangement was successfully challenged in 1774 by the upwardly mobile wealthy mine and landowner William Lemon, (a Whig), and sixteen years later by Francis Gregor (Tory), whose boldness was partly inspired by his wife's very large inheritance.[15] Despite these successful interventions one feature did not change from Lemon onwards: the clear wish of the county to be represented at Westminster by a Whig and a Tory. Following Lemon's death in December 1824 Sir Richard Vyvyan upset this, with disastrous consequences for the Tories. They were still being felt by the party in 1868—when Pendarves Vivian was the unknowing beneficiary of them.

Opposing the Tories' ham-fisted attempt in 1825–6 to monopolize the two seats were the county reformers, led by John Colman Rashleigh, William Peter and Edward Pendarves. Their rise and successes from 1809 until the 1830s have been described elsewhere,[16] but there has been relatively little attention given to their long term impact on county politics in the Eastern and Western divisions after 1832. Members of the group may be categorized as lesser gentry, so the clashes over representation were within the gentry, the wealthier members of which traditionally controlled the representation, while the upstart reformers were determined to vigorously contest this as part of their campaign for parliamentary reform. The latter were relatively small landowners in the eastern region of the county, but their influence was county-wide, not least in the West.

From the time of their formation as a political pressure group the Reformers were a thorn in the side of those Tory magnates who considered county politics to be *their* business. While there was no direct challenge at elections until 1825–6, the reformers used the forum of county meetings to harass the Tories over such topical questions as reform, commutation of tithes and Roman Catholic Emancipation. They boosted their support by insisting the meetings be open to inhabitants, as well as freeholders, a move which dismayed the Tories.[17] The *West Briton*, the reformers' newspaper, was virulently anti-Tory, building up a keen rivalry with the *Royal Cornwall Gazette*. The result was the surprising election of Pendarves in 1826, replacing the Tory, John Tremayne. Five years later Pendarves and another Whig, Sir Charles Lemon, son of the late county member, thrashed Vyvyan and Viscount Valletort in a hard fought election.

For some time beforehand there had been visible rifts among the

Tories; consequently this unsuccessful and very expensive contest proved to some of them that active involvement in electoral politics was best left to others. Significantly, too, by December 1841 Lord De Dunstanville, and his rival (but not in political terms) the fourth Viscount Falmouth, were dead. They were the natural Tory leaders to whom others looked for guidance, and no-one was ready to replace them, not least their heirs. After his crushing defeat, plus his huge expenses at Bristol in 1832 and 1835, Sir Richard Vyvyan showed no interest in regaining a county seat, so it was only the second rank Tories who were likely to be interested—and they were not, keeping their purses tightly closed. Other deterrents after 1835 were the western Whig-Liberals' organization, and the cost of fighting elections. Thus in West Cornwall the legacy of the reformers was a divided, disinterested opposition, and an absence of contests, so long as the western Tories could be satisfied that one of the division's representatives was an appropriate spokesperson for the agricultural interest, while the other could represent the miners. If this balance was preserved, there was almost no chance of a contest, despite periodic murmurings.

Another legacy of the reformers, which indirectly affected circumstances in West Cornwall in 1868, was the farmer-reformer alliance beginning in 1815 and petering out in the mid 1830s.[18] Currency, tithes and the Corn Laws were very much agriculturists' issues before 1830, and the reformers enthusiastically took the farmers' side. Not surprisingly, the farmers were also persuaded that many of their concerns might be addressed by a reformed House of Commons, so an influential alliance was formed, in which the farmers were often outspoken partners of the reformers. Apart from their electoral influence (which was considerable), the farmers, led by Penhallow Peters, J.M. Bligh and several others, began a tradition of independent activism, choosing their political allies mostly on the basis of self interest. This was their hallmark in East Cornwall for more than a half a century—supporting Whig-Reformers until 1837, then swinging over to the protectionist Conservatives in 1841, electing their own candidate, Nicholas Kendall in 1852, forcing his withdrawal in 1868, and in later years throwing their electoral weight behind the Conservatives once again. Based on the evidence of almost half a century, East Cornwall politics were farmers' politics, to the great discomfort of many Conservative landlords. The protectionist Nicholas Kendall's victory in 1852 was a huge slap in the face for them, causing bitterness which lingered on for almost two decades besides reducing the West

Cornwall Conservatives to electoral impotence, to Pendarves Vivian's subsequent benefit.

By the 1860s Cornwall electoral politics still displayed some similarities to the 1820s and 1830s, although there were also substantial differences. Three of the boroughs, Launceston, St Ives, and Liskeard never varied from the pattern of representation beginning in 1832: the first two elected Conservatives, the third, Liberals. The Duke of Northumberland made sure Launceston was his pocket borough, and the degree of control by Sir Richard Vyvyan at Helston in the 1840s and 1850s was much the same. Before the Reform Act Penryn's venality had been notorious; afterwards the combined towns of Penryn and Falmouth were little different. Meanwhile Bodmin was regularly contested by the two political parties plus a third group of scheming townsmen whose votes and influence were often decisive. Nevertheless, despite these vestiges of the unreformed system, everywhere elections were far more open, political issues aroused fierce discussion and partisanship was increasingly obvious. Political modernization was appearing, even if at an uneven rate in the different boroughs.[19]

County politics, too, were a mixture of old and new. Feuding and rivalries still pre-occupied the gentry, especially in the wake of Kendall's success. Probably due to the activism of the farmers, in East Cornwall contested elections were the rule rather than the exception. In the West, it was the opposite. What was strikingly new in both divisions was a transition in the process of control. For example before 1832 the gentry, particularly the wealthy gentry, usually dominated county politics. By the 1860s their poorer counterparts had replaced them as wirepullers, together with upwardly mobile men of comparatively new wealth such as Michael Williams and Richard Davey. There is a strong impression that by the 1850s and 1860s a shift in power was underway, land no longer being so important as a basis for political eminence. This change may have arisen from the vacuum left by disenchanted Conservative landowners who, totally lacking leadership, had no impact in either division. This was an enormous help to Vivian in 1868, but those backing him also knew the potential strength of the Conservatives. Leadership and a good candidate could produce a very close election.

III

West Cornwall, the constituency which Vivian represented for 17 years, was one of the most unusual in England: it was never contested from the day of its creation in 1832, until it was finally split into three in 1884–5. The solitary Conservative member, Lord Boscawen Rose, eldest son of Viscount Falmouth, represented the division for less than a year in 1841–2.[20] So West Cornwall was Liberal country, a division where the party never had to face the expense of a contest, and where there was little difficulty in finding eligible candidates—so it seemed. Boscawen Rose's success was an aberration, one never repeated, suggesting the Conservatives regarded their position as near hopeless in a region where Methodism was rife. However, West Cornwall electoral politics should not be accepted at face value. There were surprising differences between appearances and reality.

One starting point for an understanding of the division's politics is an analysis of the disposition of landed property. In the 1860s Viscount Falmouth (25,000 acres), the Basset family (16,000 acres) and their descendants were the largest land and mine owners in West Cornwall, together with Sir Richard Vyvyan (10,000 acres).[21] All three were Tories/Conservatives, and all were active in county electoral politics. Earlier Lord De Dunstanville (Francis Basset) was one of the foremost opponents of the county reformers, dabbled in local borough politics throughout his long life, and backed John Tremayne in the 1826 county election. The fourth Viscount Falmouth too was deeply involved (how could he fail to be when Truro was his pocket borough?), and he also controlled one seat at nearby Mitchell. In 1826 Falmouth, one of Vyvyan's principal backers, fought hard against reform in the House of Lords, and in the 1830s quietly worked to see his son elected for West Cornwall, succeeding in 1841. Vyvyan, by far the youngest of the three, had been elected for the county at twenty-five years of age, and quickly became one of the most articulate of the ultra-Tories who strenuously opposed the first Reform Bill. Thereafter Vyvyan never attained the same prominence at Westminster, but, having lost his county seat in 1831, and representing Bristol until 1835, he was elected for Helston in 1841, retaining the seat until retirement in 1857. Three wealthy, politically active families, plus Conservative members for St Ives, Truro and Helston (boroughs within the division), suggests the party enjoyed more than a little popular support. What fatally weakened it were internal divisions and squabbling: as a result, by the 1860s the Conservatives were in no position to bring forward a candidate to oppose the Liberals.

The explanation for this lies in a conjunction of events after 1850, when the West Cornwall members were an elderly and ill Pendarves, together with Sir Charles Lemon whose tenure since 1832 had been

Representation, West Cornwall (1832–1885)

Year	Candidate	Party
1832	(3,353 voters)	
	Sir Charles Lemon	L
	Edward Pendarves	L
1835	(3,612)	
	Sir Charles Lemon	L
	Edward Pendarves	L
1837	(4,928)	
	Sir Charles Lemon	L
	Edward Pendarves	L
1841	(5,040)	
	Lord Boscawen Rose	C
	Edward Pendarves	L
*1842	Lemon repl. Boscawen Rose	
1847	(5,259)	
	Sir Charles Lemon	L
	Edward Pendarves	L
1852	(4,649)	
	Sir Charles Lemon	L
	Edward Pendarves	L
*1853	Michael Williams repl. Pendarves	L
1857	(4,542)	
	Michael Williams	L
	Richard Davey	L
*1858	John St Aubyn repl. Williams	L
1859	(4,897)	
	John St Aubyn	L
	Richard Davey	L
1865	(4,615)	
	John St Aubyn	L
	Richard Davey	L
1868	(8,168)	
	John St Aubyn	L
	A. Pendarves Vivian	L
1874	(7,323)	
	John St Aubyn	L
	A. Pendarves Vivian	L
1880	(6,987)	
	John St Aubyn	L
	A. Pendarves Vivian	L

* By-election resulting from death of Viscount Falmouth (1841), and sitting members (1853 and 1858).

only briefly interrupted by Boscawen Rose. The Lemon and Tremayne families had intermarried; the latter being Conservatives, with John Tremayne senior being a county MP from 1806 until 1826. Tremayne's oldest son (also John) was frequently spoken of as a likely county candidate. There was talk of this in 1851 when Pendarves' poor health brought on discussion of the probable vacancy. The trouble with this suggestion, if it was pursued through to the next general election, was that Tremayne could not be seen to be in a contest against his uncle Sir Charles Lemon. Eventually the plan collapsed when the Liberals made it clear that should Pendarves' seat fall vacant, they would support Michael Williams, who was prepared to spend £10,000 to win it, and then would obviously fight to retain his position at the following general election.[22] Such financial resources were beyond the

Tremaynes, so the Conservative revival, apparently to be built upon a wholesale party shake-up, never eventuated. When Pendarves died in 1853, Williams succeeded him without fuss.

These fruitless discussions among the West Cornwall Conservatives indicate a longstanding problem which persisted into the 1860s. Neither the Basset nor Boscawen families could produce a credible candidate; Sir Richard Vyvyan was not prepared to leave the security of Helston where the expense of maintaining his seat was far less than the sums needed to fight county elections, so the Tremaynes were the next choice. But their family ties to Sir Charles Lemon made it very awkward for the Conservatives to fight a county election.

Meanwhile the political feuding endemic in Cornwall electoral politics further complicated the Conservatives' situation. Nicholas Kendall of Pelyn, a member of the lesser gentry and with estates worth no more than £2,500 per annum, was elected in 1852 by the East Cornwall farmers as a protectionist MP for that division. His success was surprising to many, because almost all of the county's aristocracy (Earl Mt Edgcumbe was an exception) opposed him, as did the powerful gentry families. Interestingly, Sir Richard Vyvyan was a Kendall supporter; however, the outcome of Kendall's victory over the sitting Conservative, William Pole Carew (supported by the same elements opposed to Kendall), was a serious fracturing of the party, which became obvious at the 1857 general election.[23]

Events at this time appeared to be running the Conservatives' way. Beforehand, Sir Charles Lemon announced he would retire, creating a vacancy. Since 1832 there had been a longstanding view that Lemon represented the division's agricultural interest, and Pendarves, and later Michael Williams, the mining sector. The Tremaynes were regarded by the agriculturalists as 'one of us' and so John junior was a very eligible candidate, in fact an ideal choice. Meanwhile the Liberals were not prepared to acquiesce in the likely loss of a seat, however eligible Tremayne was, so they persuaded Richard Davey, agent for the Williams family's Consolidated Mines, to come forward. The stage was now set for a contested election, the first since 1831. What followed was a disaster, bringing into the open the tensions arising from Kendall's 1852 success. Tremayne's election committee was chaired by Gordon Gregor of Trewarthenick, and the latter, quite naturally, wrote to Vyvyan asking for his support (Tremayne and Vyvyan took opposing viewpoints over Kendall's 1852 candidacy).[24] Vyvyan declined to join the committee, and was pleased he did so for he found out that Tremayne was to have been the chairman of Carew's Committee in the East (in fact Carew decided not to stand). Tremayne, it seemed, was working far harder in the East to defeat Vyvyan's friend Kendall (a fellow Conservative!) than for himself in the West. Vyvyan wrote to Gregor demanding Tremayne's neutrality in the East, but the request remained unanswered. All this occurred before Davey's candidacy was announced. When it appeared in the local press, the pro-Conservative *Royal Cornwall Gazette* was highly critical. While the *Gazette* acknowledged Davey's wealth, it stated that he was unsuitable for several reasons: firstly, the mining interest was already represented (by Michael Williams); secondly, Davey was 'new' landed wealth; and, thirdly, 'we know not of any pretensions he can advance to the distinguished trust of a county member'.[25]

Undoubtedly, Davey would have been vulnerable in the event of a well-organized Conservative challenge, but it did not come about. Vyvyan, receiving no answer from Gregor about Carew's position in the East, chose to give his very considerable support to the Liberal, Michael Williams, ruining Tremayne's chances. When he published his withdrawal he bitterly referred to those 'who still call themselves Conservatives [who] have withdrawn from me their support in the Western Division', pointedly ignoring, of course, the problems he had created for himself.[26]

A slightly different version of events may be found in the election notebook of Sir William Jolliffe, the Conservative party's chief whip at the time. Joliffe's source is unknown; nevertheless the entry again highlights the Conservatives' problems:

> Last election Mr Williams and Mr Davey started on the Liberal interest and Mr Tremayne on the Cons. Mr Williams was favourable to Tremayne, but instead of splitting his votes with Mr Williams so as to prevent the necessity of that gentleman coalescing with Davey he [Tremayne] solicited plumpers and asked Cons who had before supported Williams to withdraw from him. Williams whose known Cons tendencies, would have sensed the arrangement placed him at the foot of the poll, was thus actually as he explained to me driven to split 1300 votes with Davey and Mr Tremayne's party, seeing the mess they had made, withdrew their candidate.[27]

Whatever the reason for the withdrawal—and there is the possibility that Tremayne retired because he did not wish to spend the money on a contest he had not anticipated—in 1857 West Cornwall's Conservatives displayed a stunning degree of ineptitude.

One year later there was talk of J.M. Williams replacing his recently deceased father, but this idea was dropped when Sir Richard Vyvyan intervened again, this time on behalf of John St Aubyn, another Liberal.[28] It appeared no-one of sufficient stature was prepared to confront Vyvyan, certainly not members of the Basset or Boscawen families, so while Kendall retained his seat in the East, Vyvyan played the role of spoiler in the West.

Another factor overlooked by the Conservatives was their surprisingly consistent lack of attention to the electoral registers—the registers of eligible voters. The party had sympathetic solicitors working on its behalf in St Ives, Truro and Helston, making objections to Liberal claimants or those already on the rolls, and assisting potential Conservative voters to register. Success here was not mirrored in the county where the registers provided the foundation for the Liberals' confident domination of the Division. The reality was that no potential Conservative candidate possessed the inclination and/or the wealth to make a serious onslaught on the registers. As revealed in the Pendarves Vivian papers this necessitated the establishment of a committee, hiring of solicitors, and organization. The Conservatives were simply not capable of such effort.

After the 1858 by-election everything was peaceful, despite the Conservatives' usual speculation and rumours. By 1864 it seemed to be accepted that neither John Tremayne nor his brother Arthur, Sir Charles Lemon's heir, would be candidates until after Lemon's death, so the potential opposition came from a new quarter, William Williams, J.M.'s uncle. In January 1864 he decided to sound out Sir Richard Vyvyan about his son Frederick contesting West Cornwall at the next general election.[29] Simultaneously, Williams also wrote to Lord Churston, who oversaw the party's interests in Devon and Cornwall, asking how such a move would be regarded by 'gentlemen of influence' in the Division.[30] Two days later Vyvyan replied to Williams, pouring cold water on the idea. The same day Vyvyan informed Churston of several realities: registrations, as usual, had been ignored by the Conservatives for several years; the Liberals therefore had a majority; and John Basset said he was willing to be a candidate. As a representative of the mining interest Basset had infinitely greater credibility than Frederick Williams, who was relatively unknown in the Division. Nonetheless, Vyvyan thought Basset too would be unsuccessful.[31] In a follow-up letter he repeated the problem with the registers, accompanying this with the rumour among some circles of Williams senior starting. Nothing happened.[32]

As expected, West Cornwall's Conservatives did not lift a finger in 1865. The pro-Conservative *Gazette* criticized the party's indifference in the Western Division, taking no interest in the registers at a time when it believed conservative opinions were becoming popular.[33] Interestingly, John Rogers of Penrose wrote to Vyvyan expressing the view, 'I quite think it would not be desirable to put J.M.W.'s monkey up by proposing his uncle Wm' [Williams].[34] This suggests that with his great wealth John Michael Williams was regarded as the most influential of West Cornwall's Liberals, and a very dangerous opponent who should not be provoked.

The significance of these tentative moves could not be ignored four years later, when Pendarves Vivian was selected as a Liberal candidate. Besides Basset and the two Williamses, in 1864 there was also talk of John Rogers or Major S.M. Grylls being nominated by the Conservatives. No longer was the party relying on the Tremaynes—and all those mentioned above were potential candidates in 1868. Certainly by then little had changed with the registers, except that the Second Reform Act gave both parties equal opportunities to recruit new voters, leaseholders and £12 occupiers in particular. This meant that with diligence and effective organization the Conservatives could seize the initiative, even to the point of eliminating the Liberals' advantage. It was a once-in-a-generation chance. The likelihood of a candidate in 1868, especially Basset, and the uncertainty about the registers, motivated the Liberals to leave no stone unturned in their endeavours to retain both seats.

IV

As the Vivian correspondence reveals, foremost among those instrumental in electing Pendarves Vivian in 1868 were John Michael Williams and his wife, Elizabeth Maria. Both worked tirelessly from May until November, encouraging support from friends and acquaintances, bringing potential problems to Vivian's attention, and introducing him to the aristocratic and gentry networks upon whom he relied so heavily. They also played a pivotal role in the negotiations leading to Vivian's eventual candidacy, but before discussing why the two Williamses were in this position, who were the Liberal power brokers in West Cornwall at this time?

The correspondence does not provide a clear answer. On the other hand what it does suggest is that Lord Falmouth and Thomas Robartes' approval for a prospective candidate was essential, presumably because as two of the wealthiest men in Cornwall, their money would be needed to fight a contested election. Yet the days when two rich land and mine owners could recommend a candidate, expecting the rest of the party to fall into line, were over. Vivian's letter to J.M. Williams (PV 35/6/1–2) on 5 June reveals that Falmouth and Robartes were happy to allow the party to elect a candidate: 'they could not wish to appear as having taken any part in my selection'. Three days later H.M. Grylls (PV 35/9) re-iterated this point to Pendarves Vivian. 'It is deemed very desirable that nothing should transpire previous to our meeting on the 16 Inst that can be construed into the semblance of a wish on the part of a few, however influencial [sic] to dictate in the election of a Candidate'. Falmouth and Robartes discreetly gave their approval, the process beforehand being initiated by J.M. Williams.

Williams, a comparative newcomer to the county political scene, could be labelled new wealth—from mining, copper smelting and banking.[35] Although he lacked the status of Falmouth and others, he more than equalled their wealth, most of it from non-landed sources. And it was *his* helpers, Theophilus Downing, Henry Grylls and the others who were prepared to bend their backs to see Vivian succeed. The composition of Vivian's election committee, and the crucial 16 June party meeting, suggest that candidate selection was far more consultative, and electoral organization more middle class in character, than in the 1830s. The days of the powerful, politically domineering county magnates were over.

J.M. Williams and his wife personified the family networks important in Cornwall electoral politics for more than a century. The Williams family's upward social path, based originally on a mining fortune, commenced in the 1820s when John Williams (1753–1841) and several of his sons 'established a manufactory of copper and yellow metal at Burncoose, the firm being Fox, Williams, Grenfell & Co. and the partnership for twenty one years'.[36] The firm endured various changes of partners, metamorphosing by the 1850s into Williams, Foster & Co., with operations in several English cities, plus Swansea in Wales. By then the family consisted of two branches, one headed by Michael Williams (1785–1858) a son of John Williams, and the other by Michael's brother William (1791–1870). With sixteen children between them, Michael and William Williams, and several of their sons, were partners in the smelting business, and the Cornish Bank—Tweedy, Williams & Co.[37] Geographically, the family was concentrated in the mining area between Gwennap and Redruth, until 1854 when Michael Williams purchased Caerhays Castle in the Veryan district south east of Truro. At this time the Williamses were outwardly united in business and politics, with Michael Williams's position as a Liberal county MP symbolizing the steady upward mobility enjoyed by a family which could never have aspired to such a position 50 years earlier.

Michael Williams's remarkably moderate opinions meant many Cornish Conservatives were happy for him to represent them, especially those with mining interests. His sons John Michael and George were members of the Reform Club, as were William Williams and his eldest surviving son Frederick, so when Michael died there was a possibility of one of the family succeeding him. The leading prospects were John Michael perhaps, or one of his younger brothers.[38] At this point another family/political connection should be mentioned. In 1852 John Michael had married Elizabeth Maria Davey; seven years later his younger brother George married her sister Charlotte. The Davey sisters were nieces of Richard Davey, the West Cornwall Liberal MP from 1857 to 1868. Michael Williams' death in 1858 precipitated great activity—by Liberals and Conservatives. With their party activist Samuel Triscott as broker, the latter attempted the almost impossible task of persuading the electorate to accept J.M. Williams as a Conservative replacement, and the remainder of the family to join the party, apparently in an attempt to exploit their wealth and position in several borough seats in the next general election.[39] A West Cornwall Conservative recovery, par excellence! Triscott's machinations failed: grief stricken and disgusted by the opportunistic manouvering, John Michael refused to join the Carlton Club (although the remaining family members did so), or contest the by-election. George and his uncle William were involved in discussions on the vacancy, but these proved pointless, owing to Richard Vyvyan's intercession. As usual he played the role of spoiler—ruining the Conservatives' chances. Vyvyan persuaded the 'Tory Squires' of John St Aubyn's suitability: he was the descendant of a long-established family, several of his ancestors having been county MPs; and, because he held moderate views, he, like the late Michael Williams, would be an appropriate representative at Westminster.[40] Also in St Aubyn's favour was his more obvious connection with agriculture. It was drawing a very long bow to suggest J.M. Williams fitted this bill—or his uncle or brother!

Samuel Triscott had his own cynical interpretation of events. Writing to Sir William Jollife after the 1859 general election he suggested:

> Mr J.M. Williams of Caerhays has suffered his beautiful wife to lead him after a shadow; she fancies her husband's enormous wealth should command what I once wrote you about from Caerhays: and Davey her uncle [Richard Davey], a creature of Lord Palmerston's, has to my knowledge been inflating her with hopes that Lord P is if he comes in to make her Duchess of Hyde Park or some such thing, and this obtuse gull of a Croesus, her husband, fancies it will be so.[41]

These may have been the bitter remarks of a frustrated party activist; in 1871–2 when several Cornish Liberals were pursuing a peerage for Williams, he emphatically discouraged the move—at a time when it had far more chance of success than in 1859.[42]

The implication by Triscott of Elizabeth Williams's role in her husband's non-defection, creates the impression of a persuasive, even powerful woman. Without any evidence, except her letters to Vivian in 1868 and 1874 when she revealed her political astuteness, Triscott's opinion must be problematic; nevertheless, besides her marriage into the Williams family, Elizabeth's family connections help explain why she was involved in Vivian's 1868 election. Her grandfather, William Davey (?–1841) was the manager of Consolidated Mines, part of the Williams's industrial and commercial empire. Davey had two sons, Stephen, born in 1785 and Richard who was 14 years younger. The family's wealth, based on their mining connections, allowed the sons to purchase landed estates, and by the 1830s they were Deputy Lieutenants and Magistrates.[43] Equally significant was their direct involvement with the organization of the West Cornwall Liberals, and earlier, their links with the parliamentary reformers. Richard Davey never married, but his brother, with whom he was a partner in the firm, Richard and Stephen Davey, Mine Agents, did, and had at least three children, Elizabeth, Charlotte, and William Horton. It was William Horton Davey who inadvertently widened the split in the Williams family.

Already divided politically (at least insofar as J.M. Williams was separated from most of his influential male relatives), the business empire now ruptured.[44] For some years J.M. Williams had been actively managing Williams, Foster & Co., with the assistance of his brothers. Finding their help insufficient, in 1861 he proposed that Davey, the firm's agent, should be admitted as a partner, with some of J.M. Williams's shares being transferred to him. George and William Williams rejected the plan. One year later J.M. then successfully gave notice to dissolve the partnership. The same happened to the Cornish

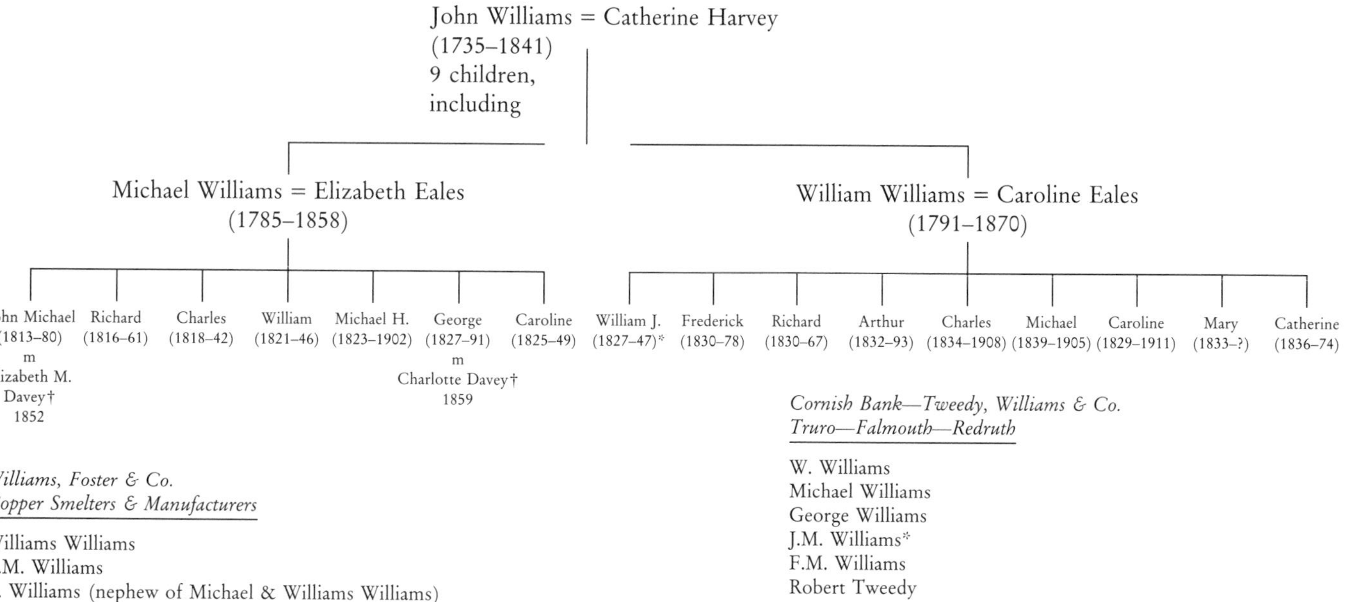

* He successfully petitioned in 1861 to dissolve the partnership, the defendants being the remaining directors, including his brother George. He retired in 1862, taking the Redruth branch as his share. It was re-named the West Cornwall Bank.

† The Davey sisters were daughters of Stephen Davey whose brother Richard was Liberal MP for West Cornwall 1857–68. As mine agents Stephen and Richard were linked through business to the Williams family.

Bank, and the family's tin smelting business, with J.M. profiting by these actions. The schism, it seems, was complete.

J.M. Williams, his brother and uncle henceforth were rivals in politics, and business. In 1859 Sir Charles Lemon, Richard Davey and Reginald Hayter (the Liberals' former Chief Whip) had persuaded Williams to retain his membership of the party. By 1864 his immense wealth, plus his commercial and family contacts, could be employed to thwart those family members who considered standing for the county, as William and brother George did. It would be surprising if Richard Davey did not encourage him to do so, just as it was logical for Davey to have informed his niece and/or her husband sometime early in 1868 of his plans to retire at the next election. Conjectural as these various links are, they do provide an answer as to why J.M. Williams and his wife were energetic in encouraging Arthur Pendarves Vivian to become a candidate for West Cornwall. Knowledge of Elizabeth Williams's family connections assists in explaining why she was such a valuable member of Vivian's 'team' during 1868.

Why then did J.M. Williams take the unheard of step of going outside the county for an appropriate candidate? Such a person would inevitably be criticized for being a non-resident, and be regarded as the breaker of a longstanding county tradition, for county seats, unlike the boroughs, were not available to carpetbaggers. In fact Vivian could not really be labelled an outsider.

His grandfather John Vivian of Truro (?–1820) was a Cornish mine-owner. Like some of his counterparts in the 1770s and 1780s, Vivian was concerned about the precarious financial situation in which many copper miners found themselves at that time. One difficulty was periodic over-production and fluctuating prices; another was operating costs, especially coal, needed to fuel the massive steam powered pumps; a third was the Welsh smelters and their near monopoly of purchase; and lastly, beginning in 1768 there was competition from Anglesey mines which had much lower production costs chiefly because geological conditions allowed them to employ open cut mining. Add to these problems the contentious position of Matthew Boulton and James Watt who supplied steam engines to a number of mines in return for lucrative financial rewards which substantially reduced the adventurers' profits, and the difficulties were obviously formidable.[45]

To overcome several of them, in 1785 Boulton and John Vivian formed the Cornish Metal Company, described by John Rowe as 'an attempt to create a monopolistic cartel controlling the marketing of copper'.[46] Vivian was Deputy Governor of the Company, the

Governor was Sir Francis Basset, and there were 36 directors. From his conspicuous position it may be assumed John Vivian was prominent and respected in Cornish mining circles.

Eventually the Company was unsuccessful, primarily because of the attitude of John Williams, controller of the Anglesey mines. Although agreeing to the Company's formation, he did not always co-operate fully—increasing production of copper and beginning his own smelting works. This was 'an example John Vivian did not forget'.[47] He had some association with Welsh smelters, and this probably motivated Vivian to be the driving force behind the move in 1810 by his sons Richard Hussey Vivian and John Henry Vivian to start the Hafod Copper Works at Swansea. 'The copper industry was becoming closely integrated; what the adventurers lost as miners they more than recovered as smelters.'[48]

By 1812, when John Vivian became Sheriff of Cornwall, the family had diversified interests inside and outside the county. Richard Hussey Vivian, later first Baron Vivian (1775–1842), and John Henry Vivian (1785–1855) appear to have agreed with their father that different branches of the family should have primary responsibility for different business interests, the basis for the divide being geographical. From the 1820s Richard oversaw activities in Cornwall, leaving John to manage the copper smelting and coal mining near Swansea; however, the two were interconnected, just as different family members occasionally crossed the locational boundaries. In time, as their wealth and status rose, the Vivians extended their careers into politics, a trail followed later, as we have seen, by the Daveys and Williams. Richard Vivian, after a distinguished army career, was twice elected for Truro, once for Windsor, and ended his political life as MP for East Cornwall.[49] His eldest son Charles was twice elected for Bodmin, in 1835 and 1841, before succeeding his father. Meanwhile John C. Vivian, Richard's second son, at various times represented Penryn & Falmouth, Bodmin and Truro, where the family name obviously carried great weight. The estate of Glynn near Bodmin gave this branch a landed base in the county.

John Henry Vivian's residence was at Singleton near Swansea, the borough he represented in the House of Commons for 23 years (1832–55). His eldest son Henry Hussey (or Baron Swansea as he became in 1893), began his parliamentary career at Truro (1852–7), then shifted to Glamorganshire (1857–85) and later Swansea District (1885–93), a span of 41 years. So, with one of the original John Vivian's sons and two of his grandsons all representing Truro in West

Cornwall, the family name was well known in local politics. No objections about where he lived were raised when Hussey sat for Truro—but it was a borough. His younger brother Pendarves Vivian was invited to contest a county seat—a very different proposition.

In county divisions there were thousands of voters, compared to the hundreds in most Cornish boroughs who could be 'managed' in various ways, and, county elections were much more open. All of the West Cornwall MPs since 1832, and their predecessors stretching back through the eighteenth century, had been Cornishmen who lived in the county. It was a matter of pride to the inhabitants that their county members—the Knights of the Shire—knew and understood the economic and social nuances of the county. Many in 1868 believed Pendarves Vivian did not meet this requirement and his status remained controversial for years afterwards.

Clearly there would have been an argument for Williams to approach another member of the family, rather than a third son who had never lived regularly in the county. Why not John C. Vivian, for example? By 1868 he had been a Truro MP for three years, after two previously unsuccessful attempts at election. The answer is that there was no reason for him to retire from a relatively safe seat for the possible anxiety and expense of a county election. Pendarves Vivian's oldest brother Hussey, another former Truro MP, now represented a Welsh county and was happy to continue. The process of elimination left the wealthy younger brother, someone who bore the name of one of Cornwall's longest serving county members, Edward Pendarves.

J.M. Williams must have known Pendarves Vivian through their common business interests—copper smelting and coal mining. In 1855 at the age of 21 Vivian succeeded his father as manager of the family's Hafod copper smelting and rolling works at Taibach, plus the Morfa Colliery at Port Talbot. Until 1861–2 Foster, Williams & Co. had a branch in Swansea, and some time previously they had sold their Morfa colliery to the Vivians.[50] Thus the two families were linked by business interests (Morfa coal was exported to Cornwall for use in the Williamses' mines); and Pendarves Vivian was wealthy, successful, and, if necessary, prepared to bear the expenses of a contest. Add the Vivian family's well known Liberalism and it is easy to understand why Williams decided the advantages outweighed the principal disadvantage of non-residence. Moreover, if the candidacy was speedily approved by the West Cornwall Liberals, it would deter any likely Conservative opponents, as well as providing impetus for the critically important work of registering new voters.

V

Many of the letters to Pendarves Vivian in July and August 1868 are concerned about voter registration, a concern made greater by the fact that the 1867 Reform Act had changed the county franchise qualifications. Downing, Grylls and others therefore had at least three reasons for making every effort to gain an advantage over the Conservatives in 1868: firstly, they hoped to establish a decisive margin over their opponents by enrolling more new voters thereby deterring any challengers; secondly, the registers were badly out of date so there was now an opportunity to rectify this; and thirdly, money, time and effort spent on recruiting and registering voters would possibly stop the Conservatives from contesting the division in the foreseeable future.

Analyses of the post 1832 electoral system have frequently pointed out that in early and mid-Victorian Britain the annual registration of voters, coupled with public voting and the occasional publication of pollbooks, sometimes combined to render the actual elections pointless in specific constituencies. One party or the other, having established a decisive superiority on the registers, would therefore reap the electoral rewards. Throughout the 1830s, and particularly after 1835, Liberals and Conservatives acknowledged this new reality, the outcome being the establishment of party organizations for registration purposes in many constituencies, Cornwall being no exception. Naturally, being out of office and almost annihilated in 1832, the Conservatives probably had a far greater incentive to register friendly voters, and this was evident in East and West Cornwall. The West Cornwall Reform Association came into existence in 1835, the primary object being 'to watch over the registration', and one year later the Conservatives joined the race, although their Protestant Conservative Association had a much shorter life.[51] Despite this, between 1835 and 1841 almost 1,480 voters were added to the Division's registers, while in East Cornwall the total was nearer 1,600. There, no Conservative Association existed until after Lord Eliot's victory in the 1837 general election. Then, their justification was clear: 'The contests for the representation of this county have been very expensive to the Conservatives, arising from want of organized plans, the consequences of all arrangements being left until the verge of the election and of general want of attention to the Registration since the Reform Act'.[52] Like the western Liberals they chose a three tier structure: central committee including representatives from each polling station, an agent to work in each district, and at the lowest level, parish leaders.

Not only in Cornwall, but throughout England and Wales this attention to the registers assumed a yearly rhythm, but gradually after 1841 the machinery became neglected as enthusiasm waned. Industrious committees lost their momentum, leaving local party magnates to employ solicitors to look after party interest. Generally, this was the pattern in the 1850s and 1860s although there were, as always, exceptions to the rule. Of course alteration to the qualifications provided an incentive for parties to make an effort in 1868, and this is certainly what happened in West Cornwall. Still, the *process* of registration was much the same as it had been since 1832, and because it is referred to so frequently in the correspondence it needs some elaboration.

Charles Seymour provided a clear picture of the system in *Electoral Reform in England and Wales*.[53] It commenced at parish level, with the overseers of the poor who were responsible for compiling the rate book, because it was assumed they knew who were residents or occupiers in their parishes. By 20 June each year overseers were required to notify all qualified persons (potential new voters) to forward to them their notification of claim. In county divisions no claimant could be registered until he proved his qualification, and once entered on the list of voters his name remained there, unless an objection was lodged by an existing elector, or claimant. On or before 31 July the overseers were required to compile a list (open for public inspection) of all existing voters and claims, making up the register for the coming year. If they (the overseers) doubted a claimant's qualification they could place 'objected' alongside the name. Once the lists were available to the public, further objections could be made—to the claimant, and overseers, by 20 August.

The lists of objections were then published in the first week in September, and as well they were supplied to clerks of the peace in counties, and the courts. From mid-September to the end of October, 160 revising barristers spread out to all corners of the country to adjudicate on claims and objections (for example in Cornwall they sat in each of the boroughs, and also in one or two other towns). The lists were then corrected, through a process of the objectors appearing in court, or being represented through agents. Then, once the lists were finalized, they became the voting registers for the coming year. Seymour wrote:

> These registers were considered evidence of the elector's franchise, and at the time of the election there was no further enquiry, except as to the identity of the voter, the continuance of his qualification, and whether or not he had voted before at the same election.[54]

Inevitably weaknesses emerge in any newly created system, and this was no exception. The system of claims and objections meant an apathetic public could happily allow the work to be done by an election agent working for one or other of the parties. These men, it was soon realized, could create or delete votes, and in extreme cases, by their industriousness or lack of it, even decide elections. The overseers of the poor changed constantly, meaning they did not necessarily know all ratepayers of a parish; nor were all of them well educated, at least to a point where they could make out the initial lists. This problem did not disappear, Hanham claiming that the overseers 'were totally unqualified, and had become by 1870 a by-word for inefficiency, ignorance and illiteracy'.[55]

Minor changes were made to the system in 1842–3. Parliament was aware of a rash of problems and so the Peel government asked Sir James Graham (in 1831–2 a Whig, and drafter of the registration section of the Reform Act, but now a Conservative), to submit legislation to improve the system. Among the changes was the responsibility given to clerks of the peace and town clerks to prod the overseers into action in June–July, and the power given to revising barristers to award costs against 'frivolous claims and vexatious objections'.[56]

In 1864 a Select Committee reviewed the county registration procedures. This was in response to complaints that persons entitled to vote could be called annually to substantiate their qualification. Frequently speculative objections were made by party agents on the chance that those objected to would be unable or unwilling to respond. And, of course, there was always the possibility of non-qualified voters being included on the registers—no objection meant a successful claim. Nothing happened. 'In the last resort the county members and their supporters always closed rank against any suggestion which might have broken the secrecy surrounding the ownership of property.'[57] The overseers could not demand that landowners produce title deeds, nor could farmers be required to provide their leases, so the status quo remained in 1867–8.

The passage of the Second Reform Act in 1867 brought several of these problems into the spotlight again. The reason was that changes to county voting qualifications meant thousands of potential new voters could be registered. These were predominantly the £12 occupiers: 'The Act allowed a man to vote in a county who was "the occupier", as owner or tenant, of lands or tenements within the county of rateable value of £12'.[58] The Act also gave voting rights to those who were copy holders or leaseholders of lands or tenements of £5 yearly value. Originally the Conservatives were committed to a £15 occupier franchise, but conceded the Liberals' lower figure. Yet the outcome still favoured the former, and 'the £12 county occupation franchise did not have the liberating effect that Liberals intended, since suburban middle class voters came to display propensities as strikingly Tory as those of old voters'.[59] Nevertheless, as new voters the £12 occupiers had the potential to hold the balance of power in many constituencies.

Not knowing whether or not he would be opposed by a Conservative challenger, Vivian was rightly concerned about the West Cornwall registration. How could he not be when his eldest brother Hussey and his cousin John were sitting members who also had to confront the issue? Registration is first mentioned in Downing's letter of 6 July (PV 35/45/1–3), less than a week after the overseers' lists were compiled. He reassured Vivian that the work was already under way in the towns and villages, being managed not only by professional men, but others skilled in the task. 'In addition to this all our large properties are being worked up by the Stewards and Lord Falmouth's rental alone will show an immense number of new voters.' Three days later Vivian expressed his desire to see 'our efforts should be continued with the utmost vigour', so the process should be thorough. 'Afterwards the Expence [sic] of keeping it up properly will be trifling and that our great safeguard will be in this' (PV 35/47). These efforts were very successful, almost 4,000 voters being added to the registers, over 2,700 of them Liberals. Voters in West Cornwall totalled 8,168, compared with 4,615 three years earlier. The story was much the same in East Cornwall, an increase from 5,781 to 8,107.[60] As far as the West was concerned Vivian's goal of overwhelming the Conservatives, and so discouraging serious challenges in the near future, was achieved.

VI

Of all the nuances of West Cornwall politics with which Vivian had to familiarize himself, the one having the greatest *potential* impact on his position was the linkage between East and West. This may be seen early in the correspondence, when Brydges Willyams was spoken of as a prospective candidate in the West. Whatever his true intentions they collapsed by the end of May, the reason being uncertainty about who would pay his election expenses (see PV 35/4). Willyams was obviously an attractive candidate for he had represented Truro from 1857 to 1859, enjoyed a degree of popularity in the West arising from his father's long association with Cornish Liberalism, and had banking interests. Eventually, though, he decided to try his luck in East Cornwall where Thomas Agar Robartes (Liberal) chose to retire. Before Willyams finalized his position complications emerged in the Division. Since 1852 the Conservative Nicholas Kendall had been Robartes' political partner; in 1867–8 his future was uncertain because he had made himself very unpopular with the eastern farmers (his one-time supporters), over a local issue.

It was J.M. Williams (PV 35/43) who first explained why Vivian should carefully watch developments in East Cornwall:

> There is a very strong feeling gaining ground daily—that Mr Kendal [sic] should be allowed to retain his Seat for East Cornwall and if the Liberals attempt to bring forward a second candidate—a second conservative will I have no doubt be started—as well as an opposition in the Western Division—the other side may allow us to return three but never quietly four, the whole of our County members.

The danger to Vivian was therefore obvious—two Liberal candidates in the East would probably mean Conservative opposition in the West. Sir John Trelawny had already signified his intention, so if Willyams joined him there would be repurcussions. The unknown factor, as always, was the unpredictable stance of Sir Richard Vyvyan; if Kendall's seat was attacked would he (Vyvyan) decide to contest the West? He was a wealthy man with an annual income of at least £10,000, but he would almost certainly remain an onlooker if he knew the Liberals would be untroubled to take both East Cornwall seats (PV 35/71/1–3).[61] By 25 July Willyams had finally taken the plunge (or at last his father Humphrey had agreed to pay his expenses), which meant Downing's total attention was now given to Vivian's election.

Aware of their weakness, especially in the West, the Conservatives pursued their usual course of inaction. It was not surprising that Henry Grylls informed Vivian on 8 August (PV 35/85) 'The Liberal cause is very hopeful in the Eastern Division. I do not think Mr Kendal [sic] has any chance of success. This is very gratifying—to retain our position in the "West" and rescue a seat in the "East" is glorious'. Grylls's judgement was correct; after campaigning for more than four months, during the course of which Kendall faced countless hostile audiences who taunted him over his vote to increase the salary of the governor of Bodmin Gaol (implying Kendall favoured an increase in the county rate—something the farmers bitterly opposed), he withdrew in early November, just before the poll. Ostensibly this was because a thorough canvass of the division revealed he had little chance of retaining his seat, but correspondence in the Kendall papers suggests he may have been looking for an excuse to back out. For most of the year Kendall had been seeking a position of some kind from the Conservative government, so that he could shut Pelyn, reduce his expenses and begin a process of financial rehabilitation.[62]

While Vivian found in 1868 that politics in one division had the potential to create problems in the other, he was fortunate that J.M. Williams and his wife were aware of this, keeping him informed of developments, whereas his running mate John St Aubyn offered no advice, perhaps because he was less concerned about Vivian's success than his own.

VII

After 1832 West Cornwall's Conservatives could best be described as a dormant political force. Judging by the successes achieved in the registrations of 1838–40, culminating in Lord Boscawen Rose's 1841 election, they could, with some effort, always seriously threaten the Liberals. Landlord influence could not be dismissed as irrelevant, the Conservatives were strong in the three boroughs in the division (Truro, St Ives, and Helston), and there was no shortage of sympathetic solicitors ready to assist the party. Offsetting these favourable circumstances, however, were longstanding and ultimately fatal weaknesses, most notably the unwillingness of anyone of sufficient wealth and status to be a willing candidate—and equally importantly, to organize a concerted attack on the registers over a year or two. The old-style politics of casual arrangements among gentlemen were a thing of the past. Besides leadership and the registration of voters two other difficulties occasionally deterred Conservative candidates—the strength of Methodism in the Division, and the feuding among the gentry, originating in Kendall's defeat of his fellow Conservative and one of the sitting members, William Pole Carew, in 1852.[63]

In January 1868 the *West Briton* announced that John Basset of Tehidy would offer himself as a Conservative candidate for West Cornwall whenever a vacancy occurred. 'There is no doubt that the "sinews of war", in a political sense, will be amply forthcoming, and that the Liberals of the western division must prepare themselves to enter upon a strong contest.'[64] This was a repetition of similar rumours and announcements over the previous 35 years, and the *West Briton* knew it; later in the same article it was pointed out that Tory candidates had always retired before polling day, and we have seen earlier how John Tremayne managed to do so in 1857. 'Sinews of war?' The Bassets of Tehidy were among the wealthiest families in the county, but were they prepared to spend money *before* the election? Ignoring that for the moment, why did the Conservatives have a leadership problem, and a lack of suitable candidates?

On the basis of his successful campaign to seat his son in 1841 it might be thought that the fourth Viscount Falmouth would have provided leadership. Unfortunately he died in December 1841; his only son, the former Lord Boscawen Rose, did not marry, and although he was prepared in 1850–1 to help finance a suitable Conservative candidate, this was the limit of his contribution. Following his death in 1852 he was succeeded by his cousin who, as the papers reveal, was a Liberal. Earlier in the century Lord De Dunstanville was a towering figure in Cornish mining, society and politics—and he was a Conservative. When he died in 1835 his massive estates were inherited firstly by his wife, and later by his nephew's sons, none of whom revealed serious inclination to stand for parliament. The rumoured 1868 candidacy was typical: indeed it may have been no more than a 'beat-up' by the paper to spark the West Cornwall Liberals into action.

Among the gentry there were several likely contenders who, if the circumstances were right, could have been candidates. As we have seen, one was John Tremayne; another his brother, Arthur. However, their problem was membership of what has been referred to elsewhere as the 'Lemon Connection'. The Lemon family's seat was Carclew near Truro, and by the 1840s Sir Charles Lemon, as a longstanding Liberal county member, was a powerful political figure in the west. Two of his sisters had married into the Basset and Tremayne families, providing the opportunity for Sir Charles to sometimes neutralize potential candidacies from among these families. After the debacle of 1857 he seems to have used his influence to prevent either John or Arthur

Tremayne from standing, an embargo ending with his death in 1868. The Tremaynes were attractive candidates because their father John (a Tory) had been a well-respected county member from 1806 to 1826, because the family estates were spread through both divisions, and because they were involved in mining. Both entered parliament in the 1870s and 1880s.[65]

The other possibilities were John Rogers of Penrose near Helston (Sir Richard Vyvyan advised him in 1865 to wait and watch rather than being hasty!), and William, George, or Frederick Williams. Rogers served one term (1859–65) as member for Helston, but with Vyvyan advising him it was problematic whether he would ever risk the much greater expense of a contested county election. The Williams family had the wealth required for a serious bid; their disadvantages were what today would be referred to as their 'lack of profile' in the Division, coupled with the certainty that if one of them agreed to stand, he would face fierce opposition from his very wealthy relative J.M. Williams. One other potential candidate was Vyvyan, but once he retired from Helston in 1857 he preferred to play an idiosyncratic, behind-the-scenes part in county politics. He was still doing so in 1868, to the detriment of the Conservatives.

Without leadership or credible candidates it is hardly surprising that the Conservatives therefore rarely attempted to build up a strong position on the voting registers, leaving their opponents to do little more than required to maintain their advantage—at least until 1868. The process, as described earlier, demanded an organization stretching from divisional to parish levels, with competent people overseeing it and motivated by the imperative need to be successful. All these hallmarks were displayed by the Liberals, Downing eventually reporting to Pendarves Vivian that the total of new claimants was:

Total Claimants	3876
Liberals	2762
Conservatives	1114

These figures were approximately the difference in the official size of the electorate between 1865 and 1868; what is surprising about them is the number of Conservatives who made successful claims, because few of the party's usual solicitors were engaged to attend to the registrations. Quite clearly the politicization of the middle classes was proceeding rapidly, even in a county division dominated by the Liberals.

VIII

Just as Liberal voters' names recorded on the registers were a tangible reminder to the Conservatives of a crucial obstacle to be overcome, another arose from the sight of the hundreds of non-conformist chapels in the towns and dotting the low green hills and scarred mining landscapes. Whereas the spires or steeply pitched roofs of the parish churches seemed to be reaching upwards to an Anglican heaven, the squat chapels were closer to the ground and to the lower classes, many of whom they attracted. West Cornwall in particular was 'Methodist country', and most notably Wesleyan Methodist. The nexus between Dissent and Liberalism, strong in several English counties, was especially so in Cornwall, although it should not be presumed that the county was therefore a Liberal stronghold for most of the nineteenth century. After the First Reform Act (when the county's total representation was 14 MPs) until 1874, the Conservatives rarely won fewer than five seats, and eight in 1841 and 1852.

Nevertheless, in West Cornwall the strength of Dissent was perceived to give the Liberals a substantial advantage. It sprang from several possible causes. When John and Charles Wesley first visited the county in the mid-eighteenth century they seemed to make their biggest impact in the distant parishes of the Penwith peninsular—Zennor, Morvah, St Just and Sennen. These were among the most remote parts of the sprawling diocese of Exeter, areas where the Church of England's hold was tenuous and many of the poorer people were greedy for religion. Absentee clergy and overworked and uninterested curates combined to leave the Church vulnerable to a populist appeal of the kind preached by the Wesleys.

By the 1820s the Reverend Grylls, vicar of Crowan near Helston was writing 'we have lost the people. The religion of the mass is become Wesleyan Methodist'. Pondering the reason for the failure of the established Church the clergyman Richard Tyacke offered a unique explanation:

> the roads that led to the Methodist chapel were thronged in every direction. My religious sentiments are not uncharitable, but Methodism I am convinced is not the only notice that calls them to this conventicle. The greater portion are the young of both sexes, the time is at night most suited to assignations and the secrets of love. These are causes that will attract members, and if religion has a share, there is a secondary object that claims a share also.[66]

It would be fair to say this was far from being the single reason for the Church's loss of popularity, whatever the Reverend Tyacke's thoughts. He recognized this several weeks later when he observed that in his parish members of the lower class preferred Methodist meetings to the Established Church: 'perhaps prejudice may in some degree effect this and another inducement the preachers of the persuasion are generally selected from their own sphere in life'.[67] Methodism's appeal also lay in its organizational flexibility, and the preparedness of its preachers to recruit members in the small, isolated fishing villages and mining settlements, often some distance away from a parish church where notions of social hierarchy remained important to a core of attendees.

Because so little electoral information has survived for the West Cornwall division between 1832 and 1868, it is therefore impossible to prove the religion of many of the registered voters. Even so, there is no scarcity of links between Dissent and Liberalism in the three boroughs, Truro, Helston and St Ives. One example from Truro illustrates the point. Several days before the December 1832 general election, the radical candidate William Tooke explained to his wife, 'I am to hear Mr Moore who is a most agreeable man, as also is Mr Clark with whom I drink tea on Monday to meet Mr Moore, the Reverend Mr Steadman and the two Wesleyan ministers Mr Martin and Mr Boot. They and all their congregations support one most strenuously'.[68] Martin, Boot, Moore (Congregationalist) and the Baptist minister Edmund Clarke all duly voted for Tooke. Many of their congregations would have followed their lead, helping Tooke to win a seat in what proved to be a tight contest.

Thirty years later in a letter to Lord Churston who oversaw the Conservative party's fortunes in Devon and Cornwall, Sir Richard Vyvyan mentioned 'the prevalence of dissent' in West Cornwall—with good reason.[69] The 1851 Religious Census proved what many had long suspected—Wesleyan Methodism had swamped the Church of England.

Over the whole of the county, Methodism was strongest in the west, particularly in Truro, Redruth, Helston, and Penzance, each the centre of thriving mining districts nearby. Add Bible Christians plus the followers of what was termed 'Old Dissent' (such as Baptists and Congregationalists) and the Church of England's relative position was even worse than indicated below. Consequently it is not surprising that the Conservatives were wary of the forces apparently ranged against them.

Places of Worship, 1851. (Bracketed figures show total worshippers at most numerously attended service.)

Division	*Church of England*	*Wesleyan Methodists*	*Bible Christians*
St Austell	18	31	27
	(1920)	(4568)	(2531)
Truro	31	59	21
	(4634)	(10,034)	(2484)
Falmouth	10	13	4
	(2312)	(3635)	(260)
Helston	21	36	19
	(2194)	(3198)	(650)
Redruth	19	54	7
	(2030)	(8964)	(1350)
Penzance	22	58	16
	(4315)	(9628)	(1039)

Source: P. Hayden, Culture, Creed and Conflict: Methodism and Politics in Cornwall, c. 1832–1879, unpublished Ph.D. thesis, University of Liverpool 1982, p. 56, and *British Parliamentary Papers, 1851 Census Great Britain: Report and Tables on Religious Worship, England and Wales, 1852–53*, LXXXIX.

At an election meeting in 1868 a Penzance Wesleyan remarked that:

> although the great Wesleyan body throughout the kingdom was in no sense, in a public and aggregate capacity, a political body, yet it had been a great pleasure to him to see for a great number of years past that Liberal opinion had been making very distinct and rapid progress among its individual members.[70]

By this time West Cornwall Liberals were sure this religious factor gave them a considerable edge, although obviously many Methodists were not Liberals, and of those who were, some were either not qualified to vote, or qualified but not on the registers. This is why Downing, Grylls and their helpers were careful not to take the Methodist vote for granted. When Irish Church disestablishment emerged as one of the principal election issues Henry Grylls urged Vivian to publicly declare his support for Gladstone's proposal (PV 35/26). 'On this latter point [disestablishment] we are here very strong. All the sections of the Methodist Body and other dissenters have these views, besides many good Churchmen.' Later in June 1868 Vivian explained to St Aubyn (PV 35/31) 'the Wesleyans have supported me throughout and indeed the Methodists and we have experienced no opposition anywhere'. Downing (PV 35/60/1–2) thought most of the farmers in the Lizard area were Wesleyans, and part of a total of 20,000 in the entire Division. He emphasized to Vivian the 'vast importance' of this, a point not lost on either Vivian or St Aubyn.

IX

After 1868–9 Pendarves Vivian's electoral career was relatively uneventful, at least until the end of the 1870s. When Gladstone took the sudden decision to go to the polls in February 1874, both local parties were taken by surprise, although as usual Downing, T.S. Bolitho and J.M. Williams refused to be complacent; on 24 January Downing wrote, 'I don't think there will be a Contest but of course we must be cautious and careful'.[71] Despite rumours of a last-minute nonconformist candidate, everything proceeded smoothly, a large crowd attending the nomination. Afterwards J.M. Williams, who as usual took a prominent 'behind the scenes role', explained to Pendarves Vivian's brother Hussey,

> If Providence will continue Mr P.V. his usual health—no one here will stand a chance of being above him—we have several men to the West—plenty [of] money & violent Politicans—whom I have caused to be looked after—for some time Past—quite ready to start if the Colonel at Carclew [Arthur Tremayne] had moved—but no … .[72]

The only fly in the ointment was a totally unjustifiable £50 claim by the solicitor Henry Rogers of Helston, who wrongly believed he had been 'retained' for the election.[73]

In the years that followed Pendarves Vivian and St Aubyn faced few problems, and this led to the gradual decay of the J.M. Williams-inspired organization put in place in 1868. Minimal attention was paid to the registers because the Conservatives were not a serious threat, so the advantage established in 1868 remained. At that time there were 8,168 voters, but by 1880 the total had fallen to 6,987, a change reflecting not so much attempts by the Liberals to eliminate bad votes from the registers, as the decline in population caused by the near disastrous downturn in tin and copper mining, and the accompanying migration out of the county. Between 1861 and 1881 Cornwall's population, defying the national trend, fell from 364,848 to 330,686, a 10% decrease.[74] Many of the emigrants were out of work miners, more than willing to take their 'hard rock' skills to Canada, the USA, South

Africa and South Australia, leaving behind West Cornwall families dependent on regular overseas remittances.

Given these circumstances it is not surprising that in a Division where election contests were unknown, some of the population rightly believed the two MPs were remote and complacent. Towards the end of the 1870s this was manifested in vociferous demands for the introduction of public meetings where Pendarves Vivian and St Aubyn could speak on (and be questioned about) topics preoccupying parliament, listen to complaints, and gauge dissatisfaction with an atrophied party organization still reflecting the heyday of the miners, bankers and other middle class men of 1868. As usual the Conservatives took advantage of the discontent; in October 1879 Vivian wrote in his diary

> Downing came over to St Michael's Mount to see J.St A & myself about the proposal which had been made by Cornish of Penzance to St. A to the effect that the Tories meant to bring forward Col.Tremayne to attack my seat, that if St. A would not coalesce with me only one Tory would be run, but if he joined with me, two Tories.[75]

This time the Conservatives even had a committee (Jonathan Rashleigh of Menabilly was the Chairman), but as so often in the past, nothing eventuated.

What *had* changed was the popular mood in the Division. Privately, St Aubyn was disturbed by this. He was certain he and Vivian would be re-elected in 1880 'but I don't feel quite so sure about the next Election afterwards and trouble then is more likely to come from our side than the other'.[76] Meanwhile, in a near revolutionary step, in February 1880 the Conservatives held a closed meeting at Truro, to attempt to address their perennial problems.[77] This stung the Liberals into action, Downing and others acknowledging that the party's organization had grown decrepit, and that there should be discussions about the best way to strengthen it. Over the remaining months of 1880, and continuing into 1881, a complete restructuring, with some changes of personnel, was quietly accomplished.

The Conservatives too remained active after the 1880 general election—something unheard of for almost half a century. One reason was Vivian's continuing vulnerability as an outsider, someone whose business interests required him to be absent from the county for long periods. Secondly, there was his and St Aubyn's reluctance to hold public meetings; at a time when people wanted to hear and see their members more often, they were disappointed. Finally, there were signs of the Liberals splitting between men whose moderate opinions were at odds with those held by the radicals in bigger towns such as Redruth and Camborne. Taking heart from these difficulties the Conservatives applied themselves to mounting serious opposition, even going so far as to encourage the formation of several registration associations. The effort was in vain; in 1881 the Liberals more than maintained their superiority, confirming this by canvassing voters in most districts.

Yet the pressure continued to mount on Pendarves Vivian and St Aubyn, who were now without the money, networks and energy of J.M. Williams who died in 1880. They were confronted by two prospective Conservative candidates, firstly Carew Davies Gilbert, and secondly H.J. Atkinson, a Wesleyan outsider. Both held a series of public meetings, and Atkinson in particular played a crucial role in politicizing the electorate.[78]

The ways in which Pendarves Vivian and St Aubyn grappled with the onset of public politics in West Cornwall has been discussed elsewhere.[79] Throughout the years from 1880 to 1885 tensions in the Division continued to mount, more so for the 'junior' member who was always the most vulnerable of the two. Even though he took charge of the Cornwall Sunday Closing Bill, and attempted to build support among the Wesleyan Methodists, Pendarves Vivian could do little to dispel the perception that he was identified with the Whig rather than the radical wing of the party.

In 1885 when West Cornwall was split into three divisions, St Ives, Truro-Helston, and the Camborne or Mining Division, he was left with no choice but to contest what potentially was the most radical of the three, Camborne where an old-fashioned Liberal would be regarded critically by voters and non-voters alike. Unfortunately for Pendarves Vivian he and his supporters were confronted by Charles Conybeare, a radical Chamberlain follower, who skilfully and successfully exploited his weaknesses. 'Conybeare For Ever' became the campaign catch cry as Vivian's meetings were broken up by interjectors or bullies, and his supporters beaten up in the streets of Camborne.[80]

In keeping with the preceding weeks of turmoil the election itself ended dramatically. On the evening of polling day a violent mob smashed the doors of Tabb's Hotel, Redruth, where Vivian and his wife were staying. Windows were broken elsewhere in town, and so potentially dangerous did the situation become that early the next morning the Vivians left for the peacefulness of Helston where they received by telegram the final result: Conybeare 2,926, Vivian 2,577.

According to his canvass Vivian believed he would have a majority of more than 1,000, so broken pledges added to the bitterness of his defeat.[81]

Vivian was deeply scarred by the Camborne experience. Although agreeing to serve a term as Sheriff of Cornwall (1889), he had no desire to regain his lost parliamentary seat. In 1890, when C.R.M. Talbot, the long-serving Liberal member for Glamorgan's Mid Division, died, Vivian refused to contest the vacancy.[82] Earlier he was approached to consider standing for Truro-Helston, and again refused, preferring, as he said, to remain independent and not help widen the breach in the Liberal party. In 1895 the lifelong Conservative John Tremayne believed Vivian was a Unionist, and therefore wrote asking for his help in Truro-Helston in the forthcoming general election. The reply, after the normal expressions of friendship, was blunt:

> As regards the present political situation, I have taken no part whatsoever in politics since my contest in the Camborne Division. I was disappointed then at the course taken by some would be friends from whom I looked for support and who absolutely did nothing for me against my blackguardly opponent. In the present Contest in the Truro Division ... I do not want to take any part.[83]

Thereafter Vivian appears to have had little more than a passing interest in national political affairs, preferring instead to contribute to many local organizations. Besides serving as Sheriff, he was a member of the Glamorgan County Council from 1892 until 1901, and later of the Cornwall County Council. Closer to his Bosahan estate, he chaired the Manaccan and St Anthony School Board, and the Parish council. He sat regularly on the Helston bench, and was also President of the Helston Cottage hospital. After outliving his brothers and cousins Vivian died at Bosahan on 17 August 1926.

X

Beginning in June 1868 and concluding in March 1869, the election correspondence may be grouped into several phases, beginning with the obvious first step of candidate selection. Until that process was finalized on 16 June, most of the letters are concerned with the uncertainty about whether Brydges Willyams or someone else would succeed Richard Davey as the West Cornwall Liberals' nominee to partner John St Aubyn. At the same time the electoral links between

East Cornwall and West complicated matters. Yet, despite the apparent uncertainty of his position, Pendarves Vivian had to commence introducing himself to influential figures in and outside the county. These included the Earl of Kimberley, who owned extensive property in Falmouth where there were voters who were not qualified for the borough franchise, and were his tenants. As a newcomer to the county Pendarves Vivian needed to build support throughout the community. One obvious and vital contact was the newspaper, the *West Briton* (the voice of Cornish Liberalism since the beginning of the century), with which he was to have a strained relationship when the paper's final accounts were submitted after the election.

In this first phase it is also apparent that Pendarves Vivian was being managed by J.M. Williams, in the sense that it was Williams and his wife who did most to ensure that he began moving quickly to build on the historical advantage the Liberals always enjoyed over their opponents. Williams's letter of 9 June (PV 35/12) is full of advice about who to contact (mine managers in particular), and steps needing to be taken quickly, even though Pendarves Vivian was a week away from being the 'endorsed' Liberal candidate.

From mid-June and into July, the introductions and string-pulling continued, but they were to some degree superseded in importance by the business of registration of voters. Thus a new and important dimension enters the correspondence, namely, the working relationships between Pendarves Vivian and men such as Theophilus Downing (in particular), Henry Grylls, Thomas Bolitho, and others. Wealthy middle class professional men or relatively small land, mine and property owners by comparison with Robartes, Falmouth, or J.M. Williams, their world was much more that of the local towns and villages where they could oversee the build-up of Liberal support. So the second phase of the election campaign is characterized by organizational matters such as forming an Election Committee (PV 35/34/1–2) and establishing the best possible way to handle the registrations. From his brother Hussey and other family members Pendarves Vivian must have received well meaning advice about this, only to be informed by Downing that there were other ways of achieving the same goal. '[Local?] Committees are all very well in their way but with them it is much more talk than real work. ... But in every parish almost there can be found some man who at former Elections has done good service and from being a parish officer or having been one in former years understands something of the business' (PV 35/45/1–3).

Apart from putting in place a structure with tentacles in every parish in the Division, the correspondence reveals an ongoing concern with the likelihood of a Conservative opponent appearing, the continuing complications flowing from affairs in East Cornwall, and securing support from influential landowners. On day to day matters Pendarves Vivian relied very heavily on Downing, while J.M. Williams and his wife Elizabeth Maria were strategists with a much broader view of the campaign. Their letters to the candidate indicate the lengths to which they were prepared to go to ensure Pendarves Vivian's successful election. Indeed they adopted an approach suggesting a Conservative candidate *would* appear, rather than assuming the opposite and therefore running the risk of complacency throughout the party. The letters in this phase also convey the unmistakable impression of the ongoing need for Pendarves Vivian to be educated about the various complexities of West Cornwall electoral politics.

By August, the commencement of the third phase, the registrations were being finalized, producing an impressive Liberal majority, so much so that by this time conjecture about likely opposition gradually died away. Because his address had been published and re-published for almost two months, Pendarves Vivian was now sufficiently familiar, and probably certain of election, for requests to be made for him to become more closely involved in the life of the community. Consequently the first of the letters (PV 35/88) seeking subscription to local organizations began to roll in, followed by requests to read papers before such bodies as the Royal Cornwall Polytechnic Society (PV 35/94). Furthermore, as the earlier frenetic pace began to slow, Pendarves Vivian found himself enmeshed in the complexities of selecting someone to propose and second him on nomination day, a task eventually performed by Richard Davey and Charles Fox.

The aftermath of the election, the final phase, from December 1868 through to late March 1869, is highlighted by the problems over payment of accounts. Between them St Aubyn and Pendarves Vivian split the major account of more than £1,000, but there were questions asked by the latter over the amounts *he* was charged by the *West Briton* for the continuous publication of his address, and the expenses incurred by Downing as his agent. Additional difficulties arose with other solicitors who were paid retainers but also billed Pendarves Vivian for additional work. Letters from Downing emphasize the point that extra expenses were incurred because this was Vivian's first election, and therefore he had to 'present' himself to the electorate. Furthermore, the first serious attempt for many years to update the registers of voters was costly, but would not be repeated on such a scale in the near future. Vivian's response to this, in fact his longest piece in the correspondence (PV /53), reveals someone careful with his money, prepared to argue his viewpoints, and to seek advice from elsewhere, specifically his brother Hussey who was re-elected without a contest at Swansea District in 1885. Inevitably valuable comparisons could be made, and were!

By early 1869 Pendarves Vivian was 'off and running' as one of West Cornwall's Liberal members. Widely recognized as being junior to St Aubyn in the political sense (St Aubyn was also five years older), he was in demand as a subscriber to numerous bodies, the recipient of requests for patronage, and someone who knew from the previous years' campaigning that he should never neglect his supporters, particularly the Methodists. Downing, the two Williamses and others had successfully introduced him to Cornwall political life, and in doing so ensured West Cornwall remained the Liberal stronghold it had always been since the 1830s.

NOTES

1. E.K.G. Jaggard, 'Political continuity and change in late nineteenth century Cornwall', *Parliamentary History*, 2, 3 (1992), p. 233.
2. The biographical details may be found in the *West Briton And Cornwall Advertiser*, 26 August 1926, and the *Cornish Post*, 21 and 28 August 1926.
3. [C]ornwall [R]ecord [O]ffice, Pendarves Vivian MSS, PV 290/12: see election correspondence for October 1885, for details of the family's business interests.
4. R.M. Fitzmaurice, 'A Chapter in Cornish Banking History', *Journal of the Royal Institution of Cornwall*, New Series, 2, 1 (1991), p. 42.
5. See Michael Stenton, *Who's Who of British Members of Parliament Vol. I 1832–1885* (Hassocks; Harvester, 1976), p. 392.
6. Jaggard, 'Political continuity and change', p. 231.
7. C.R.O., Pendarves Vivian MSS, PV (290)/17 and *Cornish Post*, 21 and 28 August 1926, for details in this paragraph.
8. C.R.O., Pendarves Vivian MSS, PV 38/61, Summary of correspondence and meetings between APV and S.T.G. Downing, entry for 12 February.
9. A. Pendarves Vivian, *Wanderings In The Western Land*, (London: Sampson Low *et al.*, 1879), p. 426.
10. *Cornish Post*, 21 and 28 August 1926.
11. Both residences attracted criticism. Downing thought Place House was too out of the way in St Anthony-in-Roseland, although he later retracted this opinion. When he purchased Glendorgal APV closed several 'public' footpaths, arousing very strong feelings in nearby Newquay.

12. See E. Jaggard, *Cornwall Politics in the Age of Reform 1790–1885* (Suffolk: Boydell Press, 1999), chapter 3.
13. E. Jaggard, 'Small boroughs and political modernization, 1832–1868: a Cornwall case study", *Albion*, 29, 4 (1997), pp. 622–42.
14. John A. Phillips and Charles Wetherell, 'The Great Reform Act of 1832 and the political modernization of England', *American Historical Review*, 100, 2 (1995), pp. 411–36.
15. C.R.O., FS/3/1126/2, Memoirs of Loveday Sarah Gregor, pp. 195–200.
16. See Brian Elvins, 'The Reform Movement and county politics in Cornwall 1809–52', unpublished MA thesis, University of Birmingham, 1959, and E. Jaggard, 'The Parliamentary Reform Movement in Cornwall 1805–1826', *Parliamentary History*, 2 (1983), pp. 113–30.
17. *Ibid.*
18. *Ibid.*
19. Phillips and Wetherell, 'Great Reform Act', and Jaggard, 'Small boroughs'.
20. He was elected in July 1841, and the by-election arising from his move to the House of Lords was held in February 1842.
21. John Bateman, *The Great Landowners of Great Britain and Ireland*, reprint (Leicester: Leicester University Press, 1971).
22. C.R.O., Kendall MSS, KL, Nicholas Kendall to Dr Clement Carlyon, 5 April 1851.
23. See Elvins, 'The Reform Movement', for a careful analysis of the 1852 East Cornwall election, and the ensuing problems.
24. C.R.O., Kendall MSS, KL, Sir Richard Vyvyan to Nicholas Kendall, 31 March 1857. In this long letter Vyvyan detailed the correspondence between himself, Tremayne and Gregor.
25. *Royal Cornwall Gazette*, 20 March 1857.
26. *Ibid.*, 3 April 1857.
27. [S]omerset [R]ecord [O]ffice, Hylton MSS, DD/HY/24/23, Sir William Jolliffe's Election Notebook, part 1: 'West Cornwall'.
28. A description of Vyvyan's interference may be found in S.R.O., Hylton MSS, DD/HY/24/17, Samuel Triscott to Sir William Jolliffe, 23 June, 1858.
29. C.R.O., Vyvyan MSS, BO/46/13, W. Williams to Sir R. Vyvyan, 9 January 1864.
30. *Ibid.*, Lord Churston to Vyvyan, 4 January 1864.
31. *Ibid.*, 46/15, Vyvyan to Churston, 6 January 1864.
32. *Ibid.*, 46/14, Vyvyan to Churston, 7 January 1864.
33. *Royal Cornwall Gazette*, 7 July 1865.
34. C.R.O., Vyvyan MSS, BO/46/5, Rogers to Vyvyan, 13 June 1865.
35. Brief details of Williams's business interests may be found in G. C. Boase, *Collectanea Cornubiensia: A Collection of Biographical and Topographical Notes Relating to the County of Cornwall*, (Truro: Netherton & Worth, 1890), *cc.* 1249–54.
36. *Ibid.*.
37. *Ibid.*.
38. S.R.O., Hylton MSS, DD/HY/24/17, Triscott to Jolliffe, 23 June 1858.
39. For an account of these manoeuvres see E. Jaggard '"The Age of Derby" outside Parliament: new orthodoxy for old?', *Journal of the Royal Institution of Cornwall*, New Series, 10, 1 (1986–7), pp. 62–83.

40. S.R.O., Hylton MSS, DD/HY/24/17, Triscott to Jolliffe, 23 June 1858.
41. *Ibid.*, HY/24/19/37, Triscott to Jolliffe, 31 May 1859.
42. C.R.O., Pendarves Vivian MSS, PV 290/17, Notebook on Cornish matters, entry on 'Peerage, J.M.W.'.
43. Elvins, 'The Reform Movement', chapter 4, footnote 21 for details on Davey family.
44. Boase, *Collectanea Cornubiensia*.
45. Information about John Vivian and late eighteenth century Cornish copper mining may be found in John Rowe, *Cornwall in the Age of the Industrial Revolution*, reprint (St Austell: Cornish Hillside Publications, 1993), chapter 3.
46. *Ibid.*, p. 82.
47. *Ibid.*, p. 83.
48. *Ibid.*, p. 121
49. The brief details of his parliamentary career may be found in Stenton, *Who's Who*, p. 393.
50. Boase, *Collectanea Cornubiensia*, and C.R.O. Pendarves Vivian MSS—Introductory note on A.P.V.
51. Jaggard *Cornwall Politics*, p. 93.
52. *Ibid.*, pp. 94–5.
53. Charles Seymour, *Electoral Reform in England and Wales*, reprint (Newton Abbot: David & Charles, 1970), chapter 12. Additional details may be found in William Leader, *The Franchise: A Manual of Registration Election Law and Practice* (London: Reeves and Turner, 1879).
54. *Ibid.*, p. 115.
55. H.J. Hanham, *Elections and Party Management: Elections in the time of Disraeli and Gladstone*, reprint (Hassocks: Harvester, 1978), p. 399.
56. John Prest, *Politics in the Age of Cobden* (London: Macmillan, 1977), pp. 72–3.
57. *Ibid.*, p. 123.
58. D.C. Moore, *The Politics of Deference*, (Hassocks: Harvester Press, 1976), p. 373.
59. Hanham, *Elections and Party Management*, p. 217.
60. British Sessional Papers, House of Commons, *Return of Number of Electors 1865–66*, 1866, LVII, 23; J. Vincent and M. Stenton (eds), *McCalmont's Parliamentary Poll Book 1832–1918* (Brighton: Harvester Press, 1971), p. 70.
61. Bateman, *Great Landowners*.
62. C.R.O., Kendall MSS, correspondence between Colonel Taylor and Kendall, January–July 1868.
63. Much of the feuding after this 1852 fiasco, arose from the belief among many leading Conservatives that Kendall had agreed to be the *second* Conservative and therefore would not endanger Pole Carew's seat.
64. *West Briton*, 16 January 1868.
65. John Tremayne was a Conservative member for East Cornwall from 1874 to 1880 and South Devon 1884–5, while his brother Arthur represented Truro from 1878 to 1880.
66. C.R.O., AD 715, diary of Richard Tyacke 1826–9, entry for 5 April, 1829.
67. *Ibid.*, 17 May 1829.
68. C.R.O., FS/3/1289/5, William Tooke to Amelia Tooke, 13 December 1832.

69. C.R.O., Vyvyan MSS, V BO/36/46, Vyvyan to Lord Churston, 6 January 1864.
70. Peter Hayden, 'Culture, creed and conflict: Methodism and politics in Cornwall c.1832–1979', unpublished Ph.D. thesis, University of Liverpool, 1982.
71. C.R.O., PV 38/5–6, S.T.G. Downing to PV, 24 January 1874.
72. *Ibid.*, 38/41, J.M. Williams to Hussey Vivian, 3 February 1874.
73. *Ibid.*, 38/12–49 for occasional correspondence between Downing, P.V. and Rogers.
74. British Parliamentary Papers: *1881 Census of England and Wales: General Report*, 1883 [C. 3797] vol. LXXX.
75. C.R.O., Pendarves Vivian MSS, PV 17/11, diary entry 25 October 1879.
76. *Ibid.*, 41/4, St Aubyn to P.V., 1 February 1880.
77. *Ibid.*, 41/7, St Aubyn to P.V., 5 February 1880.
78. See Jaggard, 'Political continuity and change', pp. 226–7.
79. *Ibid.*.
80. *Ibid.*, pp. 228–30.
81. C.R.O., Pendarves Vivian MSS, PV 53, notebook on elections—see entry for 1885.
82. *Ibid.*, 290/14 P.V. to ? Stalbridge, 9 February 1890.
83. *Ibid.*, A.P.V. to John Tremayne, 16 July 1895.

The 1868 Election Papers of A. Pendarves Vivian, M.P.

PV 35/4

J.M. Williams Memoranda

May 29 1868

Question

In the event of a Contest will Mr Hy Willyams[1] undertake to meet the Balance of the Expenses over and above the Subscriptions?[2]

Answer

May 29 1868

I asked Mr Hy Willyams the above question several times at Carnanton in the presence of Mr Henry Grylls[3]—Mr Humphrey Willyams distinctly and absolutely declined to meet the Balance of Expenses over and above the subscriptions, but he again offered to subscribe. Mr Brydges Willyams[4] accompanied Mr Grylls and Mr Downing[5] from Truro to Carnanton and was present at the discussions on the above question and answer.

Mr J.M.W. met Mr Hy Willyams etc at 1 Dean St May 16/68

Mr J.M.W.[6] saw Mr Hussey[7]—Graham[8] and Pendarves Vivian at Belgrave Square—immediately after the Meeting of 16—at Dean St.

? met Mr Brydges Willyams at Truro—May 21—but could ? satisfactory reply about Balance of Expenditure.

In consequence of the foregoing facts as stated over—Mr J.M.W. agreed with Mr Hy Grylls and Downing to meet Mr Brydges Willyams at the Falmouth Agricultural Meeting—on Wednesday the 3rd of June—to press for a definitive answer either to undertake the residue of Expenses (above subscriptions) or retire as the Liberals of West Cornwall were determined to bring forward a Liberal—as successor to Mr Davey[9] without further delay—Mr Brydges W said he could not deviate from his Fathers [sic] decision at Carnanton—on the previous Friday and must therefore retire in favor [sic] of any other Person that would come forward.—Mr J.M.W. had conversation with

Mr B.W. who expressed himself much gratified with [?] the support and assistance that had been offered him. B.W. also promised to write Mr Robartes[10] and Lord Falmouth[11] by the following Post Thursday announcing his retirement ...

[the remainder fragments]

---

1. Humphry Willyams (1792–1872) of Carnanton, Liberal MP for Truro 1849–52, Sheriff 1860. Senior partner in the Miners' bank at Truro and St Columb.
2. This referred to the practical issue of who would be responsible for Brydges Willyams's election expenses if the subscriptions by wealthy Liberals were insufficient to cover them.
3. Henry Grylls of Redruth and his son Henry Grylls junior were solicitors, the younger Grylls being a member of Paige, Kelly and Grylls, solicitors.
4. Brydges Willyams (1836–1917) of Carnanton, J.P., D.L., and Liberal MP for Truro 1857–9, 1880–5, and East Cornwall 1868–74.
5. Samuel Theophilus Genn Downing, solicitor in practice at Redruth. Barrister of Lincoln's Inn 1881. Downing became A.P.V.'s 1868 election agent.
6. John Michael Williams (1813–80) of a Caerhays Castle, D.L., D.W., Sheriff 1865, was a very wealthy mineowner, copper smelter and banker who owned extensive estates in mid Cornwall, as well as numerous properties in Redruth. His father, Michael, was Liberal MP for West Cornwall 1853–8.
7. Henry Hussey Vivian (1821–94), A.P.V.'s eldest brother, was MP for Truro 1852–7, Glamorganshire 1857–85, Swansea 1885–93. Baronetcy 1892, and cr. Baron Swansea 1893.
8. William Graham Vivian (1827–1912), was A.P.V.'s youngest brother.
9. Richard Davey (1799–1884) of Bochym House, Helston, J.P. and D.L. MP for West Cornwall, 1857–68. J.M. Williams's wife was the eldest daughter of his brother Stephen.
10. Thomas James Agar-Robartes (1808–82) of Lanhydrock owned estates totalling more than 20,000 acres throughout Cornwall, and was Liberal MP for East Cornwall 1847–68.
11. Evelyn Boscawen, sixth Viscount Falmouth (1819–99), of Tregothnan, owned more than 30,000 acres and with extensive mining interests was one of Cornwall's wealthiest aristocrats. Unlike several of his predecessors he supported the Liberal party.

PV 35/5

E.M. Williams[1] to A.P. Vivian (London)

Pengreep, Perranarworthal, 4 June 1868

Dear Sir

Mr Brydges Willyams has now decided not to stand for W.Cornwall so Mr Williams telegraphed to you this morning as follows: 'Are your views about West Cornwall the same as when last saw you? The Gentleman then contemplated has now fixed not to stand.' A similar message was sent to yr brother at Park Wenn and we shall now wait to hear from you and also to know what Lord Falmouth and Mr Robartes advise, before taking any further steps. Mr Williams fully hopes to write to you himself but as he has an engagement after the Ticketing, he wished me to send you a few lines, in case he was unable to do so by this post.[2] We shall be very glad to hear that you are still willing to represent W.Cornwall and will do all we can to help you and we feel sure that you will meet with a hearty welcome from the Liberal party whenever you come among us!

1. Elizabeth Maria Williams (nee Davey) (1832–84) was the eldest daughter of Stephen Davey, brother of Richard, Liberal MP for West Cornwall. Together with her husband, John Michael Williams, Elizabeth played a leading role in A.P.V.'s eventual election.
2. Ticketing refers to the Cornish system for marketing copper ores. It was instituted early in the eighteenth century, and details of the system are described in John Rowe, *Cornwall in the Age of the Industrial Revolution* (Liverpool: Liverpool University Press, 1953), pp. 21–3.

PV 35/7

J.M. Williams to A.P. Vivian (London)

(telegram)

Redruth, 4 June 1868

Are your views about West Cornwall same as last saw you gentleman [sic] then contemplated has now fixed not stand.

[Handwritten note by Pendarves Vivian]: My view unchanged from when I saw you will be down at once whenever you may deem desirable.

PV 35/6/1–2

A.P. Vivian to J.M. Williams (copy)

London, 5 June 1868

Dear Mr Williams

I received your telegram this morning and replied to it. ... [rest of page undecipherable]

Since replying to the telegraph Ld Falmouth and Mr Robartes have called here. We had a long conversation on the subject. They give me to understand that though they could not wish to appear as having taken any part in my selection yet in the event of Liberal party requesting me to stand I might count on their support. Nothing could be kinder or more cordial than they were. [gap] am here at your disposal [gap] as expressed in my telegram go down whenever I might be required, but it seemed to be the opinion of Ld Falmouth and Mr Robartes that it would be better unless specially requested by the Liberal Leaders to remain passive until elected by the party as their candidate.[1]

1. Throughout early June West Cornwall's wealthiest Liberals were very concerned not to appear to be high-handed, but rather consultative, in the selection of a replacement for Richard Davey.

PV 35/8/1–2

E.M. Williams to A.P. Vivian

Pengreep, Perranarworthal, Cornwall, 5 June 1868

Dear Sir

Mr Williams desires me to thank you very much for your Telegram and letter of yesterday and to tell you how pleased we are to find that your views remain unchanged. Mr Williams regrets again to depute me to write for him, but he thinks that he will best promote your interests by seeing as many influential electors as he can during the next few days, so he has started for Marazion and Penzance this morning and may not arrive at the latter place before post-time. Yesterday he had most satisfactory interviews with Major Bickford, Dr Smith and other important people around Camborne and Redruth and he sent you a Telegram to that effect this morning. Lord Falmouth and Mr Robartes consider Redruth, Camborne and Penzance to be the <u>most</u> important districts in W. Cornwall, so if my Husband and those who are acting with him should be as successful today with Messrs Bolitho[1] of Penzance and Mr R.R. Michell of Marazion as they were with the Camborne magnates yesterday, we hope that you will have little or no trouble in the all important western district. I am going to Enys this afternoon to make an appointment for Mr Williams to see Mr and Mrs Enys[2] tomorrow when we hope that he will obtain the promise of their support and of that of Mrs Gilbert[3] for you. It will give us much pleasure to receive you here whenever you decide to come to Cornwall and if Lady Augusta Vivian will accompany you, we shall be delighted to welcome her. We generally live at Caerhays now but it is rather out of the way for electioneering purposes, so we hope that you and Lady Augusta[4] will not mind 'roughing it' here under the circumstances.

P.S. Mr Williams wished me to write to you fully as to what had been done and I could not do so without troubling you with a great many strange names, but perhaps you may hereafter find it useful to have heard of them!

---

1. Thomas Simon Bolitho (1808–87) of Trengwainton, J.P., D.L. Married in 1838 Elizabeth, daughter and co-heiress of Thomas Robins of Liskeard. Bolitho was Sheriff of Cornwall in 1867, and his eldest son Thomas Robins Bolitho (1840–1925) J.P., D.L., was Sheriff in 1890.
2. John Samuel Enys (1796–1872) of Enys, J.P., Sheriff 1824. Married in 1834 Catherine, eldest daughter of Davies Gilbert of Cornwall and Eastbourne.
3. Mrs Gilbert was the wife of John Davies Gilbert (b.St Erth 1811, d.1854). She was the Hon. Anna Dorothea Shapland Carew (b.1822 and married 1851).
4. Lady Augusta Emily Wyndham-Quin, daughter of the third Earl of Dunraven, was A.P.V.s first wife. They were married in March 1867, and she died in February 1877.

PV 35/9

H.M. Grylls to A.P. Vivian

Moreton House, Redruth, 8 June 1868

Sir,

As Chairman of the Committee of Liberal Electors of West Cornwall it devolves on me to take rather an active part in the coming election of a Liberal Member for this Division.

It is proposed to have a Meeting of Electors at Camborne on Tuesday the 10th Instant to nominate a Candidate to succeed Mr Davey, one of our present members and though I have not the honor of a personal knowledge of you yet, from all I have heard of your political opinions as being in the main in agreement with Mr Gladstone's—and knowing your election is desired by some of our principal landowners, and Mining and Commercial men of the Division—I fully believe there will be a very general call on you from the Meeting to become a candidate for our suffrages at the next election. And I beg to say it will give me and my son great pleasure to promote your return in every way in our power.

Mr Davey has left Redruth this morning for his parliamentary duties and will readily give you any information of our movements if you think well to call on him at 11 St James Place, St James Street.

It is deemed very desirable that nothing should transpire previous to our meeting on the 16 Inst that can be construed into the semblance of a wish on the part of a few, however influencial [sic], to dictate in the election of a Candidate. I will therefore thank you to consider this letter as private.

PV 35/10

T.J. Agar Robartes to A.P. Vivian

Park Lane, London, 9 June 1868

My dear Sir

I am happy to say that I have this morning received a letter from Mr Brydges Willyams in which he announces decidedly that he does not mean to be a Candidate for W. Cornwall at the present time, and in readiness to assist the Liberal Cause there.

PV 35/11

T.S. Bolitho to Hussey Vivian

Penalberne, Penzance, 9 June 1868

My Dear Sir

Some days since I intimated to J.M. Williams and I have since then said as much to Lady Falmouth[1] that if your brother shd be a candidate for West Cornwall I should vote for him and that I thought some of my family would do the same, but that there were many shades of Politics among us and that therefore I did not think it likely that any of the name wd take an active part in the next election.

I would venture to say more to you than I did to J.M.W. except that I am satisfied that none of our family will vote against Mr Pendarves Vivian—not that I am authorized to pledge others.

It is of course difficult to form an opinion as to how far the cause of your Brother would be affected by his not being resident in Cornwall but my own private opinion is that he would have a majority of votes in this district.[2]

1. Mary Frances Elizabeth Stapleton (?–1891) married Evelyn Boscawen, sixth Viscount, in 1845. She succeeded her grandfather in 1889 as Baroness le Despencer.
2. Vivian became Cornwall's first non-resident county MP. Throughout his career from 1868–85 he was criticized for this, despite buying several residences in the Western Division, e.g. Glendorgal, Newquay, and later Bosahan near Helston.

PV 35/12

J.M. Williams to A.P. Vivian (London)

Burncoose, Cornwall, 9 June 1868

My Dear Sir,

I am much obliged for your letters of yesterday's Date and return you enclosed Mr or Capt J. Vivian's letter[1]—you will kindly excuse my suggesting that you try to ascertain what he has heard from Mr Brydges W. (since Wednesday last) with regard to his retiring from coming forward as Mr Davey's successor for West Cornwall—my object is to strengthen our claim on him—to fulfil his pledge to us on Wednesday last—viz to retire from further candidature, and give assistance to the Gentlemen of Liberal Principles whoever the Electors might bring forward. I would suggest that you have some communication made to Mr Heard[2] of Truro as from your self or family, asking his support. Mr Downing saw Mr Heard on Saturday and informed him of what was going on.——

There are several Managers of Mines resident in London whom I think you should call on and ask their support—such as Mr Noakes of Great Wh[l] Vor near Helston—and Mr Edw King of Austin Friars—manager of many mines—Great North Downs etc—and Messrs P.W. Thomas & Sons
48 Threadneedle St
W.P. Thomas the Senior well known to Mr Edw Budd—(Chairman of Devon Consols) and manager of many mines about Redruth—Messrs Taylor who have management of several mines about Redruth—their Representative in West Cornwall is a Mr Bennetts of Falmouth—a good Liberal and will me [sic] one of your best men of business and supporter in that neighbourhood.—

There are several other Managers of Mines resident in London—who have Offices in the City—whom I would suggest you finding out and seeing.—As I have only a short time for Post—I enclose copy of what I write Mr Robartes by this Post—which please return.—

[PS] Earl Kimberley's[3] (late Lord Woodhouse) [sic] influence for the votes of his property in the neighbourhood of Falmouth—should if possible obtained, Lord Falmouth—Mr Robartes or Mr Hussey Vivian can perhaps assist you.—Earl K is a decided Liberal—but his agent in Cornwall is Mr P.P. Smith[4] = Mr Bassett's[5] [sic] leading adviser.

---

1. John Cranch Walker Vivian (1818–79) of Truro, second son of the first Baron Vivian. Captain in 11th Hussars, Liberal MP for Penryn & Falmouth 1841–7, Bodmin 1857–9, Truro 1865–71. He was a cousin of A.P. Vivian.
2. Heard and Son, Truro, printed and published the *West Briton*.
3. Earl of Kimberley (1826–1902), succeeded his grandfather as 3rd Baron Wodehouse, 1846, and raised to an earldom in 1866. He owned 342 acres in Cornwall, producing an annual income of more than £8000.
4. Philip Protheroe Smith (1810–82), admitted solicitor 1832 of Roberts and Smith, and then in 1838, Smith & Wm Paul, Truro. Truro councillor, alderman, and mayor, and leader of the town's Conservatives.
5. John Francis Basset (1831–69) of Tehidy, who was a possible Conservative candidate for West Cornwall. His 17,000 acres plus extensive mining interests meant Basset, a nephew of Baron De Dunstanville, was one of the most influential West Cornwall Conservatives.

PV 35/13

G. Clyma[1] to H.H. Vivian

Truro, Cornwall, 11 June 1868.

Dear Sir

A few minutes before I received your letter I was called on by a Gentleman belonging to the *Cornwall Gazette* office, to know if it was true that a few Gentlemen met yesterday at the Royal Hotel, for the purpose of bringing forward one of the Vivians of Swansea for the Eastern Division of Cornwall, but for that question your letter would have given me the first intimation. I have had several interviews with Mr B. Willyams and also with Mr Cornish[2] of Penzance, Mr St Aubyn's solicitor, respecting the subject[3],—but about ten days ago I feared that Mr W. would resign in consequence of the great expense it was likely to cost,—I had engaged with Mr W. should he stand to accompany him as far as I could throughout his canvass,—therefore Mr W. having resigned, if my feeble ability will be of any service to your brother, I shall be ready to do for him as if it was for yourself or Mr W. and very much delighted I shall be to see him one of the MP's for Cornwall,—this reminds me of his accompanying us for a short time when you was [sic] a Candidate for Truro.[4]

With respect to Truro, everything of a Political character seem [sic] quiet,—sometimes it is said that A S[5] intends to come forward,—and then I have heard it said that he is ready to do so if a requisition should be sent him,—I know nothing of the movements of either party, having of late kept aloof.

---

1. George Clyma (1802–82), J.P. and Mayor of Truro on three occasions.
2. Thomas Cornish, of Rodd & Cornish solicitors, Penzance. In 1868 he was town clerk, registrar of the County Court, superintendent registrar of births, deaths and marriages, etc.
3. John St Aubyn (1829–1908) of St Michael's Mount, Cornwall, grandson of the 5th Baronet, J.P., D.L. Liberal who sat for West Cornwall 1868–85, St Ives Division 1885–7. Succ. to Baronetcy 1872, and created Baron St Levan, 1887.
4. This refers to Hussey Vivian's successful 1852 candidacy when he and John E. Vivian (Conservative—and no relation) defeated Augustus and Montague Smith. Hussey Vivian remained Truro's MP until 1857.
5. Augustus Smith (1804–72) of Tresco Abbey, Scilly Isles, J.P. and D.L., Liberal MP for Truro 1857 to 1865.

PV 35/14

R.M. Sampson[1] to A.P. Vivian

Devoran, Cornwall, 11 June 1868.

Dear Sir

A report is afloat that a member of your family is coming forward for the Western Division of this county. Mr Brydges Willyams has been solicited to stand in the room of Mr R. Davey M.P. but no arrangement can be effected as to electioneering expense, on the Liberal side to meet the opposition of Mr Basset, Tehidy. Mr Humphry Willyams will not spend more than £2000, Mr Robartes and Mr Jno M Williams with another will guarantee £1000 more which is considered not to be sufficient by £2000 or so.

It will be a smart contest no doubt at the same time I think the chances are in favor [sic] of a Liberal, and if Mr Brydges Willyams do not stand, I have heard of no other party named in his stead except as stated in the former part of this note.

---

1. Richard Michell Sampson of Devoran near Truro, copper mine agent.

PV 35/15

Heard & Sons *(West Briton)* to A.P. Vivian

Truro, 11 June 1868.

Dear Sir

You will observe by the *West Briton* of this evening (a copy of which we address by this post) that all is apparently going on well, and we have thought that you may perhaps wish a copy sent to you weekly: this paper arrives in London on Friday evening.[1]

1. Obviously by this time the inner circle of West Cornwall Liberals (including Heard) were aware of A.P.V.'s candidacy, more than a week before the electors' meeting.

PV 35/16

Henry Grylls to A.P. Vivian

Moreton House, Redruth, 11 June 1868

Dear Sir

I duly received your favor of the 9th Instant—and am happy to find you will so cordially respond to any call that may be made on you by the Electors at the Meeting to be held in Camborne on Tuesday next.

It will be very desirable for Capt Vivian,[1] your relative member for Truro, to be at the meeting. You are unfortunately not personally known amongst the Electors but he is well known and speaking on your behalf would have great weight. Everything that has transpired since I last addressed you tends to confirm my conviction that your name will be well received at the meeting and your subsequent election as safe as any contingency can be.

I beg to enclose dft of resolutions to be proposed on Tuesday, and we shall be glad if you will make any alterations you think desirable.

[P.S.] The *West Briton* of tomorrow will contain Mr Davey's letter to the Electors and the announcement of the Public Meeting for Tuesday next.

1. Captain J.C.W. Vivian, MP Truro 1865–71.

PV 35/25

J.M. Williams to A.P. Vivian

Burncoose, Perranarworthal, Cornwall, 11 June 1868

My Dear Sir

I am much obliged for your letter of yesterdays date and very pleased to hear you were so successful with Lord Kimberley and Mr Hawkins[1]—it tends so much to strengthen our confidence in our own strength—I have great faith that our meeting on Tuesday will be a great success.—I think it right to send you in confidence—the copy of a letter from a Mr Cornish of Penzance to Mr Grylls a Tory Solicitor—retained by Mr St Aubyn, and the Copy of a letter I have by this Post written to Mr St Aubyn. Also copy of a letter from Mr St Aubyn to Mr Grylls. We hope to get Resolutions passed on Tuesday and such a requisition in your favour that we shall have to ask you to come down as promptly as possible. I shall send you a Telegraph message from Camborne on Tuesday as promptly as possible.

Will you kindly consider and write to Mr Grylls by tomorrow's Post such a letter, expressing your Political views in a general way, as he can read to the meeting—it may surprize you—but it is the fact—that if we are asked your views, on different Political subjects—there is no one down here acquainted with them—you can however easily write a letter—expressing Liberal views in a general way—and with an offer to explain them more fully hereafter.

[P.S.] Will you kindly return the enclosures in course—I think Mr Hussy [sic] Vivian should be acquainted with their contents. It appears as if Mr St Aubyn—hesitates whether to act in concert with you or not—until after he has heard the result of Tuesday's Meeting.

We saw Mr Peter of Chiverton[2] yesterday—he will attend the meeting and I think heartily support you—If you see Mr Robartes tomorrow—mention I spent an hour yesterday with Mr Shilson (his confidant and adviser on all important matters)[3] that I explained and consulted him on our proceedings—that he gave me much sound suggestions and quite approved of our general proceedings.

---

1. Christopher Henry Thomas Hawkins (1820–?) of Trewithen, J.P. and D.L., and Sheriff 1846. Hawkins was a nephew of Sir Christopher Hawkins Bt (1758–1829) the notorious borough monger, and owned almost 12,000 acres in the Division.

2. John Thomas Henry Peter (1810–78) of Chiverton, J.P. and D.L., and Sheriff 1866. Eldest son of the county reformer William Peter, he was a small landowner.
3. William Shilson (1806–75) of Tremough, admitted as a solicitor 1828. Chief partner in Shilson, Coode & Co., bankers and solicitors, St Austell.

PV 35/17

Edward Heard to A.P. Vivian (Private and Confidential)

Truro, 12 June 1868

Dear Sir

I am favoured with your letter of yesterday's date and beg to assure you that no effort on my part shall be wanting to ensure your success.

Last evening we sent out over 2000 of the accompanying bills to be distributed throughout the Western Division of the County so as to have, if possible, a large and enthusiastic meeting.

You will see by the *West Briton and Cornwall Advertiser* of this week the articles on the West Cornwall Election. The seed thus sown is already bearing good fruit. I send you a few copies herewith, that you may if desired, mark and send them on to your personal friends.

I have just come back from Redruth from seeing your zealous and indefatigable friend, Mr Downing; also Mr Henry Grylls and Mr William Grylls[1]—all heart and soul with you.

Everything that can be done, you may rely on will be done. I presume that should the meeting on Tuesday next be an enthusiastic one, we shall see you here on the following or at the latest on Thursday morning. Probably your address may appear in that day's County Papers.

I need scarcely add—the names of Pendarves[2] and Vivian are both dear to me; and when I first heard of your candidature I resolved that no stone should be left unturned on my part. I first heard your name in connection with West C last week. I was to have left Truro for London on Monday and had secured two reserved seats for my wife and myself for the Handel Festival at the Crystal Palace, the rehearsal taking place today.

It only shows what short-sighted mortals we all are. Instead of listening to the sweet sounds of the music of the greatest composer ever known, I am at my letter desk thinking of how best your seat can be secured.

1. William Grylls was secretary of the Redruth Literary Institute 1847–70, President 1870–8. He left Redruth in 1878 to become a partner in Williams, Williams & Grylls, Bankers, Falmouth.
2. E.W.W. Pendarves (1775–1853), A.P.V.'s godfather, was Liberal MP for Cornwall 1826–32 and for West Cornwall 1832–53.

PV 35/27

Edward Vivian[1] to A.P. Vivian

Woodfield (?), Torquay, 12 June 1868

Dear Pendarvis [sic] Vivian

I am informed, confidentially, that you have consented to obtain the support of the *Western Morning News* in your favour as soon as it may be discussed.

Mr Saunders, its principal proprietor, is an old friend of mine, and has been one of my firmest supporters for St Ives. He would consider it a compliment if you would give him an early intimation, and although on many points a neutral paper they would, I venture, support you as heartily as they have me on all the leading points of its Liberal creed.

I shall be at the Camborne Meeting on Tuesday next, and need not say how rejoiced I am that you propose to canvas [sic] West Cornwall. I can promise you some good liberals from the St Ives district, which, in addition to the town, embraces about 20 square miles of agricultural population.

If, as I understand, the Liberal party engages Rodd and Cornish of Penzance as their leading Election Agents you will strengthen my chance for St Ives and make it almost a certainty, as Mr Cornish has hitherto been our principal difficulty being Land Agent for Mr Tyringham and Mrs Davies Gilbert's properties the whole of whose tenants have been compelled to vote against me, although Liberals, Dissenters, Teetotallers and of all advanced civilizations.

I send you a *Western Morning News* with report of my last meeting at St Ives. It was copied into the *West Briton* and other papers. The *Western Morning News* has by far the biggest circulation in the county.

It might be of mutual advantage if I could meet you when you canvas [sic] St Ives.

[P.S.] Could you pay me a passing visit on your way to Cornwall?

1. Edward Vivian (1808–93) of Torquay, a partner in the Torquay bank, was the unsuccessful Liberal candidate for St Ives in 1865. He became a Vice President of the United Kingdom Alliance in 1862, serving in the position until at least 1879.

PV 35/26

Henry Grylls to A.P. Vivian

Moreton House, Redruth, 13 June 1868.

Dear Sir

I am in receipt of your favor of yesterday. We are glad to hear that if Capt Vivian cannot come to help at the canvas [sic] etc your Brother will accompany you : but we think it is a Sine qua non that some-one should be able to state what your political opinions are to the Electors on Tuesday next. I believe a general declaration in writing to be read to the meeting that you approve of Mr Gladstone's[1] politics—Specially with respect to the Irish Church would be sufficient. On this latter point we are here very strong. All the Sections of the Methodist Body and other dissenters have these views, besides many Good Churchmen. But we still think Capt Vivian's presence at the meeting would be the right course—and as far as his election at Truro may be influenced by his help to you I think there can be no doubt it will improve his position. A very influential elector of that Borough, and hitherto a Staunch Supporter of Capt Vivian, said yesterday that his advocacy of you would strengthen him in Truro—and knowing as I do (in confidence) that Lord Falmouth wishes you success I am of the electors' opinion.

1. William Ewart Gladstone (1809–98). Entered the House of Commons in 1832 as a Tory, but in the 1850s moved to the Liberal party. Chancellor of the Exchequer 1852–5, 1859–66, then Prime Minister 1868–74, 1880–5, 1886, and 1892–4. Paramount among Gladstone's policies in 1868 was Irish Church Disestablishment.

PV 35/24

H.S. Stokes[1] to A.P. Vivian

Bodmin, 15 June 1868.

My Dear Sir,

I wrote to you yesterday with an outline of topics for your guid^{ce} in preparing an address.

I should have gone to Redruth today, but for my engagements here on County matters. But I have written Mr T.S. Bolitho, and Mr H.M. Grylls with suggestions.

Today I received a note from Brydges Willyams, stating the grounds of his withdrawal.

So soon as practicable, after you receive a resolution inviting you to stand, your address should be ready, and you should arrange with Mr St Aubyn that it sho^{d} appear simultaneously with his, say on Thursday next in *West Briton*, *Cornwall Gazette*, *Western Morning News*, and *Plymouth Mercury* [sic]. The two last named papers have a very large daily circulation in the County.

Your next step will be to present yourself to the Electors, arranging head places for meeting and addressing them. As to this also, you must act in concert with Mr St Aubyn. Possibly he will think this shd be delayed till the sittg^{s} of parliament are over. But you must be guided chiefly by what Mr Grylls and his friend recommend.

The undertaking will require a strong effort on your part. I hear the fact of your not having a resid^{ce} in Cornwall much commented on.

It has occurred to me that the house in which I resided in Prince's Street, which was built by one of your ancestors, and which is now shut up, might be obt^{d} from Lord Falmouth on very easy terms. There are offices attached which would well suit for the business of your firm, and the rooms of the house are large and handsome.

When you decide on coming down, I hope to be able to be with you occasionally.

---

1. Henry Sewell Stokes (1808–95), of Bodmin. Solicitor at Truro 1832–65, Mayor 1856, Town Clerk 1859–65. Clerk of the Peace for Cornwall, at Bodmin 1865 until his death.

PV 35/23/1–4

A.P. Vivian to Henry Grylls (Letterbook)

London, 15 [?] June 1868

Dear Sir

I have received your letter of the 13 inst. and am much obliged to you for the interest you have taken in the question of my possible candidature of West Cornwall. I beg to say that I shall accept the position of one of the candidates for that Division of the County, if I am decided on by the Meeting on Tuesday next, with much gratification.

My political opinions are comparatively unknown to the Division it is right that I should state them shortly and categorically in such a manner as will enable you to make them known to the Meeting.

I approve of and should support Mr Gladstone's policies, especially in respect of the Irish Church which I believe to be simple but long deferred justice correcting a grievance to which the Irish have submitted only as a conquered nation and calculated in no way to inquire, but settles on its contrary to advance Protestantism in that country.

I should support Mr Gladstone as the Minister more likely than any other to effect sound Financial and Economic Reforms. I base this opinion on his past measures to which much of the development of the commerce of this country is due and to his frequently expressed opinions on the necessity of Economy. Both imperial and local expenditures have reached a point at which remedial measures must be attempted and I hope that the action of Ratepayers may be brought most directly to bear on County expenditure. I view with satisfaction the large extension of the Franchise which has taken place. I regret only that it has been unaccompanied by protection for the Independent voter: and measures such as the ballot, calculated to attain that object would receive my support.

I believe that a well considered System of National Education is now more than ever needed and I hope that it will receive the earliest attention of the new Parliament.

I should support all measures calculated to remove disabilities based on religious belief such as the Tests which now exclude non-conformists from the enjoyment of the fruits of their well earned University Honors: I am a conscientious churchman but I hold that others have Equal rights with myself to their conscientious convictions: and I also hold that in these days the true interests of no class or institution can be based on repression. By such well considered changes alone can the peace, security and advancement of this great country be secured. To such has it been due in the past and from the past we may learn to know the future.

Perhaps I may be allowed to allude to the fact that commercially the interests of Cornwall and my own are most intimately associated: my education at the Mining College at Freiberg in Germany and my experience since, will I hope and believe, enable me to understand and efficiently to represent the great Mining interests of Cornwall.

Although I do not reside in the County I can claim to be the son and grandson of Cornishmen whose memories I believe have not faded from the recollections of many of those who I seek to have the honor [sic] of representing.

PV 35/22

J.C. Vivian[1] to A.P. Vivian

London, 16 June 1868

My Dear Pendarves,

You know, I am sure, how heartily I wish you success in the West not alone on yr own account but especially in the interest of the Liberal party and how glad I shall be to wear [?] my humble efforts to promote the return of St Aubyn and yourself in every way in my power.

Mr Grylls who urges my presence at the meeting today seems to think that a Member of Parliament can leave London at any moment. Idle members may. But those who work have business always on hand which cannot be closed in a moment or neglected without damage to the Public Interest. Ex : gra : I am at this moment a Member of a Royal Commission appointed to enquire into the system of Courts Martial and Military punishments. I was put on that Commission as representing the views of those who wish to abolish flogging and Reform altogether our Military Code. We are now (having closed our Evidence) discussing the basis of our report. On that Report will depend the future prospects of our Army so far as discipline and justice are concerned. It would be manifestly a gross dereliction of duty were I on any pretext to leave London until the labors of this Commission are closed. After that I have told Hussey[2] that I shall be ready to tender you any assistance in my power. I shall be very much obliged if you will take an opportunity of making the contents of this letter known to Mrs J.M. Williams and in short to <u>all</u> who are interested in the good cause. For I would not be liable to a charge of supineness or neglect of duty to my constituents or friends in Cornwall.

---

1. Although the letter was signed H.[?] Vivian, it was written by Captain J.C.W. Vivian, MP for Truro, who was a member of the 1868–9 Royal Commission as described above.
2. Henry Hussey Vivian, A.P.V.'s eldest brother.

PV 35/36

J.M. Williams to A.P. Vivian (London)

(telegram)

Camborne, 16 June 1868

Very large and influential meeting invitation for you unanimous—Hope see at one o'clock on Thursday

PV 35/37

Henry Grylls to A.P. Vivian (London)

(telegram)

Redruth, 16 June 1868

Sent you telegram when third resolution was passed every resolution passed no dissentient[.] Hall full triumphant meeting five pm

PV 35/38

Henry Grylls to A.P. Vivian (London)

(telegram)

Camborne, 16 June 1868

Resolutions carried unanimously. You will be received most cordially.

PV 35/39

Henry Grylls to A.P. Vivian (London)

(telegram)

Redruth, 16 June 1868

Your address most satisfactory perhaps the words such as the ballot may be prudently omitted for the present shall I bring it with me omission retaining the remainder of the sentence were yes or no

PV 35/21

Lord Kimberley to A.P. Vivian

18 June 1868

Dear Mr Vivian

I am very glad to hear that you are accepted as our candidate, and shall be most happy to give you my support. I will not fail to write to my agent as I promised.

PV 35/3/1–4

To the Electors of the Western Division of the County of Cornwall[1]

5, Buckingham Gate,
London
June 1868

Gentlemen

In compliance with the invitation conveyed by the resolution of the meeting of Liberal Electors of West Cornwall held at Camborne,—I beg to offer myself as a candidate for the seat about to be vacated by your greatly esteemed member Mr Richard Davey.

My political opinions are I believe generally in accordance with those of that Gentleman and of the many and distinguished Liberals who have represented the Western Division of Cornwall, as well as with the traditional tenets of my own family.

I hold that the greatness and prosperity of this country can only be secured by the judicious adoption from time to time of measures calculated to keep pace with our moral, social and commercial developments. A stationary policy must in my judgement lead to retrogression. I have closely watched the course pursued by Mr Gladstone, and I believe him to be a worthy leader of the Liberal Party.

I coincide in & should support his proposal relative to the Irish Church. I hold that it is a measure of simple justice to the great mass of the Irish people: The existence of a grievance so well founded, cannot but tend to rouse feelings of animosity and disloyalty while its removal is calculated to re-unite those ties of amity and loyalty which should bind together all sections of a great nation. As a conscientious churchman I cannot believe that the interests of the Church are advanced by the imposition of her tenets on an unwilling people, nor as a Protestant can I hold that my faith needs the aid of the bayonet to sustain it and to propagate its truths. I can admit of no analogy between the position of the church in Ireland and in England nor can I believe that to deal with the one endangers the other. I hold that all disabilities consequent on religious belief should be abolished and I should heartily support the measure proposed by Mr Coleridge for the removal of those tests at universities which prevent nonconformists from enjoying the fruits of their well earned honours.

I should support a measure for securing a more complete system of Education, having regard always to the religious feelings of the various denominations.

Our national expenditure must engage the most serious attention of the next Parliament with a view to its reduction. How this is to be effected, with due regard to the safety of our country and our commerce, is a problem most difficult to solve, but I look forward with hope to the efforts of Mr Gladstone in that direction on his next advent to power: his opinions on the question of retrenchment have been frequently and earnestly expressed. Any judicious measures from whatever quarter calculated to effect economy will have my cordial support.

I trust that the principles of non-intervention in the affairs of other nations will continue to prevail. Such a policy would have my hearty concurrence.

The burden of local Taxation has become very heavy, and I should advocate the adoption of such a system as will insure representation to the ratepayer by the establishment of County Financial Boards. I rejoice that so large a measure of Reform has received the sanction of the Legislature. As the Act now stands much amendment is ~~in its present form that measure requires much amendment~~ required and I should support proposals calculated to afford protection to the dependent voter and to remove the inconvenient and useless restriction with which the Act is trammelled

Although not resident among you I am proud of my Cornish descent, and from my earliest days have been taught to entertain feelings of deep regard towards Cornwall.

Commercially my interests are intimately bound up with your own, and I may venture to hope that I should be able efficiently to represent them in their technical and commercial bearings

x see below

In conclusion, Gentlemen, I can only say that I shall now gratefully appreciate your cordial invitation and I need not add, should I succeed in obtaining the distinguished honour of representing you, no endeavour shall be wanting on my part to justify your choice, and to deserve your continued confidence

I am, Gentlemen,
Yr faithful servant
Arthur Pendarves Vivian

x I will also to the best of my ability study all questions affecting the great agricultural industry of the County, an industry which I will know is second to no other in the land.

1. This election address, dated 24 June 1868, appeared in the Cornish press with the final sentence included immediately before the paragraph beginning, 'In conclusion ...'.

PV 35/20

John St Aubyn to A.P. Vivian[1]

London, 20 June 1868

My Dear Vivian

Many thanks for your note. I explained my views about the future course of proceedings in a note to Mr Grylls of the 18th which he has doubtless shown you—and I am glad to see by a letter from him this morning that we are all entirely agreed on the subject. Mr Cornish my agent is in town, on other business—he returns on Wednesday, and I have told him to attend your meeting on Thursday and also on the following days should you wish it. He will also immediately put himself into communication with Mr Downing.

I am quite sure that you will have a most successful week—and my belief is that the Tories will think several times before they attack so well defended a position. Always let me know if there are any directions I can give that will be of use to you and believe me ...

1. There appears to have been no correspondence between St Aubyn and A.P.V. before this date, suggesting that the former was wary of committing himself to assist until he was sure of his fellow Liberal's politics.

PV 35/19

H.S. Stokes to A.P. Vivian

Bodmin, 21 June 1868

My dear sir,

I have sent on copies of the Register[1] to Mr Downing. While at Truro Friday mg. Mr Smith wished to see me but I had not time to see him, and my partner, Mr Paul[2] [?] delivered me to the station. All he said was respecting the present Register and the future and he desired copies. From this and other information I consider that there will be a contest. Sir Wm Wms[3] is (I fancy) pledged to contest the division. So be prepared accordingly, and do not stint the needful in agencies etc. I shall be happy to confer with you whenever you may think it of any use. Heard was away when I was at Truro, but I have since conferred with Mr Hooper[4] of the West Briton.

You must get help through Mr Ed. Vivian, from the *Western Mg News*. The circuln of the City papers is very small in comparison.

Don't forget Agriculture. You must stand up for the farmers. County Rates are the topic for them. Improved culture is also a topic. Could you bring some of your chemical skill to bear on our soils?

But as regards County rates don't overdo it. All the County rates on gaol, militia stores [?] police etc. only amt to 6^{d} in the £. The 3/or 4 per annum rate collected in the name of poor rate, embraces nigh every rate and poor rate, and also the County rates—all lumped together. The whole subject demands revision. County Boards, if desirable at all, are rather on the ground that the Ratepayers should have a voice, on the old principle of taxation and representation going together.

P.S. I think you should be at the different towns on the Market days, and have someone in each place, to introduce you to the farmers. Try Truro next Wednesday and get Mr Geo. Clyma to introduce you to Mr Trethewy and other farmers in the market place. You would do yourself no harm in dining at the ordinary at 2 o'clock that day.[50] So in Redruth, Camborne, Penzance, Helston, Falmouth, etc. dine at the Ticketings.

---

1. The register of qualified voters for counties and county divisions such as West Cornwall, was reviewed each year. The process began in June when the overseers of the poor asked qualified persons to send them notification of their claim, and ended in September–October when revising barristers heard claims and objections before correcting the register.

2. Robert Macleane Paul (1840–?), son of W.H. Paul, solicitor of Truro, who was P.P. Smith's partner. R.M. Paul was admitted as a solicitor in partnership with P.P. Smith in 1866.
3. William Williams (1791–1870) of Tregullow, uncle of J.M. Williams, was from 1859 a prospective Conservative candidate for West Cornwall. He received a Baronetcy in 1866.
4. William Frederick Hooper (1820?–82), editor of the *West Briton* from 1862.
5. A meal provided for farmers attending Market day.

PV 35/18/1–2

Henry Eliot[1] to A.P. Vivian

22 June 1868

My Dear Vivian

You are mistaken in supposing that I have any influence with Carmarthen.[2] I know him, but not intimately and my speaking to him would be more likely to do harm than good. However I have done all my little possible to help you, by speaking to Freddy Leveson,[3] who has great influence with him, and who is a staunch Liberal and a Cornish Member. He tells me that he is already working on your behalf and is in great hope that the Duke will support you.[4] Carmarthen, he tells me, is a violent Tory, but fortunately has nothing to do with it, so if a merciful Providence will only spare His Grace till after the election, I hope you will be all right.

Whether you succeed or not, I suppose the election will bring you down into our parts a good deal, and I hope you will find time on one of your visits to drop in at Port Eliot. It is close to the Station, and makes a convenient halting place on the journey. I shall not be there before September but my father will probably be going down next month, and will I am sure be glad to see you. Charles[5] and his wife will be there too.

If you can come in September I hope there will be a few partridges to kill. The accounts so far are very good, but you know Cornwall is not much of a game country. Wishing you all success in your electioneering ...

---

1. Henry Cornwallis Eliot, 5th Earl of St Germans (1835–1911), D.L. and J.P. Cornwall, served in the Navy 1848–53 and in the Foreign Office 1855–81.
2. George Godolphin (1828–95), Marquess of Carmarthen and later ninth Duke of Leeds.
3. Hon. Edward Frederic Leveson-Gower (1819–1907), Liberal MP for Bodmin, 1858 to 1885.

4. George Godolphin (1802–72), eighth Duke of Leeds. Until 1841 the representation of Helston was controlled by the Godolphin family, which owned property in the borough.
5. Charles George Cornwallis Eliot (1838–1901), younger brother of Henry Cornwallis Eliot, 5th Earl of St Germans. His wife, Constance Rhiannon, was the 4th daughter of Sir Josiah John Guest (1785–1852) of Dowlais, Wales, MP for Merthyr Tydvil 1832–52.

PV 35/28

H.A. Bruce[1] to A.P. Vivian

London, 23 June 1868.

My Dear Vivian

I only received Hussey's letter yesterday on my return from the Isle of Wight. I send you the[?] Educn Bill by this post. You will find it somewhat hard to decipher without a guide thro' the Labyrinth. The main principles are:

1. Not to interfere where there are sufft Schools already.
2. to allow the Act to be voluntarily adopted.
3. to impose its adoption, where need for it has been proved upon due inquiry.
4. The School—Committee to be elected for every district except Municipal boroughs, where they will be passed by act of the Council.
5. The Rates to [be] levied as a supplement to the Government Grant, and fees.
6. All existing schools, on fulfilling certain conditions on efficiency, and on giving good secular educn, to be aided from the rate, without interfering with their managers, or their denominational character.
7. The School Committee to determine the character of any new Schools built by Local Rates. It ? denominational, unsectarian, or secular, as they may determine.

The Bill will, after a Statement, be withdrawn by me this Session.

I rejoice to hear that your prospects are so good. We want an infusion of good looking, straight-going men in our ranks.

---

1. H.A. Bruce, 1st Baron Aberdare (1816–95) of Duffryn, Co. Glamorgan, J.P. and D.L. MP Merthyr Tydvil 1852–68, Renfrewshire 1869–73, Under Secretary for Home Dept 1862–4, Vice President Education Board 1864–6.

PV 35/29

Arthur Tremayne[1] to ? Vivian

Carclew, Penryn, Cornwall, 26 June 1868

Dear Mr Vivian,

I arrived here from London late last night, and found your letter. I have been in town on and off for the last 4 months, but I did not call upon you for I thought you had probably forgotten all about me; and indeed also I have been so out of heart and health for two years past that I have hardly gone anywhere. I return to Claridges for a day or two next week, and if I have a moment I will do myself the pleasure of calling upon you. I go abroad the end of the week, and have some Lawyer's business that will occupy most of my time in London.

My politics (such as they are) differ so widely from Mr Arthur Vivian's that if it comes to a Contest, as I think it will, I shall vote against him. I shall vote for the Candidate who goes most against Gladstone, and if I have a 2[d] vote to spare it must go to my old friend, and Schoolfellow, John St Aubyn. I cannot understand Mr Hussey Vivian's theory expressed in a speech recently made in this County that no man must need elect either Gladstone or Dizzy as his Leader. I wish there were more strictly independent men in the House. I think too that if we must have two Gladstonites, we should have two Cornishmen.[2] I am sure you will like to hear the whole truth and nothing but it from me.

---

1. Arthur Tremayne (1827–1905) of Carclew, Cornwall, Lieutenant Colonel in 13th Light Dragoons, and son of John H. Tremayne, MP Cornwall, 1806–26. Arthur Tremayne, inherited Carclew on the death of his uncle Sir Charles Lemon in 1868, and was Conservative MP for Truro, 1878–80.
2. Pendarves Vivian's non-residency was obviously of concern to Tremayne, as it was to other Cornishmen.

PV 35/35

Tryphena Pendarves[1] to Mrs Vivian

Tristfowel[?] Harburton[?] South Devon, 26 June 1868

Dear Mrs Vivian

Any interest I may possess will of course be given to a Liberal Candidate who if <u>well known</u> in the County, might very likely beat Mr—B[2]—who is a Tory—

Your son being quite unknown has a very poor chance with such a formidable opponent—who with such a property must possess considerable influence—and in my opinion will succeed—In the present state of our Government I would not throw away one sixpence in contesting a County.

1. Tryphena Pendarves (nee Trist) married E.W.W. Pendarves, member for Cornwall and later West Cornwall, 1826–53.
2. The reference is to J.F. Basset of Tehidy near Camborne.

PV 35/30

H. [J.C.] Vivian[1] to Hussey Vivian (Private and Confidential)

House of Lords, n.d.

My Dear Hussey

I am confined to this room as Member of R^L^ Commission on C^ts^ Martial or I wd call on you. For I think it right that you sh^d^ know without loss of time that Brydges Willyams is hesitating about announcing his withdrawal!! notwithstanding that he has been pressed to do so. This is thought by those in London to be most unfair both to the party and to Pend: and a letter will go to Brydges by this Post saying in definite and unmistakable words without any arguments that his claims are considered finally closed and at an end. You sh^d^ see to this at once.

Enys of Enys is all right—Glanville Gregor[2] to my surprise and regret is the reverse.

I leave town for Folkestone at 4.30. West Cliff Hotel

1. This was Captain J.C.W. Vivian, MP for Truro.
2. Glanville Gregor (?–1876) of Trewarthenick near Truro. He was a Conservative who chaired Lord Boscawen Rose's 1841 election committee.

PV 35/31

A.P. Vivian to John St Aubyn (copy)

Pengreep, Perranarworthal, Cornwall, 27 June 1868

My dear St Aubyn

Very many thanks for your letter which reached me some few days ago, but rapid movements and frequent meetings have prevented my acknowledging it earlier for which I must apologise—You will no doubt have received the daily County papers, and news [of] what we have been doing in the way of meetings. My reception has been most cordial everywhere, even at Camborne, so close to opposition Head-Quarters,[1] but the Wesleyans have supported me throughout, and indeed the Methodists, and we have experienced no opposition anywhere.

No movement has yet been made to my knowledge by the other side, but we hear occasional rumours.

We returned yesterday from a short visit to Mr Bolitho at Penzance—the meeting there, very strong and influential.

We had an interview with Mr Cornish, when he stated your introductions, as he did also before the public at the meeting at Penzance and St Just.—You may rely on my doing all I can to carry out our perfectly satisfactory understanding. Today a meeting at Helston.

1. The reference is to Tehidy, John Bassett's mansion near Camborne.

PV 35/32

H.S. Stokes to A.P. Vivian

Bodmin, 29 June 1868

My Dear Sir,

I wrote a letter to yr brother[1] on Friday, which has probably followed him to London. It was to express my entire approval of the Address, and to congratulate you on your entire success. At the same time I urged that as little as possible should be said or written to annoy Mr P.P. Smith of Truro, or Mr Augustus Smith, having regard to Capt. Vivian's position at Truro, whom I know both you and Mr Hussey Vivian would be most reluctant to prejudice in his somewhat precarious position.

I hope the *West Briton* will be careful on the same points.

I should hardly think it necessary for your address to be continued from week to week in the papers.

Say twice more, and then suspend the advtmt. But you will be guided by yr cmtee. These advtmts run up to a large sum.

1. Probably Hussey Vivian, whom Stokes assisted when the former was M.P. for Truro.

PV 35/34/1–2

Document in P.V.'s hand

Committee

Charles Fox	—	Falmouth
Robt Broad	—	"
J.M. Williams	—	
T.S. Bolitho	—	Penzance
Henry Grylls	—	Redruth
Major Bickford	—	Camborne
Brydges Willyams	—	Truro
Sydney Davey	—	Redruth
Alfred Jenkins [sic][1]		
James B. Read	—	Penryn
H. Trethewey	—	Grampound (Hawkins)
Rich[d] Davey	—	
Capt Hay	—	Redruth
C.F. Topham	—	Trevour
Enys of Enys		
Newton	—	St Agnes
Grenfell	—	St Ives
Trembath	—	St Just
Robt Blee	—	Secretary
Edw[d] Michell	—	Truro
J.T.H. Peter	—	Chiverton
Henry Williams	—	Tredrea
R.R. Mitchell	—	Marazion

Principal Agents

Cornish	—	Penzance
Downing	—	Redruth

Ld Cowley's[2] [sic] and Kimberley's agents to be written to

We the undersigned being the candidates elected to contest the western division of Cornwall in the Liberal Interest at the ensuing general election hereby pledge ourselves to abide by the decisions of the General Committee chosen to conduct the said Election for the Liberal Party in all and every matter relating to that election.

1. Alfred Jenkin (1792–1872), steward to Anna Maria Agar of Lanhydrock, and later to her son T.J. Agar Robartes. An elder of the Society of Friends, Jenkin was also an agent for Pascoe Grenfell & Sons, copper smelters and manufacturers.
2. Henry Richard Wellesley (1804–84) cr. first Earl Crowley 1857. The family owned property in St Ives.

PV 35/41

Henry Grylls to A.P. Vivian

Moreton House, Redruth, 2 July 1868

My dear Sir

I received your telegram this morning and one from Mr Jenkins[1] Penryn informing me that the arrangements for this Evening's Meeting were completed and that he had written you by messenger to the same effect. Will you allow me to suggest that St Agnes and Grampound are worthy your consideration?[2] Unless you visit these places you will scarcely have fully covered the ground and removed all cause of complaint.

No doubt Mr Downing can make the way plain for you at St Agnes if you think well of it. Many of Mr Enys' tenants are in that vicinity—and as there is some vague feeling about that gentleman's help a visit to St Agnes might remove it.

Hoping you will have a good meeting at Penryn. I remain my dear Sir

1. David James Jenkins (1824–91) merchant, shipowner and partner in Jenkins & Co., London. Liberal MP for Penryn & Falmouth 1874 to 1880.
2. St Agnes and Grampound were villages in the northeastern and eastern extremities of the Division. The voters in and near both had a well developed sense of their political importance.

PV 35/42

William Bolitho[1] to A.P. Vivian

Penzance, 2 July 1868

My dear Sir,

Many thanks for your good wishes about St Ives. I received a visit from the Liberal Deputation today and have promised them a definite answer on Monday. Pray say not a word about the infinitesimally small service I may have rendered you. I spoke that evening for the first time and can only claim the indulgence never refused to a maiden effort as an Excuse for my Shortcomings.

1. William Bolitho (1815–95) of Polwithen, Cornwall, J.P., brother of T.S. Bolitho of Trengwainton.

PV 35/45/1–3

S.T.G. Downing to A.P. Vivian

Redruth, 6 July 1868

Dear Sir

I only succeeded in getting a decree on Friday and so could not leave Town until Saturday. I am very sorry for this as I find you are very anxious about the Registration and I should have liked to have personally explained how the matter stood and that you need have no fear on that score.[1]

Before I left for London (in fact my last 24 hours in Cornwall I devoted entirely to the work) I made every arrangement so far as the greater part of the division was concerned for getting the work done economically but at the same time effectively.

Committees are all very well in their way but with them it is much more talk than real work and on the other hand to rely on professional men solely is to pay very dearly for very little. But in every parish almost there can be found some man who at former Elections has done good service and who from being a parish officer or having been one in former years understands something of the business. These men for a very small sum will do everything we want and do it well too. Courtney at Truro Bryant at St Agnes, Carne in Kenwyn, Huthnance in Gwinear, Berryman at Hayle, Bottral [sic] at Camborne etc. have been hard at work (altho' of course quietly) during the last week, and I will now see that the same course is pursued in the other parishes. Cornish promised me that Penryn should be attended to and I will see him tomorrow and ascertain that he is really doing all that is necessary.

In addition to this all our large properties are being worked up by the Stewards and Lord Falmouth's rental alone will show an immense number of new voters: the same may be said for Mr Robartes' property and that of others.

The sub committees shall also be asked to assist forthwith so that everything they can do will be done. All this you will find will in its result be much more satisfactory than the course our friends are taking in the Eastern Division.

How do we stand with Mrs Pendarves, has she been seen since I left Cornwall? Mr J.M. Williams has an appointment with me for this afternoon but he has not yet arrived and I am consequently somewhat ignorant of what has been done.

Roberts[2] (Smith and Roberts Truro) and Hill[3] (Grylls and Hill Helston) were the Solicitors opposed to me in the Cause that took me to town and I thus had an opportunity of sounding them—I confess that from all they said I believe you will have an easy victory—in fact an uncontested return.

---

1. Before the last day of July the overseers had the responsibility for compiling the register for the new year (i.e. 1868–9), including current voters, claims and objections. As little money had been spent by parliamentary candidates updating the registers in the previous twenty years, Vivian's particular concern was to register new Liberal voters.
2. Joseph Roberts (1815?–77), solicitor, Truro.
3. Frederick Hill (1807–74), solicitor, Helston, and onetime Town Clerk of the borough. His son F.V. Hill, also a solicitor, was in partnership with him and F.V.H.'s uncle.

PV 35/46/1

A.P. Vivian to S.T.G. Downing (copy)

London, 7 July 1868

My Dear Sir

I was very sorry not to see you before leaving the County but felt that I could be down again in a few hours if required and that our meeting had all been accomplished as far as was deemed sufficient.

I am very glad to hear you are proceeding as rapidly as possible with the organisation for registrations. We have but a very limited time for carrying it out and it is of the utmost importance to see that no parish is passed over or insufficiently dealt with.

I quite agree with you that where this latter cannot be dealt with satisfactorily by voluntary assistance as of local committee men, paid persons must be employed. What must be arrived at is every individual parish being effectively registered. Mr Williams[1] will no doubt have told you of my satisfactory interview with Mrs Pendarves.

---

1. The reference is to J.M. Williams of Caerhays Castle.

PV 35/51

A.P. Vivian to J.T.H. Peter

London, 7 July 1868
Copy of a letter by APV

Dear Sir

I have to acknowledge receipt of your letter—the 4th inst.

The historical facts you allude to, I am of course not personally acquainted with. I cannot but regret both for my own sake and for that of the cause that they should indispose you to give me your valuable countenance but gathering as I do from your letter that for personal rather than political reasons, you do not wish to appear on a Liberal Committee I can only acquiesce in your decision and write by this post to Mr Grylls to acquaint him with the fact.

PV 35/43

J.M. Williams to A.P. Vivian (London)

Caerhays Castle, St Austell, 8 July 1868

My Dear Sir

We are much obliged for your letter of yesterday and much amused at its enclosures which we forward to Mr Grylls. There is a very strong feeling gaining ground daily—that Mr Kendal[1] [sic] should be allowed to retain his Seat for East Cornwall and if the Liberals attempt to bring forward a second candidate—a second conservative will I have no doubt be started—as well as an opposition in the Western Division—the other side may allow us to return three but never quietly four, the whole of our County Members. Mr Richard Foster—Banker[2] at Lostwithiel and Liskeard and his partner Mr Thos S Bolitho of Trengwainton were very decided in their expressions to me yesterday of Mr Kendal's merits etc—and hope that no attempt would be made to interfere with Mr Kendal's seat. I was told that Mr Fortescue of Boconnoc has announced his intention to support Mr Kendal thoroughly.[3]

---

1. Nicholas Kendall (1800–78), of Pelyn, Cornwall. Magistrate and D.L. Conservative, Sheriff 1847, MP for East Cornwall, 1852–68, when he retired to become a Police Magistrate at Gibralter.
2. Richard Foster (1808–69), partner in Robins, Foster, Coode & Bolitho's East Cornwall Branch. He was a J.P. and owned a smelting works in Truro.

3. Hon. George Matthew Fortescue (1791–1877), of Bocconoc, MP Hindon, Wiltshire, 1827–32, J.P. and D.L., Devon and Cornwall. In 1864 inherited the Bocconoc estate of 17,000 acres on the death of his aunt Anne, Lady Grenville. Fortescue's support was significant because in 1852 he had opposed Kendall.

PV 35/44

J.M. Williams to A.P. Vivian (London)

Caerhays Castle, St Austell, 8 July 1868

My Dear Sir.

I was very glad to learn by your letter from Totness the favorable report of your interview with Mrs Pendarves.—I spent some hours with Mr Downing on Monday considering with him whom should be fixed on, to attend to the Registrations in the different Parishes—(there are more than one hundred) and again we met yesterday present also the two Messrs Grylls.—Yesterday morning early I arranged for Mr Downing to go to Truro to see Mr Marrack[1] (Lord F's Solicitor) to undertake the looking after of certain Parishes in that Neighbourhood.—Mr Downing also saw Mr Rogers[2] of Helston Monday Eveng at Redruth—and made some fresh (conditional) terms with him—viz that he should make Plomer[3] and Edwardes[4] [sic] satisfied—however this will have to be attended to further.—Last Evening Mr Cornish was to come to Redruth by appointment to meet Mr Downing about the Western districts.—Today Mr W Grylls and Mr Middleton will visit five or six Parishes between this and St Mawes to see Parties and get them to undertake to attend to the Registration.—[5] Yesterday I called on Mr Trethewey—but he was not at home and I could not learn anything from his wife.—Mr Grylls was to send circulars by last post to all Members of the Committee asking their prompt attention to the Registration.

---

1. Richard Marrack, (1791–?), solicitor, Truro.
2. Possibly Thomas Rogers (1792–1876), of Helston, solicitor and head of Rogers & Son, solicitors. A partner in the Helston Banking Co. he was a Baptist, and one time Mayor of the borough.
3. John Gilbert Plomer, (1817–?) of Helston, solicitor, and Town Clerk of the borough.
4. Thomas Hyne Edwards (1800?–78) of Helston, J.P. and clerk, conveyancer and auctioneer. One-time Mayor of the borough, he too was a partner in the Helston Banking Co.
5. The parishes included Veryan, Ruan Lanihorne, Philleigh, Gerrans and St Anthony-in-Roseland.

PV 35/48/1–2

S.T.G. Downing to A.P. Vivian

Redruth, 8 July 1868

My Dear Sir

I am obliged for your favour of yesterday's date.

The Registration is proceeding most satisfactorily. We have supplemented the local Committees by paid assistance when necessary and a very good feeling exists. In fact by splitting up the Central Committee with local committees and getting each local committee to appoint its own Chairman and hon. Secretary, we have prevented jealousy and also called into existence much latent voluntary effort. The only district from which I have not yet had a satisfactory account is the Helston district. Bribery and intimidation of all sorts on the part of both parties have always been resorted to in their miserable Borough contests,[1] and they seem not to understand that anything of the kind in a County contest is perfectly absurd, however I will personally go there tonight and try to put matters on a proper footing.

At Truro Mr Marrack is doing his work most admirably. I was with him for some hours yesterday and find Lord Falmouth's interest will be most largely increased by the means that are being adopted to get his leaseholders on the register.[2]

Cornish was here this morning, he was most ready to adopt every suggestion for jointly working the registration and I am quite confident that the union between your friends and those of Mr St Aubyn is most cordial and complete, and of course we must do everything in our power to maintain the present good understanding.

Mr John Jope Rogers[3] (Penrose) has entirely failed in getting Mr Rashleigh[4] to come forward and I still think there is not the smallest chance of any opposition, but this of course must not make us relax our efforts as to the Registration, for if we now get the lists put right a very little expense will hereafter keep them so.

I am still continuing your address as an advertisement in the papers. I don't think a little money is thrown away by my doing so, for we have all the papers with us (except the Truro Gazette) and they will all be prepared to help us with leading articles if the necessity should arise.

Pray excuse my troubling you with this long letter but I thought you would like to know everything that was going on.

---

1. Bribery and intimidation were present at most Helston elections after 1832.

2. The means used to register leaseholders are unknown, but the 1867 Reform Act changed one of the leaseholder voting qualifications from £10 p.a. to £5 p.a. for any unexpired part of a lease originally granted for a term of 60 years. Hence a larger pool of eligible voters meant a possible advantage to the Liberals if they persuaded many in West Cornwall to register.
3. John Jope Rogers (1816–80), of Penrose, J.P., D.L., Conservative MP for Helston 1859–65.
4. Probably William Rashleigh (1817–71), of Menabilly, J.P. and D.L., Conservative MP for East Cornwall 1841–7. The Rashleigh estate of almost 10,000 acres was spread across both county Divisions.

PV 35/50/1–2

Henry Grylls to A.P. Vivian

Moreton House, Redruth, 8 July 1868

My dear Sir.

I am in receipt of your favor of the 7th Instant enclosing Mr Peter's letter to me and copy of one from you to that Gent. The latter I beg to enclose.

Mr Peter's movement is quite inexplicable. First cordially nominating you at the Meeting at Camborne—then declining to be on the Committee on account of alleged intended absence from home—then wavering again, then remembering some dispute of a previous generation and out of respect for his father's memory talking nonsense so that really it is impossible to determine if he wishes to be on the Committee or not. The better way now, I judge, is to let the matter rest. He is got into the mud and if he can get out again, Well.

I met Mr Downing, Cornish and my son yesty afternoon, first having a Conference with Mr J.M. Williams—and the mode of getting the voters on the registration was carefully arranged. There is to be a meeting of the Subcommittee of this District at Redruth this evening—at Penzance and Helstone etc tomorrow so that parties will be at work all over the Western Division immediately—and I have no doubt the work will be well and promptly done.

William[1] is gone to Grampound today on this matter—and will be south tomorrow and I shall be at Penzance.[2]

---

1. The reference is to William Grylls.
2. 'The south' was the region of West Cornwall including Helston and the Lizard peninsular.

PV 35/47 A.P.

Vivian to S.T.G. Downing (letterbook)

London, 9 July 1868

My dear Sir,

I am obliged by your letter of yesterday and am glad to find you are pushing on so energetically with the registration and on a system which aught to leave no parish ineffectually dealt with, but be good enough to see that it is properly carried out and that Helston and no other parish is at all slurred over. I quite concur with your views that our efforts should be continued with the utmost vigour that the Registration be thoroughly done this time. Afterwards the Expence [sic] of keeping it up properly will be trifling and that our great safe-guard will be in this. No time should be lost; it is already very limited. I saw Mr St Aubyn yesterday. He seemed to think that paid assistance was scarcely required but I told him unnecessary expence could be gone to in getting the work well done. He meant to write to Mr Grylls on the subject. I conclude Mr Cornish takes the most Western Districts?[1] I shall be very glad to hear as often as you can how you are getting on.

1. The districts referred to were those comprising the Penwith peninsula, stretching westwards from St Ives and Penzance to Land's End.

PV 35/49/1

E.M. Williams to A.P. Vivian

Caerhays Castle, 9 July 1868

My dear Sir,

We have just heard from Mr Grylls that Mr Cornish called on him about the Registration on Tuesday afternoon and that they made all the needful arrangements for prompt attention to it and that Mr Grylls had written you fully on the subject by yesterday's post, so I trust that ere this you and Mr St Aubyn are free from anxiety on this important point. Mr Marrack, Mr Grylls junr. and our Mr Middleton undertook the parishes between this place and Truro, and the latter came here last evening to report progress and a very satisfactory report it was. The increased number of voters will be very small in the rural districts, but where they had been it was greatly in our favour and what is more, the Liberals have for once been first in the field and they could hear of no move having been made by the Tories as to the County Registration, wh is wonderful as their organisation is so perfect in the Truro district. The friend to whom I wrote about Mr Paynter[1] says: 'Mr Reginald Paynter at present resides with his Mother, Mrs Paynter

38 Onslow Square
Brompton

'He is the owner of Boskenna'. Mr W Bolitho writes me word that ... [letter incomplete]

---

1. Reginald Paynter (1831–78) was the son of Thomas and Anne Paynter of Boskenna.

PV 35/49/2

NOTES WRITTEN BY A.P. VIVIAN

G Noakes Esq[r] Manager of
Gt Wheal Vor
184 Gresham House
Old Broad Street

Edward King
22 Austin Friars

P.W. Thomas & Sons
48 Threadneedle St
(Miners about Redruth)

Messrs Taylor etc
(6 Queen St Place E.C.?)
their manager in Cornwall
Mr Bennett of Falmouth

Ld Kimberley (Smith & Roberts agent)
Falmouth

Ld Cowley
his steward Tresidder
Property about St Ives

Edward Heard
West Briton Office
private
knowledge of the family
assistance of the *West Briton*

PV 35/52

H.S. Stokes to A.P. Vivian

Bodmin, 9 July 1868

My dear sir,

I am only too well pleased to be in any degree enabled to further your cause, which seems now in need of no such small assistance.

I send you a list of polling districts and places, which may prove useful to you. There should be a properly organised staff for each District.

Is it necessary for yr address to continue to appear every week? I fancy not; you will find the expence very great. You may discontinue for a time, and then advtze again. As regards Capt. Vivian,[1] I know well you would not intentionally do harm; and I believe no mischief has been done.

---

1. A.P.V.'s cousin, Captain J.C.W. Vivian, the Truro MP.

PV 35/53

Henry Grylls to A.P. Vivian

Moreton House, Redruth, 10 July 1868

My dear Sir,

I have received Mr Peters [sic] unique letter to you—and shall file it as a great curiosity—

Yesterday I was at the meetings of the Local Committees for Penzance and Hayle districts. Business was well conducted in both cases and I believe the Registration will be completed in the West within the next 5 or 6 days. There were meetings also at Truro, Falmouth and Penryn yesty—but I have not heard particulars. No doubt all will be right. We had a large and zealous meeting at Penzance—the Mayor in the Chair—Mr Cornish Secretary—Sub Committee appointed for 8 districts. I never saw better business men—and so also at Hayle Mr W. Harvey[91] in the Chair—and parties present undertook to see the three parishes registered of the District.

---

1. William Harvey (1805–?) of Hayle, J.P., partner in the mercantile and engineering firm of Harvey & Co., Hayle.

PV 35/55/1–2

S.T.G. Downing to A.P. Vivian (London)

Redruth, 10 July 1868

My dear Sir

Various Committee Meetings were held yesterday and a capital feeling was shown by all parties.

At Hayle Mr William Harvey has himself gone through the lists and there will be very large additions to the Liberal voters in that district.

I have put matters right at Helston and everything is now smooth there.

Mr Grylls was at Penzance yesterday and reports favourably and I have also heard from that quarter most satisfactorily.

The point that gives me the most trouble now, is to be satisfied that none but liberals are claimed for and this point requires great care for some of our Committee—men in their zeal would put upon the lists persons of doubtful politics with the hope that they will ultimately go right! But of course—with my knowledge of the views of the different landed proprietors and other influential persons who could bring—should there be an opposition—adverse influences to bear, I am able to correct this over zeal.[1] The time is limited but we have made and are making very great progress—in fact most satisfactory progress.

Basset having retired has been a great service to us in Illogan, Camborne and Gwinear for whilst many of his Tenants who are liberals would not have liked to have voted against him personally, they say they don't feel legally bound to vote for any other tory and as to most of them they have been already secured for you.

P.S. Do you know, or can you get introduced to, Mr T.D. Acland[2] the member for North Devon? He has a good estate in Crantock and Newlyn East (both in the Western Division) and his tenants would like to know if you have his support.

Mr H.A. Bruce would probably know Mr Acland well, as the latter is great on Education!

---

1. Because West Cornwall was uncontested from 1832 to 1885, there is no way of testing Downing's assumption that some large landowners could exert influence over voters.
2. T.D. Acland (1809–98), of Broadclyst, Devon. M.P. West Somerset 1837–47, North Devon 1865–85, West Somerset 1885–6. The Aclands owned more than 5,000 acres in Cornwall.

PV 35/54

J.M. Williams to A.P. Vivian

Burncoose, Perranarworthal, Cornwall, 12 July 1868

My Dear Sir.

I am obliged for your letters of the 10th and 11th Inst—I spent two to three hours yesterday with Mr Grylls and Downing about the Registration—I hope every proper exertion is being used—I was not satisfied about Helston and left Mr Downing with the understanding that he is to go there on Monday.—If Robartes signs a requisition to bring forward B.W. for East Cornwall and thereby attempting to turn out Kendall, I believe we shall have a very severe contest for both Divisions of our County.—I have pledged myself to support Sir J. Trelawny[1] but I do not intend to commit myself any further at present.—I understand Mr Fortescue of Bocconoc says he shall subscribe one thousand Ponds [sic] to support Mr Kendall in the event of a Contest.—We have not heard of any one attending to the Registration on the other side.—

1. Sir John Trelawny (1816–85), of Trelawne, J.P., D.L., and Vice and Deputy Warden of Stannaries. Liberal MP for Tavistock 1843–52, 1857–65, and for East Cornwall 1868–74.

PV 35/57

S.T.G. Downing to A.P. Vivian

Redruth, 13 July 1868

My dear Sir

I am much obliged for your letter

On consideration I agree with you as to the advertisements, I will discontinue them in the Daily papers on Wednesday, allowing them to appear in the weekly papers until the end of the month.

I am going to Helston this morning, our friends there want discretion and I am afraid unless watched may alarm the Trelowarren Baronet.[1]

Mr Williams had a long conference with me on Saturday and concurred in the view that on the whole the Registration is proceeding very satisfactorily. The tory party are quite '<u>still and quiet</u>' in the Western Division, but are very angry at what is going on in the Eastern.

1. The reference is to Sir Richard Vyvyan (1800–79) of Trelowarren, Sheriff 1840, ultra-Tory, later Conservative MP, for Cornwall 1825–31, Okehampton 1831–2, Bristol 1832–7, and Helston 1841–57. Vyvyan had long been one of the most powerful members of the Cornwall Conservatives, sometimes using his considerable influence *against* the party as he did in 1857 in West Cornwall.

PV 35/56

JOHN ST AUBYN TO A.P. VIVIAN

London, 14 July 1868

My dear Vivian

Will you read and return to me the enclosed which I got this morning. Had you not better yourself write a line to Cock?[1]

We cannot very well do without him at Truro as there is no one else of any importance among the liberal professional men, and Cock has always been a good friend to the cause; and we should not offend anyone if it can be avoided.

This letter is in answer to a remark from Mr Cornish that Mr Cock had returned no answer to the offer of a joint retainer from himself and Mr Downing.

1. Francis Hearle Cock, solicitor, Truro, and onetime Town Clerk.

PV 35/58

EDWARD VIVIAN TO A.P. VIVIAN

Woodfield, 14 July 1868

My Dear Cousin

I ought before this to have answered your letter saying that you had telegraphed to me your intended visit to St Ives.

I never received it [gap] have had much pleasure in accompanying you, although I had given up the contest for the borough. I was very glad to hear from Revd Mr Drake[1] and other friends there that you had so good a reception. Mr W. Bolitho declined the requisition to him on the ground of ill health. A second very eligible candidate hesitates to accept it and I think it not improbable that I may again revive my candidature having given them an opportunity of obtaining some one with local influence to set free the voters; this seems to have re-united all parties, and if I should find that I have a good chance I should be very willing to return to the borough.

My special object in now writing is to ask whether you could influence Mr Cornish (Rodd and Cornish of Penzance) who is I believe retained by yourself and Mr St Aubyn, to allow the tenantry on Mr Tyringham's and Mrs Davies Gilbert's[2] properties to vote uncontrolled. They are nearly all Liberals and Mrs Gilbert wrote to each of her tenants last time saying that she wished them to exercise their own discretion but that she should be much gratified by their supporting me. They had instructions from Mr Cornish's office to vote for Mr Paull[3] and were compelled to do so, which quite turned the election.[4]

On Thursday next the Liberal Committee are to decide upon a candidate. I strongly support one who is not yet publicly announced but if he should decline I shall probably be again invited. In either case Cornish's neutrality would be of great importance.

I hope we shall meet at least at the election. We have some prospect of a Liberal for East Devon.

---

1. Reverend Drake, B.A., Cambridge 1843, rector (?) of Halsetown 1846–73, then rector of Ruan Lanihorne 1877–?
2. Both familes owned valuable property in St Ives, and in the parishes adjoining the town.
3. Henry Paull (1822–?), contested St Ives 1852, and was Conservative MP for St Ives 1857–68.
4. The result of the 1865 election at St Ives was: Henry Paull (Cons) 233, Edward Vivian (Lib) 177.

PV 35/59

S.T.G. Downing to A.P. Vivian (South Wales)

Redruth, 14 July 1868

My dear Sir

Assuming Mr Vivian, Mr Graham Vivian and yourself to be 'Vivian & Sons' you are all enabled to qualify for the Wharf and yards at Devoran.[1] I send claims and if I am right that you are all members of 'Vivian & Sons' kindly sign yours and return it to me—and also fill in your brother's number in Belgrave Square and also the names and address of Mr Graham Vivian and request him to sign and forward the claims to me by the first post. Your Brothers might like to be able to support you by their votes, and so too, you might give a complimentary plumper to St Aubyn, receiving one from him in return if needs be.

I forwarded to you at 5 Buckingham Gate this morning a copy of Mr St Aubyn's address, lest you should have left town I now send another copy.

Your conversation with Mr Robartes did much good, for he at once wrote to Mr Jenkins [sic] (his agent) to assist me to the uttermost in the 'South Country'

Did you see Mr Acland before you left London?

---

1. Presumably 'Mr Vivian' referred to Richard Glynn Vivian, A.P.V.'s youngest brother. (See letter of 17 July 1868). Devoran was a small port on Restronguet Creek, about six miles south of Truro.

PV 35/60/1–2

S.T.G. Downing to A.P. Vivian

Redruth, 14 July 1868

My dear Sir

I am much obliged for your letter of yesterday's date.

In reply to your Enquiry as to the Registration, I think I can say that nothing can be more satisfactory than the way in which it is progressing in the Redruth Falmouth Penzance & Truro districts in most places the question who shall be asked to claim has been discussed and finally settled after anxious deliberation with the best informed persons in each locality.

With reference even to Helston I don't think there is any cause for great uneasiness, for altho our professional friends there don't agree very well amongst themselves Mr Wm Grylls (who was kind eno to go there with me yesterday) concurs in my view that the steps that have been taken to protect the liberal interest so far as the registration is concerned have been prudent and at a meeting to be held tomorrow of the Committee from each parish and the professional men I trust the names to be put on the lists will be settled: so that they will have the rest of the week to get the claims properly signed.

We have the great advantage in the 'South Country' that most of the farmers are Wesleyans and from the time that Mr W. Bickford Smith spoke at the great Camborne meeting (on the 16 June) in the name of his father and the 20,000 male Wesleyans in the division, followed as he was by Dr Lyth (the superintendent Minister) coming forward at the Redruth meeting and proposing the vote of Confidence in you, the Wesleyans have been with us to a man. I need not point out to you the vast importance of this fact.

I obtained a sight this morning of St Aubyn's address, it is not yet in print. You will find a copy enclosed.

I note that you leave tomorrow for Wales and will until further advised address you at Glanafon.

PV 35/61/1–2

S.T.G. Downing to A.P. Vivian

Redruth, 15 July 1868

My dear Sir

I am obliged for your letter of yesterday. Don't be at all uneasy either 1st as to the Registration or 2nd your Election.

On the first point every thing is proceeding admirably. I personally worked 16 hours out of the last 24 but am bound to say that in some places our volunteer committee men worked equally as long.

They at last all see too, that great care must be taken to put up the right persons only, and that the cautions I have given them on that head have not been thrown away.

Upwards of 100 votes will be added to the Gwennap lists upon Mr J.M.W's interest: and his following will be largely increased in the Redruth, Stithians, Wendron, St Agnes and other districts.

Mr Robartes' influence will be increased by 60 in Illogan and also largely in Devoran and in the South Country.

Lord Falmouth's rental will also now have its legitimate influence.[1]

But in addition to the above we have a great increase throughout the division of the independent voters, Wesleyans and others who as 12 £ occupiers will now acquire votes and who will support you thoroughly.

Coming now to the second point mainly your Election, I think you may rest satisfied that you are to have an unopposed return! My agents from all the different parishes inform me that there is not a trace up to last night of any attempt on the part of the tories to strengthen themselves on the register and in addition to this great fact, I am assured by the legal Gent^{n} who would probably hold the Retainer of any tory that there is no intention on their part to fight, of course the statement does not bind them not to oppose, but I don't think they would go out of their way to deceive us.

[P.S.] As something might turn up please keep me duly advised of your movements as I shall then know where to telegram if needs be to you.

---

1. Legitimate influence, as opposed to illegitimate influence, derived from rank, wealth, and the deferential relationship between landlord and tenant, although not necessarily one of forelock-tugging subservience. In these circumstances landlords such as Lord Falmouth could make their political preferences known to their tenants, without necessarily demanding their votes.

PV 35/62/1–2

S.T.G. Downing to A.P. Vivian (Private)

Redruth, 17 July 1868

My dear Sir

I am much obliged for your letter of yesterday.

1st as to such.

You have forgotten to send me a copy of your letter to Mr Cock. Kindly let me have it as I should like to take exactly the same grounds with him that you have taken—The fact is that Cock is the retained solicitor in the Boro of Truro of Augustus Smith and consequently all the 'advanced liberals' there are very suspicious of him. When I found this was the case I thought the right course would be to retain him but if possible to do the work by Committees and without his professional assistance. I did not however say what my plan was but simply remarked that Mr Cock was surely entitled to be treated as a 'Whig' at least, and that he would receive a retainer like the other liberal solicitors and the retainer was accordingly sent him at the same time as to the others.

The Truro meeting was got up by Blee, Reynolds and the other members of our committee there, Marrack simply attending as representing Lord Falmouth.

In the country parishes too, in which Lord Falmouth's Estates are situate [sic] it was also necessary that Marrack should attend to the registration, but in Truro itself, the work is being done by a committee assisted by the Secretary to the Truro Boro registration Society, Mr Courtney.[1]

Altho' therefore we have lost nothing by our not having employed Mr Cock in the registration still it is clearly our policy to carry every body with us and as soon as I receive a copy of your letter to him I will go to Truro and I dare say I shall be able to smooth over the ruffled feathers!

2nd. The yards at Devoran are rated at 48/- so that they will exactly support 4 votes and I enclose claim for Mr Richard Glynn Vivian's signature. As time is short will you send this claim when signed to Mr Sampson at Devoran and instruct him to hand it to the overseer of Feock on Monday without fail.

3rd Whether Mr Hussey's Truro qualification is good will depend on whether it is of such a description as to confer on him the right to vote for the Borough for if so whether his name be as a matter of fact on the Boro list or not, he can't qualify for the County. If there be a building on the Garden, the claim for the County would be bad, but if there be no building and the land is worth 12£ a year it would give—being freehold—a County Vote (Daniel v Coulstin 97 M & G 122)

All goes well with the registration—not a single move on the part of the tories up to this day and it is now for all practical purposes too late! As far as our own work is concerned you can understand the difficulty of driving (and yet not seeming to drive!) a team composed in some places of Committees—in others of honorary volunteers—in others of non professional and in the remainder of professional agents, but I trust you will be satisfied with the result when the new lists are published.

[P.S.] Sir R R Vyvyan is still talking of Augustus Smith, but no one seems to see that Gent^{ms} [sic] merits but Sir R R V himself.

---

1. Possibly Matthew Courtney (1808–80) of Truro.

PV 35/63

T. Hearle Cock to A.P. Vivian

Truro, 18 July 1868

Dear Sir

I thank you for your letter of the 16th inst. and regret that you should have the trouble to write on the subject referred to in it. I was of course fully satisfied that individually you were in entire ignorance of what had taken place, and, but for the express wishes, of some of my friends and Clients I should not have mentioned the reasons for my un [sic] acceptance of the Retainer offered. They however, feeling the slight as much as I did, considered for my own sake professionally that the reasons should be given and hence by letter to Mr Cornish. You will I am sure feel that after, in the spring of the year, having arranged with that gentleman to take the entire management of this Polling district, I had some reason to complain on finding that instead of any instruction having been given to me of the Meeting, a Solicitor of known Conservative principles was summoned to Redruth on the previous day and retained to assist in introducing you to the Meeting. My professional duties are already sufficiently onerous to make me hesitate before entering on Electioneering work but I do feel that as the only Solicitor here on the Liberal side, the compliment at least might have been paid to me.[1]

1. This, and the earlier letter from J.T.H. Peter (see 35/50/1–2 and 35/53) reveal the personal sensitivities which had to be dealt with prior to elections.

PV 35/64/1–2

S.T.G. Downing to A.P. Vivian

Redruth, 18 July 1868

My dear Sir

The correspondence between Mr Cock and Mr Grylls (copy of which—and also Mr Reynolds letter Mr Grylls has sent you) will show you the position of the matter and also why Mr St Aubyn was communicated with by Cornish—It appears that some months ago Cornish retained Cock, <u>but this could only have been for Mr St Aubyn</u>, as Cornish has never had any authority to act for <u>the Liberal</u> party.

As to Mr Brydges Willyams that Gent^{m} was very distinct in his instructions to me, which were—if he started—to endeavour to get Marrack to act at Truro. In fact entre nous, B W had a very indifferent opinion of Mr Cock and was most anxious that matters should not be placed in his hands <u>if Marrack would consent to act</u>.

The fact that Marrack has been looked upon as a Conservative Solicitor is not to the point, if he be really a liberal and if he be willing to exert his client's (Lord Falmouth's) interest to the utmost for that cause.

I have explained to you that no solicitor was consulted about the Truro meeting, Marrack attending only at Lord Falmouth's request.

Mr Cock's name was placed on the Committee at the same time as Mr Roscorla[1] and all the other solicitors and he received his retainer by the same post as Marrack received his

It never occurred to Mr St Aubyn or Cornish that we would get Marrack to act for us, or that the great influence he can exert would be thrown into our scale, and so they feel bound to protect the person to whom our retainer was offered. In fact Cornish knows that on a push if we had had a contest Marrack would lean with me for you, whilst Cock would probably lean with Cornish for St Aubyn, and at 3 o'clock on the polling day (if the Tories had been strong eno' to run us close for one seat) this might be important! However pray rely on my tact to set this matter right, in fact I trust that when Cock finds that Marrack was with me the day before the Truro meeting with reference to Lord Falmouth's rental that with reference to the public meeting, he will be satisfied!

I hardly think there is anything to report, all the claims will be delivered on Monday and the last batch is now leaving the office. For the claimants registered there is not a breath of opposition and everybody assumes that there will be no contest.

Mr Grenfell starts for St Ives, he will have a difficult and expensive fight, if Paull has money eno' to go to the poll.

---

1. John Roscorla (1798–1874), articled to E.H. Rodd, solicitor, 1838, Penzance. Later Coroner at Penzance.

PV 35/65

Henry Grylls to A.P. Vivian

Moreton House, Redruth, 19 July 1868

My dear Sir.

I received the enclosed letter from Mr Reynolds, ex Mayor of Truro, and have written Mr Cock an explanation—a copy of which I beg to hand you. I have troubled you with this Correspondence from having heard the Subject had come to your knowledge from another quarter.

The Registration is going on well, showing by letters received from several parties a great relative accession of strength to the Liberal votes

PV 35/66

Henry Grylls to A.P. Vivian

Moreton House, Redruth, 22 July 1868

My Dear Sir,

I am in receipt of your favor of the 21st Instant—and have no doubt Mr Cock will be satisfied with the explanations. Within a few days I hope to receive a return from the different districts, of the result of the labours of the Committees in reference to the Registration, of which you shall hear by first post. I have requested Mr Heard to leave out Mr Peter's name from the Committee in the *West Briton*. There has been no effort made, I believe, by the Tories to get their friends (if they have any?) on the Registration.

I believe the Registration of new voters will greatly increase the Liberal strength, which has been ever since 1832 overwhelming.[1]

1. Grylls may not have been correct in his assessment of the register, because in the late 1830s the Conservatives made a sustained effort to add voters to the registers. This may have been one reason for the Conservative Lord Boscawen Rose's uncontested election in 1841.

PV 35/68

S.T.G. Downing to A.P. Vivian

Redruth, 22 July 1868

My dear Sir,

I am obliged for your letter of yesterday's date.

I am getting out the rough estimate of the result of the registration so far as we have gone but of course the Tories may (altho' I don't believe they will) still take the field with objections![1]

You shall have the estimate at the earliest moment. In the meantime some of the larger parishes have been gone thro' and they stand roughly thus.

St Just total registered voters including the old and new qualifications 306 of which!

Liberals		255	
Tories		51	306
Penzance			500
Liberals say	400		
Tories	100		500
Redruth			520
Liberals	460		
Tories at most	60		520
Camborne			525
Liberals	— 350		
Tories	— 175		525
St Agnes			300
Liberals	200		
Tories	100		300

1. The closing date for claims and objections to be lodged with the overseers was 31 July. As the correspondence indicates, the West Cornwall Liberals were well organized from the beginning of the month, whereas the Conservatives had no organization in place—because they had no candidate and therefore no party agent or committee.

PV 35/71/1–3

E.M. Williams to A.P. Vivian

London, 23 July 1868

Dear Mr Vivian.

My Husband hopes to write to you by tomorrow's post from Redruth about Mr Cock's letter after he has shown it to Mr Downing; his own opinion is that Mr Cock's influence is so slight and his character for truthfulness so indifferent that it is not worth yr. while to take any more trouble about him, especially as you cannot possibly be accountable for any steps taken by Mr Cornish 'in the spring'. I called on Mrs Paynter yesterday but rather to my dismay she at once announced herself to be a 'decided Tory'; I reminded her that Mr Paynter had offered his support to my Father-in-law[1] and afterwards to my Husband if he would come forward so that we had some grounds for hoping that she would support you. She answered very kindly that knowing her Husband's wishes respecting my Husband, she should have felt bound to use her influence on his behalf but could not do so for any other Liberals, but that she 'wished you success' and advised me to try and secure Mr Bevan's interest (he is her tenant at Boskenna) for you, as she thought it was very great. I afterwards told Lady Falmouth[2] this and she promised to write to Mr Bevan and endeavour to make him pledge himself to do nothing, wh[ich] she says is the best we can hope for, from him. Lady F seems very pleased with the present State of things but wishes much that the election could come off now and thinks we must be constantly on the lookout, as the Carlton Club has £200,000 to spend on the elections and John Jope Rogers may be induced to come forward yet, or even Sir R^{d} Vyvyan;[3] I told her that I did not fear the latter and 'greatest evil that could happen' as she termed it, unless Sir R Vyvyan's anger was aroused by an attack on Mr Kendall's seat, wh[ich] as she knew was the cause of his refusing his support to Mr Tremayne in 1857,[4] but both she and Lord Falmouth (with whom Mr Williams has just been) have had accounts from Cornwall within a day or two wh make them believe that two Liberals can easily be returned in the Eastern division, wh we greatly doubt. Thanks to Lady Augusta's influence my uncle is exerting himself warmly and successfully to 'smooth matters' in the South Country.[5] From what Lady Falmouth told me of Mr Bolitho's somewhat peculiar letter to her, it is also entirely to Lady Augusta that you owe such support as he may give you! But Lady F thinks (and evidently wishes) that in the improbable event of there being any doubt about the return of two Liberals, your return is perfectly certain. We go to Cornwall to-night and although my Husband will spend tomorrow at Pengreep and Redruth our address will be Caerhays for the present. Please remember me most kindly to Lady Augusta and believe me,

---

1. Elizabeth Williams's father-in-law was Michael Williams, the former Liberal member for West Cornwall.
2. As this letter reveals, Elizabeth Williams and Lady Falmouth were politically astute, and influential in building support for A.P.V.
3. Apart from the success of Lord Boscawen Rose (later 5th Viscount Falmouth) in 1841, the Conservatives never contested West Cornwall between 1832 and 1885. Yet at almost every general election after 1841 there was public discussion of the likelihood of a Conservative standing—usually a member of the Basset or Williams families. 1868 was no different!

4. John Tremayne (1825–1901) Conservative MP for East Cornwall 1874–80, and South Devon 1884–5, was a shortlived candidate for West Cornwall in 1857. Sir Richard Vyvyan refused to support Tremayne after he found he was opposing Kendall's re-election for East Cornwall.
5. E.M. Williams's uncle was Richard Davey, the retiring Liberal M.P. for West Cornwall.

PV 35/73

Michael H. Williams[1] to Edward Budd

24 July 1868

My Dear Sir

I only received your note this morning and had I known yesterday you wished to see me would have called in as I was in the City.— I was in Switzerland with Mrs Williams when the little excitement was going on in Cornwall and should be there now but the illness of one of our children brought us back, so we leave tomorrow for home.

---

1. Michael Henry Williams (1823–1902) of Tredrea and later Pencalenick, J.P. and D.L., Sheriff 1879. He was a partner in Williams, Williams and Grylls, the Falmouth Bank, and was one of J.M. Williams's younger brothers.

PV 35/69

A.P. Vivian to S.T.G. Downing (copy)

Redruth, 25 July 1868

My Dear Sir

I duly received your letter of the 22nd inst and was very glad to hear the satisfactory results of the Registration in those parishes which you were able to give me. Camborne, Truro and Helston will I conclude be our weakest points,[1] & as soon as you get at any approximate results at this I shall be anxious to have them.

I do not intend replying to Mr Cock's letter as Mr J.M. Williams informed me in his letter of yesterday that you will see him and set the matter straight when you are next at Truro.

I am very glad to hear of no signs of stir on the enemy's side as yet.

---

1. Truro and Helston each had large numbers of Conservative voters, and longstanding party organization. Usually the Liberals and Conservatives shared Truro's two seats after 1832, while at Helston the latter party dominated at all elections except 1857 and 1865.

PV 35/70/1–2

S.T.G. Downing to A.P. Vivian

Redruth, 25 July 1868

My dear Sir.

Mr Williams was kind eno' yesterday to say he would write you as to Cock's letter or I should have done so. Cock very well knows that I was not aware at the time we held our Truro meeting that Cornish had previously released him for St Aubyn. I certainly never retained him for Mr Brydges Willyams! I am confident Cock will be but too glad to give us his services, such as they are, and to take the retainer, and perhaps beyond a civil line informing him that you had referred the matter to me you need not trouble yourself any further about him.

Mr B W has at last started for the Eastern division. I went up on Thursday to be with him when the requisition was presented, and to settle his address, but he is well aware I shall not act for him in the Eastern division for if a contest should spring up in the West you would require my undivided services. In view of a fight in the East B W will allow us to have all his interest (including the Miners' Bank)[1] in the West, so that to that extent his candidature in the East is advantageous.

I still think there is not the smallest chance of a Contest in the West but of course something might unexpectedly arise.

I am not yet able to send you the estimate of proportion of liberals to tories on the new lists throughout the division (the agricultural overseer takes a long time to move!) but at the earliest moment possible you shall be furnished with the figures.

1. Brydges Willyams's connection with the Miners' Bank (Truro and St Columb) is uncertain. His father was a senior partner in the Bank in 1868, and therefore the family may have enjoyed some influence with other partners and customers.

PV 35/72/1–2

E.M. Williams to A.P. Vivian

Caerhays Castle, St Austell, 26 July 1868

Dear Mr Vivian.

We thank you for your letters of the 24th and 25th Insts;—my Husband, who came here yesterday, desires me to say that he has advised Mr Downing in the strongest possible way to avoid any proceeding that might excite the anger of the Tories and not to accept a retainer in East Cornwall. As Brydges Willyams [sic] address only appeared yesterday, we cannot yet judge what effect his decision to come forward will have on the other side. I see by the papers that Mr J H Buller[1] was at the Exeter Assizes, so I have written to his cousin, Mrs Craufurd (who is the only one of his relatives that I know on the right side) to ask how we can best get at him and obtain his support for you; I mentioned that we were told that he was abroad, otherwise you would have arranged to get an introduction to him ere this. I hope that this was right, as I was not sure whether you had seen him in town? but in any case I have always understood that Mrs Craufurd has very great influence with him, so no great harm can come from my letter. Did you call on Mr Augustus Stephens[2] and have you seen the letter from him wh was read at the St Ives Meeting a-propos of Mr Grenfell?[3] Mr Grenfell is certainly much indebted to you for yr endeavours to make Mr St Aubyn use his influence with Mr Cornish and try to get him to act on the right side at the next election.[4] Mr Williams met Mr Grenfell in the Train yesterday on his way back to Town where he was summoned by his wife's illness. But he hopes to return in a few days to Cornwall; and it will probably be a very severe contest at St Ives. Mr T.S. Bolitho seems to have taken the same line with Mr Grenfell as he did with you and promised him his own vote only. We expect to return to Pengreep on Tuesday evening and remain there for two days.

1. J.H. Buller (1835–74) of Downes, Devon.
2. John Augustus Stephens (1812–?) of St Ives. Owned 1,200 acres in and near the town.
3. R.H. Grenfell (1824–1902), was a partner in Pascoe, Grenfell and Sons, Copper Smelters and Manufacturers. He was Liberal MP for Stoke 1862–8, and contested South West Lancashire in 1868 and Barnstaple in 1880.
4. See above, PV 35/27, 35/20 and 35/38.

PV 35/74

E.M. Williams to A.P. Vivian

Caerhays Castle, St Austell, 28 July 1868

Dear Mr Vivian.

Mr Williams thinks that it is very desirable that you should write to Mr Augustus Stephens and tell him that you had called on him in the hope of obtaining his support, and he thinks that you will agree in this opinion when you have read the enclosed extracts from the *West Briton* of last week and the *Mercury* of yesterday. Mr Stephens's support is the more important as the Praed or Tyringham[1] interest in the same neighbourhood will probably be influenced as Mr Marriott (who married Miss Praed) may choose and that of course would be on the Tory side.[2]

I also enclose an extract from Mr Bain's copied letter just received, tho' probably Mr Budd has written you to the same effect; it is so far satisfactory that if 'our' Henry Williams meant to support a Tory, he would scarcely have dated his letter from the Reform Club?[3] I was at St Austell yesterday, but unluckily Mr Henry Shilson and Mr Morcom were away ... [incomplete]

[page/s missing]

1. The Tyringham family owned more than 3,000 acres in Cornwall, mostly in the St Ives area. No information is available for the Praeds.
2. Edmund Marriott was the Basset (of Tehidy) family's steward.
3. This reference is probably to Michael Henry Williams (1823–1902) of Tredrea, younger brother of J.M. Williams.

PV 35/79

W. Shilson to A.P. Vivian

Tremough, Penryn, 28 July 1868

My dear Sir

I was very pleased to hear that you had received Mr Rashleigh's cordial promise of support;[1] as he possesses considerable influence in both divisions of the County.

Mr Robartes' Agent, Mr Jenkin, has carefully attended to the registration, so far as his Tenantry are concerned.

With regard to your present position and prospects I am happy to say that subsequent events have confirmed the opinion which I took occasion to express at the public meeting at Penryn, namely that there would not be any opposition to your return. I see no reason to alter that opinion; and even if I sh^{d}' be wrong, I am most fully convinced that the influential support which you have received is quite sufficient to overrun all opposition.

1. William Rashleigh of Menabilly. See 35/48/1–2.

PV 35/75

E.M. Williams to A.P. Vivian

Pengreep, Perranarworthal, 29 July 1868

Dear Mr Vivian.

I return Henry Williams's letter from wh I gather that in any case you may reckon upon his neutrality and that if anything should happen to his uncle before the election, you would have his support; I fancy that he purposely dated his letter from the Reform Club so that he might have a fair excuse for not voting for a Tory, if Sir W and George Williams should press him to do so.[1] Sir W.W. is 'putting on the screw' on behalf of Mr Paull, wherever he can, in the St Ives district, so we must not reckon upon his being too weak and infirm to interfere. Mr Williams has gone to Redruth and will I think, be in time to write you from there. We came down in the train with P.P. Smith last night and my Husband reported him to be in a very subdued frame of mind and a friend of his to whom I was talking said 'you have it all your own way in the West.'

Excuse a very hurried note and with kindest regards to Lady Augusta and yourself, believe me,

---

1. William Williams (1791–1870) of Tregullow, was the youngest brother of the Liberal MP Michael Williams. William, a Conservative, was a partner in Williams, Foster & Co., copper smelters, Swansea. He was also a partner in the Cornish Bank, along with several of his relatives including his brother George (1827–91), J.P., D.L., and Sheriff 1875.

PV 35/78

A.P. Vivian to Augustus Stevens[1] [sic]

Glanafon, Taibach, South Wales, 31 July 1868

Dear Sir.

Having been selected by the Liberal party of the Western Division of Cornwall as one of their candidates in conjunction with Mr John St Aubyn I was anxious whilst in London some short time ago to solicit your support for this purpose. I called on you at your residence but was unfortunate in not finding you at home. I trust however at some future time I may again have an opportunity of making your acquaintance.

As to my politics I feel I need not here trouble you with them, my Address having appeared so frequently in the leading County Papers, beside the reports of the various public meetings which I attended in the principle [sic] towns of the Division.

1. In 1867 John Augustus Stephens succeeded his brother Henry Lewis Stephens, who was a partner in Williams, Foster & Co., Swansea.

PV 35/81/1–2

E.M. Williams to A.P. Vivian

Pengreep, Perranarworthal, 31 July 1868

Dear Mr Vivian.

Everything continues quiet as regards W Cornwall. I met Mrs Enys on Wednesday and she asked in the kindest way for Lady Augusta and yourself and expressed great satisfaction at your 'undoubted success'; she said that Mrs Gilbert was highly indignant at Rodd and Cornish's conduct in influencing her tenants about St Ives for Mr Paull and had consulted Mr Enys as to the best way of preventing them from repeating such conduct, as she is always absent from Cornwall during the Autumn.[1] This shows that the report that the Enys interest would be against you was quite unfounded, at any rate if old Mr Enys's life is prolonged. Mrs Henry Williams[2] happened to be calling at the place where I met Mrs Enys and must have overheard some of the very satisfactory remarks that she made about you and your success, wh was lucky, as both Mr and Mrs Henry Williams are apt to 'follow the stream' and the opinions wh prevail at Enys (wh is very near Tredrea) greatly influence theirs on all points.[3]

Mr Downing seems anxious that you should come down again as soon as any public meeting of any kind offers a good excuse for doing so, as Mr St Aubyn and Brydges Willyams evidently intend to keep themselves before the public, but I shall be better able to write to Lady Augusta about this a few days hence as I am going to two or three large parties at different parts of the County where I must meet some of our way of thinking, who will give better advice than a lawyer can on that point.

Mr Williams heard nothing new at Truro where he attended the Ticketing yesterday; we both go to Caerhays this evening and shall remain there until Wednesday or Thursday. Mrs Enys took <u>practical</u>

interest in yr affairs and advised that if Mrs Craufurd could not help us with her cousin (as she is perhaps invalided by now) you should write to him yourself; she was also much pleased that you had seen Mrs Pendarves.

---

1. Obviously John St Aubyn was unsuccessful in his efforts to stop Cornish influencing Mrs Gilbert's tenants to vote for the St Ives Conservative candidate Henry Paull.
2. Michael Henry Williams' wife was Catherine Anne, daughter of Richard Almack of Suffolk.
3. Tredrea was approximately three miles north-west of Enys.

PV 35/83/1–2

E.M. Williams to A.P. Vivian

Caerhays Castle, St Austell, 2 August 1868

A. Pendarves Vivian
Dear Mr Vivian.

Your letter of the 31st has just followed us here and I have only time by this post (being Tuesday) to thank you for it and return the copy of yr letter to Mr A. Stephens who we think most judicious and likely to have the desired effect. I have heard from Mrs Craufurd and enclose a copy of that part of her letter wh refers to Mr J.H. Buller; she also says that Mr Craufurd and herself will be glad to help us further in any way in their power, so perhaps we may be glad to take advantage of her offer hereafter, as she has a great many relations and connections in this County and is a most popular person. Mr Williams desires me to send you the *Cornwall Gazette*, although it contains nothing about you individually. My Husband unites with me in kindest regards to Lady Augusta and yourself. ...

Extract of a letter from Mrs Craufurd [written out by EMW]

'I think Mr Pendarves Vivian should at once canvass J.H. Buller himself and his address is : 'Downes Crediton—Devon' and I believe he has no present intention of going abroad. I will write to him by this same post and explain the misunderstanding wh has prevented Mr Vivian seeking to communicate directly with him. I doubt whether I should do much good by attempting more in the way of canvassing him;—the last time I saw him, he did say that w[d] not support anyone who went for disestablishment, but I hope that that may have been only in the heat of conversation. Previous to this task I had thought of suggesting him to you as a possible candidate for W. Cornwall, but his views seemed so unsettled that I felt I had best not say anything about him. It is quite possible that since I saw him, he may have given careful consideration to the matter and may have seen reason to change the determination he then expressed, so I wish you to consider <u>this</u> as confidential. I am most anxious to do anything I can, dear Mrs Williams, and wish I could do more with my cousin but I know him so well I am afraid of doing more harm than good if I press Mr Vivian's merits too eagerly upon him.'

PV 35/82

A. Stephens to A.P. Vivian

London, 4 August 1868

Dear Sir

I beg to acknowledge your favour and to mention that I was not aware that you had done me the honor to enquire for me as I had apprehended that your Card had merely been left as other Cards have been under similar circumstances. Should there be a contest for the Western Division of Cornwall of which at present I am glad that there appears no sign I shall be happy to give you what support I can in conjunction with Mr St Aubyn.

PV 35/84

A.P. Vivian to Augustus Stephens

Glanafon, Taibach, South Wales, 7 August 1868

Correct copy—APV

Dear Sir

I must thank you sincerely for your kind letter of the 4th inst. When I called on you in London I was very much disappointed at not finding you at home, and loosing [sic] that opportunity of personally making your acquaintance I left a message to this effect with the servant who opened the door but can easily imagine that messages must occasionally escape their memories.

PV 35/85

Henry Grylls to A.P. Vivian

Moreton House, Redruth, 8 August 1868

My Dear Sir

The returns are not coming in as fast as could be wished, but as far as received they are most satisfactory to the Liberal cause. I beg to enclose a Copy of the Circular sent to the different districts and the returns so far show full 7/8th in your favor. You shall be furnished, either by Mr Downing or myself, with the completed Lists as soon as possible.

P.S. The 'Liberal cause' is very hopeful in the Eastern Division. I do not think Mr Kendal [sic] has any chance of success. This is very gratifying—to retain our position in the 'West' and rescue a Seat in the 'East' is glorious.[1]

1. Nicholas Kendall, sitting Conservative MP for East Cornwall, was being continuously criticized by farmers (his former allies) in particular for initiating a salary increase for the County Gaol's Governor. The farmers had elected Kendall as a protectionist in 1852.

PV 35/88

S.T.G. Downing to A.P. Vivian

Redruth, 13 August 1868

My dear Sir

Looking at the way in which the Penz^{ce} [Penzance] people have supported you—I should advise you to follow St Aubyn's lead and send them £2-2-0 for their fireworks.

St Aubyn is not generally <u>too</u> liberal and in any event on the eve of your <u>first</u> election it is better you should pay away a few guineas too much than give anyone offence. When you are firmly in the seat there will be no occasion to subscribe to many of the objects which <u>just now</u> it would be unwise to neglect. Mr Coulson Cornish is a respectable man—he is not however St Aubyn's agent who is called Thomas Cornish.

There is no reason whatever why your address should appear in the <u>East</u> *Cornwall Gazette*. In fact I propose to withdraw it from the Truro papers very shortly, probably as soon as the last day for serving notice of objection has passed.

You may rely on my looking after the expenses as narrowly as possible—in fact I should not do my duty to you if I neglected your interests in that respect. I am able to be a little bolder too in this respect, for every day renders the chance of a contest more improbable.

PV 35/87

J.M. Williams to A.P. Vivian

Burncoose, Perranarworthal, 14 August 1868

My Dear Sir.

I fear you will begin to think me neglecting your Interest. I have written so little—but I have conferred and arranged with Mrs W to do so twice or thrice every week—I made a point of attending the Ticketing last week and yesterday—as it gave me the opportunity of seeing People of good standing from most parts of the County.—I cannot learn but one continued repetition of remarks of your increasing Popularity—from People having had more time—to make enquiries since you left and I have also heard in several ways some of the old members of the Tory Party—have admitted their chance is quite gone in the West etc. Now of the two men I have thought they might have started one—J.J. Rogers late M.P. for Helston or Mr Kendle [sic] now M.P. for Eastern Division—I heard a curious story yesterday—it came to Mr Downing from a Helston man—it was to this effect—that J.J. Rogers stated that Sir R. Vyvyan had said that if Kendall were turned out of his present seat—they ought to unite to return him for Helston—now this implies that Sir R.V. thinks he Kendall would stand no chance for West Cornwall and was seeking Rogers' cooperation to return Kendal [sic] for the Borough of Helston.—I have not interfered in the Eastern Division—nor do I at present intend to do so.—I saw Mr Northy [sic][1] of St Columb yesterday he says Brydges W is safe to be returned and Kendall no chance and I think such will be the result if Sir J^{no} Trelawny will face a Contest with firmness.—I heard a report yesterday of Mr Bassett [sic][2] coming forward as the second Tory for Truro—and a Mr Brogden from Wales[3]—Large Coal Proprietor / as the second Liberal.

---

1. William Henry Northey (1824–?), Wine and Spirit merchant of St Columb, and Mayor. A very vocal Liberal, in 1868 Northey disrupted many of Nicholas Kendall's meetings.
2. John Basset of Tehidy.

3. This may have been referring to Alexander Brogden (1825–92), an ironmaster and a Liberal who sat for Wednesbury 1868–85. The link with Wales is uncertain.

PV 35/86

S.T.G. Downing to A.P. Vivian (Bridgend)

Redruth, 15 August 1868

My dear Sir,

W^s Cornwall Electors I now enclose you the estimates.

The total of voters means the net number after deducting double entries.

You will see that from some of the Parishes there have been no returns from the Committees or Agents having charge of them, but I have been enabled to make a calculation based upon the best obtainable information and on the whole I think we may fairly assume we should poll a moiety of the votes in those Parishes. The result of the return is very satisfactory for you see it gives a clear majority of 822— to the Liberals, and I believe it will be found that I have not in any instance overestimated our strength.

Mr Cornish has not the means of making so complete an estimate nor has Mr Grylls and perhaps it will be as well if we keep it for the time to ourselves. Of course I have sent Mr John Michael [Williams] a copy

P.S. I am very anxious you should not communicate the result of the returns to Mr St Aubyn.

PV 35/89

Henry Grylls to A.P. Vivian

Moreton House, Redruth, 17 August 1868

My Dear Sir,

I am in due receipt of your favor of the 15th Instant enclosing Mr Kendall's application[1] for a Subscription to the Helston Rifle Corps, and have by this post requested that Gentleman to apply direct to you. I scarcely consider myself competent to advise the sum you should give to the various attempts to draw on you. Having begun your donations you will probably have applications from all the Regattas—Rifle Corps—Sunday Schools—Cricket Clubs etc, or most of them in the Western Division and I am surprised at the want of delicacy shown in sending these solicitations till after your election—and have no doubt they are coming principally from parties who would, in case of a contest, vote against you. Kendall of Helston is certainly of the Tory party. Two guineas in such a case would, I conceive, be generous. You will no doubt see the report in the *Western Morning News* of to-day of the meeting at Bodmin, to hear the Tory members' speech. The Rev. G. Hext married the sister of Mr Peter's wife of Chiverton and probably is, as well as his Brother in law, under petticoat Government.[2] His conduct at the Meeting will, I have no doubt, help the Liberal party, instead of injuring them.

There is not the least rumour in the West of any opposition. The returns are coming in slowly and I am handing them to Mr Downing to be put in a tabular form. I should have done this myself, but that he had received some of the returns direct, and wished to complete the list. They are, as far as I can judge, very satisfactory. There is good hope that Mr Magniac[3] may succeed in St Ives and if a Liberal can be got in for Helston and two for the Eastern Division—Cornwall will have done well for the right party.

Will you allow me to direct your attention to the article in the *Western Morning News* of today, in 4th Column of 3rd page. 'Dr Pusey and the Wesleyan Conference'. This will no doubt do much good through the Country.

---

1. John Kendall (?–1872), employed by the Helston Union Bank.
2. Possibly a member of the Hext family of Bodmin.
3. Charles Magniac (1827–91), Liberal MP for St Ives 1868–74, Bedford 1880–6. Sheriff of Bedfordshire 1877.

PV 35/90

Result of Registration—1868

Parishes		New claims and including Freeholders Leaseholders & Occupiers	Probably Liberal
Creed		22	14
St Erth		53	34
St Just	x	312	200
St Hilary	x	56	30
Ludgvan	x	133	100
Paul	x	207	150
Zennor	x	64	40
Penzance	x	495	300
Marazion	x	101	75
Sennen	x	35	30
Constantine & Mawnan		94	63
Gwinear		56	56
Penryn }		70	45
St Gluvias }		37	17
Feock }		74	72
Perran }		16	16
Stythians [sic]		56	46
Tregony		6	5
Veryan		30	24
Perranzabuloe	x	195	141
St Agnes	x	316	273
Illogan	x	152	85
Camborne	x	418	250
Gwennap	x	250	171
Redruth	x	491	400
St Mary's Truro		3	2
St Clements "		39	28
Kea		61	61
St Allen			
Kenwyn		34	34

x These include old returns
[In Henry Grylls' handwriting]

PV 35/91

Henry Grylls to A.P. Vivian

Moreton House, Redruth, 19 August 1868

My dear Sir.

The returns are not yet completed: but I thought you would like to see the List as far as known. Mr Downing suggests this should not be made public, at least till more complete—and even then it will be worthy of consideration if publicity be desirable.

The total is		3876
Liberals	2762	
Tories	1114	3876

PV 35/92–93

S.T.G. Downing to A.P. Vivian (Taibach)

Redruth, 19 August 1868

My dear Sir

I am obliged for your letter of the 18th.

As to the returns Mr Grylls got some returns from the local Committees. With reference to the new claims and he will send you a copy, but as you will see they were very imperfect. In fact the only complete returns he has are for Perranzabuloe, St Agnes, Redruth, Gwennap, Illogan, Camborne, and some of the Western Parishes. The returns sent you in my letter of the 15th however were arrived at from the following data

1st My old canvass books
2nd The returns made by the Committees
3rd By my personally going thro the list of Each Parish with some person thoroughly acquainted with the voters in that particular parish and upon whom I could thoroughly rely.

The Parishes that I have marked are Parishes from which there are no certain returns, are parishes in which there was no leading local politician so that I had nothing to rely on but the old canvass books. But from my general knowledge of these parishes I think we should at least poll one half.

I am rather anxious to keep the facts we have ascertained as to the strength of the Liberal party to ourselves. For at present I believe the Tory party to be in complete ignorance of all details. I don't think they know where to look even for their own strength!

If we give St Aubyn the information nobody knows how he may use it and I am confident he cannot get it except thro' us.

PV 35/98/1–2

S.T.G. Downing to A.P. Vivian

Redruth, 24 August 1868

My dear Sir

Polytechnic

I will write in a part or two. It would be a very good card to read a paper on some scientific subject—however I will ascertain all about the matter and write you.

Rifle Corps

The volunteer feeling is strong in the County of Cornwall and whilst after your return you will be able finally to drop subscriptions to Wrestlings fireworks etc a permanent subscription to the Rifle Volunteer movement might be a very politic thing.

It seems that there is no Western division association—the association being for the entire County.

I talked the matter over today with Mr William Grylls (who is a Volunteer) John Haze (?) and others and I gather that the more popular and better course would be to forward to the adjutant Cap^{n} Carew, Penzance, a certain sum for distribution amongst the several Companies (there are Eleven) in the Western division for an annual prize for shooting and that you should state the conditions as to ranges etc. This mode would have two advantages: 1st It would give something to each corps; 2nd The total being sent to the adjutant in one sum, would look much more handsome than if you simply sent two or three guineas here and there.

PV 35/94

Charles Fox[1] to S.T.G. Downing

Trebah near Falmouth, 29 August 1868

Dear S.T.G. Downing

I had hoped that our Member Pendarves Vivian could give his personal aid to our Scientific Societies, any one of which would hail his contribution.

I am glad to hear of his intention to attend the annual exhibition in the Poly^{tc} Hall. The annual meeting of the Miners' association will be held there in the same week, when the leading miners are generally present, and boring machines in operation will probably be exhibited. It could be a most suitable time and very welcome to the Asso^{n} (of which J St Aubyn is president) to have a paper on 'German mining'. Papers read before the association are heard to much more advantage than by the buzzing mining crowd of the Polytechnic Hall, from which those who are really interested in Science adjourn to the large room of the M^{g} Asso ^{n} under the same roof. The M^{g} Asso^{n} prints the paper.

If I may venture to suggest it, I could ask for a paper on 'Coal & Coal Cutting' (a subject now much interesting the public) in the annual Geological meeting at Penzance in October (probably).

I am sure that such contributions to our local Societies would be prized and be very opportune.

---

1. Charles Fox (1797–1878) was a member of the well known Cornish Quaker family and managed the Perran foundry. The originator of the plans for the Falmouth Polytechnic, which in 1835 became the Royal Cornwall Polytechnic Society, was Anna Maria Fox, Charles's niece. The Society was at the centre of nineteenth century intellectual life in Cornwall.

PV 35/95

Edward Spender to A.P. Vivian

London, September 1868

Sir,

I propose to publish in the *Western Morning News* biographical notices of the candidates from the district in which that paper circulates. These notices will be strictly impartial. I shall be glad of any information which you may be disposed to send me.

PV 35/100

Charles Fox to A.P. Vivian

Frenchay, Bristol, 9 September 1868.

My Dear A.P. Vivian

Many thanks for thy letter which I received when about to leave for Westmoreland. The Mining Asso^{n} would have much valued a paper on German mining or Metallurgy generally, and may still hope on the occasion of another annual meeting to be favor'd with the results of thy long experience and observations

The R C Geological Society will most gladly receive a paper on Coal Mining to be read at their Annual Meeting which probably will take place in next Month (at Penzance)

I shall probably not be able to be present at the Polytechnic exhibition as I intend to remain at the home of my son in law Ed Backhouse[44]

Middleton Lodge
Richmond
Yorkshire

for several weeks.

---

1. Edmund Backhouse (1808–79) married Juliet, eldest daughter of Charles and Sarah Fox.

PV 35/96

W.V. Dymond,[1] A. Lloyd Fox,[2] to A.P. Vivian

Falmouth, 10 September 1868

Dear Sir

May we have the pleasure of adding your name to the list of Subscribers to this society.

The amount of Subscription varies, we enclose a list of Gentlemen who give £2 to £2.2 annually. The Exhibition will commence on the 29 Sept—Is there any hope of our having the pleasure of seeing you? Mr J St Aubyn the President takes the chair

---

1. W.V. Dymond, Hon. Secretary of the Royal Cornwall Polytechnic Society.
2. A. Lloyd Fox (probably the nephew of Charles Fox), also Hon. Secretary of the Society.

PV 35/97

J.F. Basset Esq	£2. 2. -
J.F. Buller: Morval	2. 2. -
Wm Carne, Falmouth	2. 2. -
J.S. Enys	2. —
Viscount Falmouth	2. 2. -
R.W. Fox—	2. —
Augustus Smith	2. 2. -
Col Tremayne—	2. 2. -
J. Tremayne—	2. 2. -
J.M. Williams	2. 2. -
Earl of Mt Edgcumbe	2. 2. -
Sir Ed St Aubyn—	2. 2. -
Jervoise Smith MP[1]	2. 2. -
R^{d} Taylor—	2. 2. -
John St Aubyn MP	2. 2. -

1. Jervoise Smith (1828–84) Liberal MP, Penryn & Falmouth, 1865–8.

PV 35/99

S.T.G. Downing to E.M. Williams

September(?) 1868

Dear Mrs Williams

I find there is to be a Polytechnic exhibition after all. It has however been fixed for the end of September in order to make the interval as long as possible between it and the B & W of England exhibition. If Mr P. Vivian could write and read a paper on mineralology or any of the other 'ogies', it would tend to keep him before the public in a very nice way, and bind the Foxes and our other 'learned' to him forever.[48]

1. This highlights Downing's concern for Vivian to become fully involved in Cornish society. Through the Royal Cornwall Polytechnic Society he would meet not only the Foxes, but other influential families in Penryn and Falmouth.

PV 35/101

Henry Grylls to A.P. Vivian

Moreton House, Redruth, 3 October 1868

My dear Sir.

I have duly received your favor of yesty^{s} and beg to return its enclosure. I was not previously aware of the application to you: and I believe the friends thought I should not have recommended it if my opinion had been asked—at the same time I am bound to say the Liberal Cause in West Cornwall has not, in my opinion, so compact and firm a class as a body as the 'United Methodist Free Church'. Liberal views in Religion and Politics is their normal character—the very foundation of their existence as a Body of Christians—and they are numerous in this Division of the County. Mr Martin and the friends I have seen request me to express their thanks to you for your kindness in which I beg cordially to unite. I regretted much not having the pleasure of seeing you on your late visit. My cold is now nearly gone.

The Tory party seems to have had a complete quietening. They have not made so good a stand as even the Spanish Royalists but ran without striking a blow.

PV 35/107

J.H. James to A.P. Vivian

St Just, 16 October 1868

Dear Sir

I am very much obliged for your present of Game (Pheasants) which duly came to hand last Evening. I was rather disappointed in your not coming to Botallack[1] as you promised and also in not having the pleasure of meeting you at Truro at the County meetings respecting a Revision of the Stannary Laws[2] about which everyone seemed to agree such a great alteration is very necessary and which I trust you will assist us obtaining

1. Botallack was a well-known tin mine near Cape Cornwall. In the eighteenth and early nineteenth centuries it was popular with visitors to the county because several of the levels were driven beneath the sea bed.

2. Stannary Laws and Courts provided a legal framework governing Cornish mining until 1894. By 1868 Cornish copper mining had almost disappeared, tin mining was declining, and emigration from former mining districts in east and west Cornwall was steadily increasing.

PV 35/104

R.H. Carew[1] to A.P. Vivian

Penzance, 19 October 1868

Dear Sir,

The shooting for your Cup came off today and was won by Sergeant Barrett of the Truro Corps with a score of only 36.

The weather was very bad, the wind which was very strong, blowing first from the left rear and afterwards across the range in strong squalls so that it was almost impossible to take the same sighting for two consecutive shots. Mr Barrett requested me to thank you for your kind present.

1. Captain Robert Carew, Adjutant of the Rifle Corps.

PV 35/105/1–2

S.T.G. Downing to A.P. Vivian

Redruth, 19 October 1868

My dear Sir

If we should want Mr Charles Fox, we shall always be able to get him, but it would not do at present to ask him specially to attend the nomination for the chances are he will not be required to speak, but when you come down we will ascertain how Robartes is and if he be unwell I can then see Mr Fox and make it right with him. Mr Robartes is at present in his usual health. I saw R[d] Davey on Saturday and he then stated his intention to be on the hustings.

Charles Bawden is an uncertificated Bankrupt and a scamp of the first water, his trade is to start worthless mines and get unsuspecting strangers to buy shares, or in other words to swindle them!

Bawden could not command a single vote; not even his own!

May I venture to tell you whilst on the subject of mines, that I consider it most important you should make a rule that under no circumstances would you hold a mine share?—unless you do this you will lose thousands and after all your loss, will find that £100 a year properly distributed amongst the public institutions, volunteers, schools etc of the division would give you much more influence and make you much more popular.

Of course you need not tell people that you have determined never to have a mine share, but pray make the determination nevertheless!

[P.S.] Pardon my writing so plainly, but I should not do my duty to you if I failed to put you on your guard against the loss any non resident must sustain, if he ventures into 'Cornish Mining'.

100£ to Wesleyan Schools would make you more popular than 10.000£ thrown away in mine shafts.

PV 35/102

John St Aubyn to A.P. Vivian

Brighton, 20 October 1868

My dear Vivian

I got your note here yesterday. I am very glad that you have secured Robartes and Davey.[1] You could not possibly have done better.

If you approve I will ask the High Sheriff[2] to fix the nomination for the Western Division on the earliest possible day. We shall thus have our business over quietly, I hope, before the excitement of the contest in the Eastern Division.

I found my wife a little better; but still far from well. I have no intention of going home before the Election.

1. Both T.J. Agar Robartes and Richard Davey were retiring Liberal county members, so their public nomination of A.P.V. would be seen as the party's seal of approval of his candidacy.
2. Edward Coode—see 35/103.

PV 35/103

A.P. Vivian to John St Aubyn (copy)

Glanafon, Taibach, South Wales, 22 October 1868

My dear St Aubyn

Very many thanks for your letter of yesterday with enclosure which I return. I have no doubt as Mr Coode[1] says that the increase in numbers of polling places will entail additional trouble, on the Sheriff, still it must be of great advantage to the candidate by curtailing vastly that fearful item in a contest in a large county. Conveyance of voters. Is not the Eastern Division far better off than the Western in this respect? and will it not be well worth consideration hereafter, viz, additional polling places in the West besides those already lately made? But this we can talk over again. I was so very sorry to hear your account of Lady Elizabeth[2] and trust sincerely that Brighton air will ere this, have again benefited her and Believe me.

1. Edward Coode (1821–94) of Moor Cottage, St Austell, J.P., D.L., Cornwall, and J.P. Devon. Sheriff of Cornwall 1868, and therefore in charge of polling arrangements.
2. Lady Elizabeth St Aubyn who married in July 1856, was the daughter of the fourth Marquess Townshend. She died in 1910.

PV 35/106

S.T.G. Downing to A.P. Vivian

Redruth, 23 October 1868

My dear Sir

I am glad to find you are so firm about mine shares and trust nothing will induce you to alter your views. You will perhaps recollect that you gave me a sovereign

[incomplete fragment]

PV 35/108

S.T.G. Downing to A.P. Vivian

Redruth, 24 October 1868

My dear Sir

Old Mr Robartes thinks so strongly about the East Cornwall Election that we must be careful not to offend him.

I advise you not to reply to the circular, but when you come down, you will see Mr Robartes at your own Election on the 18th. and you can then tell him that if he wishes or thinks your vote is really of Consequence you will go to Callington on the 21st or 23rd as the case may be and poll.[1] In any event it will be better for you to refrain from answering the circular for the present.

1. At this time there seemed every likelihood of a poll in East Cornwall, Sir John Trelawny, Brydges Williams (both Lib) and Nicholas Kendall (Cons) being the candidates.

PV 35/111

J.M. Williams to T. Agar Robartes (Lanhydrock)

Caerhays Castle, St Austell, 5 November 1868

My Dear Sir

Your letter of the 3rd Inst has been forwarded to me here and I indeed very much regret to learn its contents—viz. that you do not purpose to afford your support for West Cornwall at the Nomination Day—I earnestly hope you will reconsider this decision. Your proposing Mr Vivian will be considered a voucher for his Politics by a large number of Electors to whom he is not yet personally known and will tend greatly to prevent an opposition Candidate in the event of another Election.

PV 35/112

S.T.G. Downing to A.P. Vivian

Redruth, 7 November 1868

My dear Sir

I send you a further communication from Coode which—I think—fixes the time of our nomination

I trust Mr Robartes will reconsider his determination. I believe the real point is that Mr Robartes is very anxious that Mr Williams should propose or second one of the Eastern Candidates and if he would do so, I have no doubt Mr Robartes would come west—but this must be entre nous as on a point of that sort Mr Williams will decide for himself and do what under the peculiar circumstances of the fight in the East he may deem best.

If we miss Mr Robartes we shall have in addition to Mr Williams and Mr Davey a crowd of men we could fall back on—namely Charles Fox, R.R. Broad, Major Bickford W.B. Smith—Boase[1]—Wm Bolitho Junior[2] etc etc so that I see no reason why you should come down until the 14th for you would then have Monday the 16 · 17 and 18 to make arrangements.

I will write again the moment there is anything to communicate

1. This reference may be to Francis Boase, (1819–?) of Penzance. He was Mayor of the town on eight occasions between 1859 and 1880.
2. Possibly William Bolitho (1830–?) of Ponsandane, J.P., D.L., (an uncle of T.S. Bolitho), the son of William Bolitho (1773–1856) of Ponsandane.

PV 35/113

William Coode to S.T.G. Downing

St Austell, 7 November 1868

Dear Sir,

West Cornwall Election

I see no objection at all to having the nomination at 1/2 past 10 instead of 10 oclock and if I do not hear from you or Mr Cornish to the contrary I will fix it for that time on the 19th inst.

PV 35/114

S.T.G. Downing to A.P. Vivian (South Wales)

Redruth, 8 November 1868

My dear Sir

This morning's post brought me a letter from Mr St Aubyn, which I enclose, not having time to make a copy.

The last sentence is so friendly towards yourself that I should like Mr JMW to see it, so kindly return the letter to me for that purpose unless you are writing Mr Williams when please send it to him direct.

Mr Williams thinks Mr Charles Fox should be asked to propose failing Mr Robartes—Mr Davey being so bad a speaker in public. I still hope however that Mr Robartes may be secured. I suppose you will come down on Saturday the 14th or Sunday the 15th? I have written the County papers to re-insert your address; altho it was quite unnecessary, yet as Mr St Aubyn seems to wish it, there can be no reason for our not doing so.

If anything occurs to you, don't hesitate to command me in any way but I really think (except as to supplying Mr Robartes place if he fail us) everything is provided for.

[P.S.] Will you allow me to say that I hope you are thinking over what you shall say at the hustings. I want you to hold your own in this respect when compared with Mr St Aubyn. I know you will excuse my venturing to give you the hint, but I am very anxious on the point.

PV 35/115–116

John St Aubyn to A.P. Vivian

Brighton, 8 November 1868

My dear Vivian

I heard from Mr W. Coode yesterday that Mr Downing had suggested the 19th as the most convenient day for our nomination so I wrote to him and said that I entirely concurred, and would make my arrangements for that day.

Should you go into the County so soon as the 14th you will probably keep well clear of Truro. The place, from what I hear, will be like a cauldron from the issuing of the writ until the declaration of the poll on the 17th. I hope it will have cooled down a little by our day.

I have caused application to be made to the Mayor of Truro for the use of Townhall for the County Election. It has always been granted, saves the expense of hustings—and is a great saving to the voices of the speakers.

I shall not, unless asked to do so, go down before the Election. My wife was a little better a fortnight ago, but overtired herself and is not so well. I do not care to be absent from her a day longer than is necessary.

P.S. I said to Mr Downing yesterday that I thought our addresses had better be in the two County papers next week. The Editors have applied ? Please let me know your address when you go to Cornwall.

PV 35/117/1–2

A.P. Vivian to John St Aubyn

Glanafon, Taibach, South Wales, 9 November 1868

My dear St Aubyn.

I have just received your letter of yesterday and am very glad to hear the day of Nomination may now be considered definitely fixed for Thursday the 19th inst, and from a letter Mr Downing has sent me [indecipherable] the hour is to be 10.30 am. I am very glad too to hear from him that our addresses are to appear together in the County Papers of this week: very many thanks for your instruction to Mr Cornish on this and other matters.

You will no doubt ere this have heard whether the report which has reached me today of Kendall's retirement has any foundation in it or not.[1] I fear Truro is indeed a caldron [sic] at present but think it will have boiled over a little before our appearances in public there.

My present intention is to leave this [place?] on Friday, sleep at Exeter (as my wife is not quite up to so long a journey unbroken) and on to Pengreep, Perranarworthal

[incomplete—page missing]

1. Kendall *had* retired, after campaigning almost continuously in the Eastern Division since August 1868. Simultaneously he had been seeking preferment from the government, among the positions mentioned being governorships of Bermuda and Western Australia. Whether he originally intended going to the poll in 1868 is debatable.

PV 35/118/1

A.P. Vivian to J.M. Williams (Copy)

9 November 1868

My dear Sir

I trust now from the news contained in Mrs Williams letter to Lady Augusta (which to a certain extent was confirmed by one to me from Mr Downing) viz. Mr Kendall's retirement, will leave no doubt of Mr Robartes fulfilling the promise which he so kindly made of proposing me at the Nomination. In the event of Mr Robartes adhering to his afterthought, I trust I might have looked to you. I can assure you I should have appreciated it most deeply and nobody could possibly have given me the same pleasure, feeling as I do how much I owe to you for the very hearty and energetic interest you and Mrs Williams have taken in me throughout and to which all is due. Unless I hear by letter or telegraph to the contrary we shall leave this on Friday and be with you at Pengreep on Saturday evening, sleeping at Exeter on Friday night.

PV 35/119

J.M. Williams to A.P. Vivian (South Wales)

Pengreep, Perranarworthal, 10 November 1868

My Dear Sir.

I am obliged for your letters of the 9th Inst—and very much regret I cannot comply with your wishes to be your Proposer at the coming Election for West Cornwall—I assure you it would be a great pleasure and gratification—to me—to undertake the Position—but I am so satisfied that I am unequal to carry out the responsibility of rightly expressing the various Political views that will be expected on the present occasion—that I could not be induced to attempt what I know would fail and hence be a source of very serious injury to your progress and standing.—I have no reply from Mr Robartes to my letter to him of the 5th Inst, but in any case, will you allow me to suggest that it would be important for you to call at Lanhydrock on Saturday on your way down.

PV 35/120

H. Hussey Vivian to A.P. Vivian

17 November 1868

My Dear Pen

I have telegraphed to you that I think it most unwise to overpress Robartes: I think he would resent it: I should: I know he meant to propose you because he instructed Stokes to write to me for an account of your early training and if from illness or otherwise he does not feel up to it, it is really most unreasonable to urge it further: it might set him against you hereafter. I really cannot and will not be a party to it.

Mrs JMW wrote me so strongly to come down, that I am coming although 12 hours by night is not pleasant.

PV 35/124/1

Electors of the W.D. of C.

It is I assure you with feelings of no common kind that I desire to return you my most hearty thanks for the honour you have done me in choosing me as one of yr representatives in Parlt

To be given the P[osition] is I consider the highest position that can be attained by an English man In my case I have the great additional gratification of representing the county which of all others I would have chosen for from my earliest childhood I have been taught to look with interest upon everything connected with Cornwall and to feel proud of my Cornish decent, and of the old Cornish names which I bear and so the name of Vivian it does not become me to allude further than to express my thanks to [blank][1] for the very handsome manner he has spoken of my family [indecipherable]. As regards the name of Pendarves I may here be allowed to say I feel it an omen of the happiest kind that I should be the Godson [sic] and bear the name of one who so universally and deservedly possessed the confidence and affection of this county which he for so many years represented. it will be my earnest endeavour to follow in his footsteps as I am well aware nowhere could I find a better model of what a member of P[arliament] should be—Besides however the personal reasons I have mentioned I need hardly say what a source of pride it is to me to be one of the representatives [of] a county whose vast and varied interests second to none in the British Dominions;

Who can pass through the county of Cornwall and not be struck by the industry and enterprise displayed on all sides. Besides in the agriculture common to other English counties they are shown in the highest degree in the mining operations of various kinds which have made Cornwall a household word in every quarter of the world where mining is carried on—they are shown in the rapidly increasing China clay works and extensive granite quarries. They are shown in the sea port towns of the north and south coasts where in addition to the ordinary commerce of such towns as [sic] honest livelihood is gained by thousands of hardy fishermen who not content with the produce to be extracted from their own coast, sail to the furthest points of the British Isles carrying with them to it may be the north of Scotland or the remotest shores of Ireland a reputation not only for [?], and untiring energy but also for temperance and piety which has made the name of Cornish fishermen honoured and respected wherever it is known. Well may any Englishman be proud of representing such a county. At the same time gent. I am fully aware that the same reasons which make this county of such importance render its efficient representation in P[arliament] no sinecure. To watch over these varied interests constant attention will be required and I need not accuse you, G[entlemen], this I am prepared to give to the utmost of my powers.

And now to pass from matters of local to matters of national interest—I am not going to trouble you with a long explanation of my political views as it is only a few months since I attended some ten public meetings in various towns of W[est] C[ornwall] I then explained in the fullest manner my views on the chief political topics of the day and answered many questions which were put to me. A long political speech from me would therefore only weary you especially after the full and very able one we have just heard from Mr St Aubyn

There are however a few questions which cannot be omitted from any speech on such an occasion at this moment. The first I will touch on is that of Reform. I have long watched with the greatest interest the efforts made by the Liberal party to give to the working classes the franchise to which they were justly entitled and it is with the warmest pleasure I congratulate you the new electors, on your signal and well deserved triumph. We know that the merits of this Reform Bill are claimed by the Conservative party but what their title to these claims were worth was never better put than in the able speech of my cousin Captn Vivian which many of you had the pleasure of listening to in this town on Monday. He clearly showed you in it that out of the 61 clauses which composed the bill only 4 were part of the original Conservative Bill and of these 43 were purely technical. The Conservative claim to the Reform Bill reminds me of a woodcut in Punch some years ago. The details I forget, but the gist of it was the owner of an old picture of a horse being questioned as to the amount of restoration it had undergone assured his friends that though the head neck the hind legs then the side and part of the back had been restored yet all the rest was original work. I think we may say that although the head, the body the limbs of the Reform Bill have been retouched by the Liberal Party yet we may concede all the rest to the Conservatives.

And now Gent. to pass to the great question of the day. I mean the disestablishment and disendowment of the Irish Church. At all the public meetings to which I have already alluded I expressed my decided approval of Mr G[ladstone's] policy. Since then the question has been thoroughly ventilated by the ablest men on both sides, and all I can say is that I am more confirmed than ever in the view I have already taken. I look upon it now as I did then as a matter of simple justice due to our Irish fellow subjects. Let us, G[entlemen] consider what it is. It was a church established by Queen Elizabeth some 300 yrs ago in the midst of a people who were totally unprepared to receive the truth which it taught and which to us are so precious—to maintain this church the Ecclesiastical revenues of the whole country were taken by force from the people and the religion to whom they had belonged for many centuries so that we have no in Ireland the extraordinary spectacle of a yearly income of £580,000 devoted to the religious care of 700,000 of the people while there are more than 4½ million and these including all the poorer classes left to provide religious instruction for themselves. Remember too—G[entlemen] that the rate of wages in Ireland is very different to what it is in this country, in many parts the labourer earns but 6/- per week and hardly any over 8/-. Judge for yourselves whether it is not likely and natural that a bitter feeling should be created in the mind of the poor labourer towards his landlord when he knows that though out of his poverty he is obliged to scrape together a few pence for the maintenance of his own religion there are vast sums of money yearly spent for the benefit of the church of his wealthy landlord. It is however unnecessary to bring forth further proof of the injustice of this establishment and I think nobody is now be inclined to dispute this fact. Mr G's proposal for remedying this injustice is the very simple one of removing it altogether and now that the Report of the Commissioners has been generally allowed to be a failure and their recommendation not thought to be acceptable even to the Irish Church itself it seems to be the only defined plan in the field

Now Gent. let us consider for a moment what is the great objection which our opponents bring against this policy. The greatest is that it will be an act decidedly dangerous to the protestant religion.

Now in answer to these objections I ask what has the Established Church done for Protestantism it is now 300 years since it was first imposed on that people, and the members of this church still only number 1/8th of the whole population. In the last 100 years the number has steadily diminished until that terrible visitation the Irish Famine when the R.C. population were [sic] decimated and the tide of emigration has carried yearly so many 1000s to shores of America as to cause the relative proportion of members of ch of Ireland and RCs to remain stationary. I say therefore that the Established ch. has done nothing for protestantism in Ireland and that its disendowment and disestablishment far from injuring our religion will place it in a far higher position than it has hitherto occupied. Gent. I am too good a Protestant not to be quite content that my religion should stand on its own merits and feel convinced that it does not need the aid of injustice to maintain its footing in Ireland. Other objections have been raised to Mr G's policy, but they are answered still more easily. One is that it would render private property less secure than it now is in Ireland. To this I would say that I believe that private property would be far securer [sic] if the population could be made contented and happy, than it is now when they are full of bitterness and discontent. Another objection is that when this demand is granted another would rise up. to this I reply as Mr G did that it is much easier to refuse an unreasonable demand when a reasonable one has been granted and besides it would be a strange reason to give for refusing to act justly that we dont quite see what we are to benefit by it. Another objection and as it is I think entirely original, being made by a Welsh clergyman to myself it may I think amuse you to hear it. He was in favour of the disendowment but against the disestablishment and his reason was that in the event of the Queen going to Ireland and a public ceremony taking place she would have no recognised officials to apply to for a special form of prayer? if required. So Gent. for the sake of this extremely improbable contingency we were to run the risk of keeping Ireland in a state of continual discontent and perpetuate this blot left on our national character. I am not sanguine enough to imagine that all discontent will cease to exist, but I believe we shall have removed one of its chief causes. In concluding this subject I cannot do better than by recalling the words of Mr G. in his address ...

Nearer allied to the last subject than might be thought is that of the Reduction of our Expenditure. If Ireland could be placed in a position of less discontent we could largely reduce the military expenses in that country. at present we have 32,000 men there 20,000 all regular troops and 12,000 military police. Scotland requires only 4,000. I hope the day is not far distant when we may at least dispense with 20 of the

32th this at the ordinary computation of £100 per man per annum would be a saving to us of 2 million per year. I have already taken up so much of your time that I will not dwell longer except to point out to you one significant fact and that is since the conservatives have been in power the permanent expenditure of the state has increased 3 million. I am perfectly aware that an army and navy suitable to our position among nations must be maintained but I am distinctly of opinion that this is done now at a vastly greater cost than need be. One little fact which strikes me invariably as I go to and from Cornwall is the existence of all the old men of wars [crossed out] which we see from the r/way from the Albert Bridge at Saltash and I keep wondering why some at least of the oldest are not turned into money. there may be some good reason but it is difficult to imagine what it can be and one fears it may be only a sample of a bad system. The last subject I shall touch on is Education. I hear it is a difficult subject and requires the greatest thought. When one reads such figures as those which were given in the debate in the H of C. one sees the necessity for legislation in Merthyr Tydvil.

This is a most lamentable state of things and I shall be glad to see a well considered plan which will extend education to every poor man's door so that he may send his child to the School of the denomination to which his parents belong.

I am afraid I have trespassed long on your patience. Before concluding I must beg to tender my warmest thanks to all those gentlemen who have been kind enough to form my committee. I am extremely glad that their active services have not been required but had it been otherwise I do not feel the smallest doubt that no committee in the Kingdom would have been more efficient and that with such a committee success must have been attained. I also feel most grateful to Mr Robartes and Mr Davey who have been good enough to propose and second me. I feel what a source of great satisfaction it must be to the Liberal party of the W.D. that I who labour under the disadvantages of being comparatively unknown should have such a guarantee for my Politics as being proposed by so staunch and straight forward a liberal as Mr Robartes who after a long Parliamentary career now retires to the regret of the whole county into private life carrying with him well deserved confidence, esteem and affections of all Cornwall. In my seconder too, Mr Davey I have been most favoured, he like Mr Robartes is now retiring from Parliamentary life and I am well aware what a cause of regret it is to the county that I am now standing in his place. I am quite conscious of my inferiority in experience to him, but there is one point I will not yield the palm to him or any man. As long as you continue to send me to Parl^{t} so long will I faithfully watch over your interests and devote my time and whatever capabilities I possess to your service and I trust [?] day will never come when we have come to [?] and that it is an Earnest and hearty endeavour to do my duty to the county which has chosen me as one of its representatives.

---

1. Presumably the name of APV 's proposer was to be inserted here when his identity was known.

PV 35/121

Henry Williams to A.P. Vivian

25 December 1868

Dear Sir

On receipt of your favor 15th Inst I requested the News Agent here to forward as you directed, your papers to Adare Manor. I shall enclose the Agent's card to enable you to ensure immediate attention to any attention in the address, and will provide for the *Mercury* being discontinued at the end of the year. I must beg you will not think anything a trouble to me, at anytime in anyway I can be of service it will afford me pleasure to receive your instructions

PV 35/123

S.T.G. Downing to A.P. Vivian

Redruth, 31 December 1868

My dear Sir

I am duly favoured with your letter of the 29th.

I think the arrangement as to the Infirmary Admissions could not be better than Mr Grylls for Redruth 2/3 and Mr Sampson, Devoran 1/3. Sampson is moving about a good deal. He would of course state that it was from you admission came.

Should you come into Cornwall I think you should be here time eno' to attend the meeting at St Austell on the 15th

PV 36/1

West Cornwall Election

1868

List of claims for
Registration and
Election as separated
by Downing. but
without claims for
advertising. printing etc
West Cornwall Election 1868

An analysis of Expenses incurred on behalf of Arthur Pendarves Vivian Esq. M.P. for Registration and Election

	Registration			Election			Total		
Thomas Tabb	1	15	·	25	5	·	27	·	·
J.N. Earle	·	3	6	2	12	6	1	16	·
William Warn	9	17	9	·	·	·	9	17	9
J.S. Doidge	1	2	6	2	·	·	3	2	6
Wm Angwin	3	17	5	1	17	6	5	14	11
Joseph Newton	17	10	·	·	·	·	17	10	·
Samuel Richards	·	5	·	·	14	·	·	19	·
T.N. Roberts	·	9	11	·	·	·	·	9	11
Christopher Ellis	·	11	11	·	·	·	·	11	11
W.P. Metchim & Son	2	·	3	·	·	·	2	·	3
Hodge Hockin & Marrack	19	8	8	5	5	·	24	13	8
W.R.T. Pender	2	12	6	5	5	·	7	17	6
J.G. Plomer	5	10	1	5	5	·	10	15	1
G.A. Jenkins	4	16	5	16	11	6	21	7	11
Wm Trevenen	1	11	6	5	5	·	6	16	6
John Roscorla	2	19	6	33	10	4	36	9	10
Henry Rogers	76	9	3	34	10	11	111	·	2
Pearse Jenkin	7	14	·	·	·	·	7	14	·
John Dale	10	10	·	12	9	·	22	19	·
Matthew Courtenay	1	1	·	·	·	·	1	1	·
Edmund Michell	1	1	·	0	0	0	1	1	·
J.T. Trevena	ob	ob	·	5	5	·	5	5	·
Henry Thomas	·	·	·	5	5	·	5	5	·
W.J. Genn	·	·	·	5	5	·	5	5	·
F.H. Cock	7	17	6	5	5	·	13	2	6
W.H. Richards	8	18	9	·	·	·	8	18	9
Thomas Leggo	1	11	6	·	·	·	1	11	6
Carried Over £	189	14	11	171	10	9	360	5	8

	Registration			Election			Total		
Bro[t] Over £	189	14	11	171	10	9	361	5	8
H.M. Praed	2	12	6	·	·	·	2	12	6
Christopher Hichens	1	1	·	·	·	·	1	1	·
Samuel Harvey	1	1	·	·	·	·	1	1	·
Charles Ellis Jr	1	1	·	·	·	·	1	1	·
James Jenkin	·	11	6	8	10	6	9	2	·
W.M. Grylls	5	17	7	5	19	3	11	16	10
Thomas Nicholls	10	10	·	0	0	0	10	10	·
W.T. Tresidder	7	17	6	5	5	·	13	2	6
N.T. Trengrouse	2	12	6	·	·	·	2	12	6
J.R. Daniell	30	4	10	25	19	2	56	4	·
Heard & Sons	·	3	4	·	·	·	·	3	4
H.S. Stokes	·	13	8	·	·	·	·	13	8
R.T. Hall	·	2	6	·	·	·	·	2	6
James Tregaskis	3	10	8	3	8	6	6	19	2
Thos H Edwards	5	5	·	·	·	·	5	5	·
H.S. Stokes	·	8	·	·	·	·	·	8	·
E. Rowe	·	19	3	·	·	·	·	19	3
Beare & son	1	5	10	·	·	·	1	5	10
W. Cornish	·	15	6	·	·	·	·	15	6
T.N. Roberts	·	6	2	·	·	·	·	6	2
J.N. Earle	·	3	6	·	·	·	·	3	6
Sundry payments	5	8	10	·	·	·	5	8	10
Mr Cornish	34	9	5	·	·	·	34	9	5
Mr Downing	49	18	5	·	·	·	49	18	5
£	356	14	5	220	13	2	577	7	7

PV 36/6

HENRY TILLY[1] TO A.P. VIVIAN

Falmouth, 1 January 1869

My Dear Sir,

Owing to the results of our late election here I am obliged to trouble you as one of our County Members.

The son of one of our most active members of the Liberal Association recently formed here is an applicant for a situation in the Customs Boat at this port which has been rendered vacant by the dismissal of a man named Williams

May I therefore ask the favor of your assistance on behalf of Edward Charles Travers who is about 23 years of age.

The situation is worth from 10/8 to 20/- a week.

---

1. The Tillys were a family of Falmouth solicitors.

PV 36/10

R.M. SAMPSON TO A.P. VIVIAN

Devoran, Cornwall, 2 January 1869

Dear Sir,

I think you might remember Mr John Magor of this Parish, Feock, he was a Member of your working Committee and a very respectable influential Agriculturist he is. Mrs Sampson was at his home last evening, and he sent a message by her to the effect, that he with other of your good friends thought it very desirable you should attend the Cornwall Farmers' Agricultural Meeting at Truro next Wednesday week (I think)

He says he has heard several remarks regarding it, that Mr St Aubyn is the Farmers' friend, and that you think only of the miners' Interests.[1]

I am a member, and have therefore attended some of the meetings. It is a dinner provided at the expense of the society by each member paying 5/- yearly, very numerously attended and the County as well as Borough members have I believe always been present. Mr St Aubyn has promised as well as Col. Tremayne; I thought it best to give you an early intimation of what is going on for your guidance. I am now writing this in the presence of another member of your Commt and he perfectly agrees with Mr J^{n} Magor's remarks, that seeing you have been so recently returned, it will certainly promote a good feeling and be considered a compliment without doubt by a large and influential body of your constituents.

---

1. Sampson's comment on the public perception of APV was obviously one which would concern him, and in the years ahead he worked hard to change it, as his 1869 subscriptions and donations show.

PV 36/37

Truro, 4 January 1869

D Sir

At the Annual Meeting of the Truro Agr[icultural] Exchange for election of Officers etc for 1869 the members presuming you would become a member elected you one of the Vice Presidents and the Committee hope you will be able to favour us with your …

[fragment only]

PV 36/8

S.T.G. Downing to A.P. Vivian

Redruth, 6 January 1869

My dear Sir

Mr Williams will write you as to a letter he has received from Mr Trethewey advising you being present at the Agricultural Meeting on the 15th at St Austell.

I gather from your letter of the 2nd that you will not be in Cornwall until the 18th.

I think if you write a civil letter to Mr Trethewey (see address below) stating that you cannot attend the meeting but will be at Tregothnan[1] on the 18th and 'before you leave the county shall hope to see him' (Mr Trethewey) and ascertain the dates of any future agricultural 'meetings which if possible you would attend' etc etc You will have done all that is necessary.

I confess I don't myself think the meeting on the 15th so appreciably important to render it necessary that you should put yourself out of the way.

[P.S.] Trethewey's address is
Wm Trethewey Esqre
Tregoose
Probus
Truro

1. Lord Falmouth's seat, near Truro.

PV 36/9/1–2

S.T.G. Downing to A.P. Vivian

Redruth, 8 January 1869

My dear Sir

Mr Sampson is mistaken in thinking that there is to be any dinner of the 'Cornwall Agricultural Society' on Wednesday next (the 13th inst). There is a dinner of the Truro Agricultural Exchange, of which our old friend Peter of Chiverton is the President, but this is a very different Society from the 'Cornwall Agricultural'.

St Aubyn will probably attend and make a speech and so might you if you had been in the County but there can surely be no occasion for your inconveniencing yourself, or altering your arrangements in any way.

As to your writing the Secretary expressing your regret at not being present, I think you should do so, if you have had any express invitation from the Committee or officers to attend, but if you have not then perhaps it would be almost better that you should not write—there are other societies of the same local character, and you could not well write to one, and over look the others, for instance the week's *West Briton* contains an account of the annual dinner of the 'East Penwith Agricultural Exchange'—a much more powerful body so far as voting is concerned than the 'Truro Agricultural Exchange'—but you did not write their secretary excusing your absence?—[1]

1. Downing's observation about votes and voters suggests the strategic importance of county MPs belonging to various local organizations.

PV 36/10

William Blamey to A.P. Vivian

Pennare, Veryan, Grampound, Cornwall, 14 January 1869

A.P. Vivian Esq M.P.

The Roseland Agricultural Improvement Society will hold their annul [sic] meeting at Veryan on Thursday the 11th of February next when we offer prizes to Agricultural labourers to the amount of 40/-. May I be allowed to ad [sic] your name as a Subscriber.

PV 36/11

S.T.G. Downing to A.P. Vivian

Redruth, 18 January 1869

My dear Sir

I enclose the 'Bills'. Kindly peruse them and let me know as early as possible your views thereon.

You will see that Column 1st is solely yours, whilst of column third, you pay a moiety and St Aubyn the other moiety : St Aubyn has not yet seen the bills. Under the act of Parliament we are all liable to a fine unless we pay what we admit and deposit the vouchers with the Clerk of the Purse within a day or two!

Seeing that St Aubyn has to pay a moiety of Column 3 I doubt if it would be good policy to object to any of the accounts unseen.

I shall hope to hear from you in a day or two. The few accounts of which you have not yet the particulars are with Cornish but he will send them to me when I send them those now enclosed to you.

Of course I shall not send any of 'bills column 1st' to Cornish for Mr St Aubyn has nothing to do with them

PV 36/2
(On outside) in PV's hand

WEST CORNWALL ELECTION

1868

Final list of claims
furnished by Downing
and gone into with a view
of a reduction but
without avail (see
correspondence

West Cornwall Election

List of Claims received by Mr S.T.G. Downing

No.	Name of Claimant	Residence	Nature of Claim	A P Vivian	
1	*West Briton*	Truro	Advertizing	124	9
2	*Cornwall Gazette*	D° ”	D° ”	32	8
3	*Western Morning News*	Plymouth	D° ”	57	9
4	*Western Daily Mercury*	D° ”	D° ”	57	9
5	Thomas Tabb	Redruth	Carriage Hire etc	26	6
6	J.N. Earle	D° ”	Printer	2	12
7	James Tregaskis	D° ”	D° ”	3	8
8	W Kernick	St Ives	D°”	3	10
9	William Warn	Falmouth	Agency		
10	James Gripe	St Agnes	Printer	2	5
11	J.S. Doidge	Redruth	D° ”	2	·
12	James Jenkin	D° ”	D° ” & Advertizing	8	10
13	Banfield Brothers	Hayle	D° ”	3	4
14	James Snow	Redruth	Carriage hire	1	1
15	Thomas Angove	Camborne	Use of Hall	6	11
16	Gill & Son	Penryn	Printer & Advertizing	10	14
17	R.C. Richards	Falmouth	Printer	1	11
18	*“One & All”*	Penzance	Advertizing	12	12
19	Fred H Earle	Falmouth	Printer D° ”	13	10
20	William Tregaskis	D° ”	D° ”	1	1
21	*Cornish Telegraph*	Penzance	Advertizing	24	11
22	W Dymond	Falmouth	Use of Hall	2	13
23	Heard & Son	Truro	Printer	33	9
24	Wm Angwin	St Just		1	17
25	Joseph Newton	St Agnes	Agency		
26	John Rowe	Redruth	Bill Sticker	1	5
27	Samuel Richards	D° ”	Carriage hire		14
				435	4

ohn St Aubyn Esq			Joint			Total			Remarks
						124	9	6	Mr D will go into these
						32	8	6	” ”
						57	9	·	” ”
						57	9	8	” ”
			3	10	·	29	16	·	Will enquired into as to payment
				7	·	2	19	6	” ”
			7	1	3	10	9	9	Will rest with Mr S & A
						3	10	·	
			19	15	6	19	15	6	✓ £6 paid out
						2	5	·	St Aubyn
			2	5	·	4	5	·	”
			1	3	·	9	13	6	[Indecipherable]
						3	4	·	Passed
						1	1	·	required cut
						6	11	6	✓ so arranged
						10	14	·	according to No.1
						1	11	·	Passed
						12	12	·	according to No.1
						13	10	·	✓ printer to be checked to lowest charge
						1	1	·	” ”
						24	11	6	checked according to No.1
						2	13	6	passed & paid
						33	9	·	
			1	8	9	3	6	3	✓ St A
			35	·	·	35	·	·	✓ St A
						1	5	·	
				10	·	1	4	·	
			71	-	6	506	4	8	

No.	Name of Claimant	Residence	Nature of Claim	A P Vivian	
			Bro^{t} Over	435	4
28	W Philp	Launceston	Advertizing	1	10
29	H.S. Stokes	Bodmin			
30	T.N. Roberts	London			
31	R.T. Hall	Devoran			
32	Christopher Ellis	Hayle			
33	W.P. Metchim & Son	London	Printers		
34	W M Grylls			5	19
35	Henry Grylls			5	18
36	Hodge Hockin & Marrack	Truro	Solicitor		
37	W R T Pender	Falmouth	D^{o} "		
38	J G Plomer	Helston	D^{o} "		
39	Thos Nicholls	St Columb	D^{o} "		
40	G A Jenkins	Penryn	D^{o} "	11	6
41	Wm Trevenen	Helston	D^{o} "		
42	John Roscorla	Penzance	D^{o} "	28	5
43	Henry Rogers	Helston	D^{o} "	24	·
44	John R Daniel	Camborne	D^{o} "	20	14
45	Pearse Jenkin	Redruth			
46	Under Sheriff			39	11
47	John Dale	Helston	Solicitor	7	4
48	Matthew Courtenay	Truro			
49	Edwd Michell	Gwennap			
	Henry Thomas	Penzance	Solicitor		
	Grenfell	D^{o} "			
	T.H. Edwards	Helston			
	Genn	Falmouth	Solicitor		
	F.H. Cock	Truro	D^{o} "		
	J.J. Trevena	Redruth	D^{o} "		
	W. Yewens	Camborne	D^{o} "		
	W. Tresidder	St Ives	D^{o} "		
				579	13

ohn St Aubyn Esq			Joint			Total			Remarks
						1	10	·	to be reduced
			1	7	3	1	7	3	
				19	9	·	19	9	
				5		·	5	·	
			1	3	11	1	3	11	passed
			4	·	6	4	·	6	
			11	15	2	17	14	5	
						5	18	3	
			49	7	4	49	7	4	passed
			15	15	·	15	15	·	S & A
			21	10	2	21	10	2	✓ D° ”
			21			21	·	·	✓ D° ”
			20	2	10	31	9	4	✓ D° ”
			13	13	·	13	13	·	D° ”
			16	9	1	44	14	5	✓ D°”
8	1	10	173	18	6	206	1	3	✓
			60	19	7	81	13	9	✓ D° ” £35 over bill remainder payment
			15	8	·	15	8	·	
						39	11	3	
			31	10	·	38	14	·	✓
			2	2	·	2	2	·	
			2	2	·	2	2	·	
			10	10	·	10	10	·	
			10	10	·	10	10	·	
			10	10	·	10	10	·	
			10	10	·	10	10	·	
			26	5	·	26	5	·	✓
			10	10	·	10	10	·	
			10	10	·	10	10	·	
			21	·	·	21	·	·	
8	1	10	644	14	7	1232	10	3	Mr V 579 13 10 half of 644-14-7 322 7 3 £902 1

PV 36/12

S.T.G. Downing to A.P. Vivian

Redruth, 20 January 1869.

My dear Sir

The enclosed letter from T.S.B.[1] will show you that he proposes the 1st February for the Stannary Meeting, will that day suit you?

Bills

The question of these bills is very awkward—most of the accounts are much too heavy but I think we should pause for long, and consider well before we make any objection = From June 'till Nov was a long period and we had to take possession of the ground and cover it and so retained all sorts of people that even in a fight of 3 weeks or some short period we could have done without, but there was danger in having so many idle hands for so long a period without a retainer, and altho the course we adopted has given an opportunity to some people of which they have taken advantage, still in view of all the circumstances I think it would be unwise to raise objections that at most would save us 150 £.

There is at least this comfort that if we pay now we shall save money hereafter for the expense now will be a fair reason for declining to give many retainers or inserting advertisements freely another time.

Kindly let me have your instructions as soon as possible as I am liable to a fine of 5 £ a day for every day after today that my account remains undelivered to the sheriff!.[2]

I don't suppose anyone would sue me and the list is therefore very little, but there can be no reason for any long delay.

---

1. T.S. Bolitho.
2. The Corrupt Practices Act of 1854 required all candidates to submit their accounts for payment to Election Auditors, who, after 1863, were also the Returning Officers.

PV 36/13/1

S.T.G. Downing to A.P. Vivian

Redruth, 23 January 1869.

My dear Sir

I shall be very glad to see you on Monday. In considering the expenses we must bear in mind that you are never likely to be put to the same cost again—that your name and very existence were unknown to the 'middle class' up to the 16th of June last and that the extensive advertisements etc were almost an absolute necessity.

I am as sorry as you can possibly be, that the expenses have run 400 £ more than they aught to have done but under similar circumstances I am convinced no other course could have been taken: you will never again however want to retain the lawyers or to advertise to anything like the same extent for I trust before another election occurs you will have made yourself popular eno' to dispense with such aids but still I must urge you to consider well before you determine to object to the accounts, the 150 £ we should save would be very dearly paid for at another election Pray excuse my writing [so plainly?] [section missing, but part of Downing's name showing].

PV 36/14/1–2

S.T.G. Downing to A.P. Vivian

Redruth, 26 January 1869

My dear Sir

I enclose letters from the undersheriff and Mr Rogers. I have written Coode that he shall hear as soon as possible and I shall see Mr Rogers at Helston tomorrow.

Mr Grylls proposes to see Mr Heard and point out the exorbitant nature of his Charges. This would in my view be extremely dangerous —if we were but certain that thro' Henry Budd we could at all times prevent Mr Heard from using the columns of the *West Briton* against us.

I have not yet heard from the West. If a letter comes tonight I will forward it so that you will get it with tomorrow morning's letter

[P.S.] Mr Hussey Vivian's address contains 553 words Mr Pendarves Vivian's 744 words.[1] The *Cambrian* charged for the address of 553 words £1-4-0 which would be for an address of 744 words £1-12-0.

1. Hussey Vivian was unopposed in 1868 as one of the sitting Liberal MPs for Glamorganshire.

PV 36/15

H. Hussey Vivian to A.P. Vivian

Ibford(?), 28 January 1869

My dear Pen

£ 399-10^{s}- for Printing and Advertizing appears to me to be enormous[10]. I believe my Bill amounts to £160 which is twice as much as I ever paid before but the length of time accounts for much: in your case you were longer on the tapis but I have many more Papers to advertize in. The charge of the *Cambrian* was 24^{s}/per insertion for my address and amounted to £13-4- for 11. I advise you to leave Downing to settle with the Papers giving [?—piece torn out] him the above hints. As to Solicitors I recommend you to pay. Mr Rogers of Helston £173 seems very heavy but there may be an explanation.

---

1. See PV 36/2, Claims presented by Downing.

PV 36/16/1–2

S.T.G. Downing to A.P. Vivian

Redruth, 28 January 1869

My dear Sir

I am favoured with yours of yesterday's date.

Mr Grylls will wait the address from the *Cambrian* before he sees Heard.

I enclose a letter from Mr Roscorla which will show you that he does not seem to have the smallest idea that there is any thing in his account that would cause delay.

I find that Mr Richard Davey's first Election cost him within 250 £ of the Claims on fees and we must remember that Mr Davey only came forward 8 days before the nomination day so that his advertising expenses were almost 'nil'—there were then no daily papers circulated in Cornwall and the *West Briton* could have published the address once. Your first Election therefore leaving out the advertising would be as cheap as Mr Davey's even passing the other accounts as delivered. You are aware that Tremayne retired before the nomination so that what we call the 'contest' really did not last a week and in that time Mr Michael Williams spent 800 and Mr Davey nearly 700 No subsequent Election of Mr Davey's cost him 30 £ (?) but I cannot disguise from myself that the 100 £ he saved by 'Cutting' some of the bills would have seriously affected his chances of re-election if there had been a subsequent contest. You will gather from the above that I still think it will be unwise to question the accounts (other than the advertising) but whilst I venture frankly to reflect my views on this point I will of course carry out to the best of my ability your instructions what ever they may be.

Please let me know by what train you go to Penzance Saturday.

Would you kindly let Mr J. Williams know the contents of this letter?

PV 36/17

Henry Grylls to A.P. Vivian

Moreton House, Redruth, 28 January 1868

My dear Sir

I duly received your favor of the 26th Inst. And regret being obliged to be away yesty when you called at the Bank.

I am still of opinion that several of charges are exceedingly extravagant such indeed as any man would be ashamed to make except in Election matters. On Monday next I hope to have the pleasure of meeting you in Truro. You will no doubt have received a copy of your brother's address from the *Cambrian* when I hope we shall be able to show Mr Heard how excessive his charges are, and induce him to make a large reduction.

Some of the newspapers appear to think that the trial of the Ballot at Manchester recently between Gibson and Jones is an unanswerable argument in favor of Secret Voting. I confess it appears in quite the opposite light to me. If the adoption of the Ballot is to send such men as Jones to Parliament—and I fear it would—the county should set its face against it and would justify an alteration in the litany, to be done reverently—From plague, pestilence, famine and the Ballot good Lord deliver us. This will be my prayer till I get further lights on the Subject.

PV 36/18

Henry Grylls to A.P. Vivian

Moreton House, Redruth, 30 January 1869

My dear Sir,

I am in receipt of your favor of yesterday and Mr Downing has handed me one of the Copies of your Brother's address from the

Cambrian. We have counted words, and find the *Cambrian* address contains 553 and the *West Briton* 744 words and by a single rule of three Sum (If 553 cost 24/- how much should 744 Cost? This gives $32^{s}/3^{d}$). I think therefore that Mr Heard will be handsomely paid if he gets, say, 35^{s}/- per address instead of 56^{s}/-. Whether there has been the same excess in his charges for Supplements and other jobs it is more difficult to determine: but the probability is he made all his charges with the same high hand. I hope to have a few minutes with you on Monday before call on Mr Heard.

I have not yet been able to go through the Dfs [Drafts] of Stannaries Bill, but have seen enough to be heartily sick of it. I trust the Mining Interests will not allow their affairs to be managed by Lawyers and merchants. Our object was to become less involved in legal meshes and now it is proposed to bind us hand and foot. I write you freely in confidence ...

PV 36/19

J.M. Williams to A.P. Vivian

Burncoose, 2 February 1869

My Dear Sir.

I duly received your letter of the 31st ulto and was much surprized to learn its contents, in reference to the Joint Amts—for the late Election Expenses and tho I still think they were very exorbitant—yet think you were quite right to concur with Mr St Aubyn in passing them as he appears to have fixed to do so.—I have an appointment at the Redruth Bank tomorrow and will do my best to get Mr Grylls and Downing to have the Printing and Advertising Bills reduced.[1]

1. See PV 36/2, Claims presented by Downing.

PV 36/20/1–2

S.T.G. Downing to A.P. Vivian

Redruth, 3 February 1869.

My dear Sir

Heard promised Mr Grylls that he would write me as to the reduction he would make—This was on Monday but up to this time, I have not heard.

From what passed on Monday I gathered that Mr Heard thought we were not entitled to any reduction upon the Supplements because 1st the fees paid to the reporters 2nd the cost of distributing the papers

As to the last point of course it is difficult to say much beyond the observation that I made to Mr Heard namely that the *West Briton* unstamped is largely distributed thro' the local agents of the paper and as I should assume little expence: upon the first point I have written him by this post as per copy enclosed. I expect this will bring a decided answer, one way or the other, probably he has written Mr Budd or perhaps even yourself or it is difficult to account for his not having written me as promised on Monday. Cornish is to send me Mr St Aubyn's cheque for a moiety of the joint expenses today so that my cheques may go to the different parties by tonight's post.

I enclose a letter from the Editor of the *Mercury*, to which I shall not reply until we have settled with the *West Briton* as I shall try to put the other papers on the same rebate as we get from the *West Briton*. I didn't know whether Mr Grylls told you that Heard admitted that the scale charged by the Plymo[uth] and Truro papers is six pence a line (!) and that he also stated that all the MPs but the West Cornwall Members had paid at that rate.

PV 36/21/1–2

E.M. Williams to A.P. Vivian

Caerhays Castle, St Austell, 3 February 1869

Dear Mr Vivian

My Husband asked me thank you very much for yr letter of the 31st Ins[tance] by return of post, but I was prevented from doing so, and as he has since been at Pengreep I don't know whether he has written himself, so I think it safest to send you a few lines, just to say that Mr Williams quite thinks that you had no alternative but to act in conjunction with Mr St Aubyn about the joint expenses and that you have managed most judiciously about the advertising and other single accounts. My Husband expected to see Mr Downing to-day and will take care to repeat his surprise and disappointment at the exorbitant bills wh have been sent in to you, in the hope that this will make Mr Downing careful that his own a/c shall be a reasonable one.[1] We don't see how else to help you in this matter, but shall be delighted to do so, in any way that we can. I hope that Lady Augusta is not the worse for the fatigues of the last fortnight and for your very stormy visit to Penzance?

P.S. I forwarded a paper wh. was found in Lady Augusta's room by yesterday's post. The *W.[estern] Morning News* contains no report of Monday's Meeting, but we expected and hoped that you would make many new acquaintances there, including Henry Williams and Colonel Tremayne probably?[2]

1. See PV 36/2, Claims presented by Downing.
2. This referred to a Stannary meeting in Truro.

PV 36/22/1

HEARD & SON TO S.T.G. DOWNING

Truro, 3rd February 1869

Dear Sir,

We have thought over our conversation of Monday last, and will if Mr Vivian's Committee particularly desires it make a deduction of 5s/- on Mr Pendarves Vivian's address advertisement, in consequence of its having appeared a greater number of times than is usual, but we cannot afford to make any further reduction.

You have no conception of the enormous expenses incurred by newspaper proprietors at Elections in the way of special Editions, Reporting expenses, expresses, travelling expenses etc etc which in our case amounting to ma[n]y hundreds of pounds.

We should not be doing justice to ourselves if we did not take occasion to mention that we feel a little hurt, it should have been supposed for one moment that we should have made any overcharge against Mr A.P. Vivian

We have been rather lavish in incurring expenses of delivery in comparatively remote parts of the Western division of the County, but these are mere out of pocket expenses which we thought would be of service to Mr Vivian, bearing in mind specially that he was perfectly unknown to the County and that a few shillings expense incurred at the onset would probably be the means of saving is many pounds, and we believe the result was obtained by your special exertions, but which we had the pleasure of aiding as far as we possibly could.

PV 36/22/1

EDWARD HEARD TO S.T.G. DOWNING (COPY)

Truro, 3 February 1869

Dear Sir,

Since writing you this afternoon I have received your note of today's date respecting the expenses of the special Editions etc, and note your remarks as to our being compelled in the ordinary course of business to report public meetings: but you will I am sure remember in our case that Mr A.P. Vivian was not at all reported in the ordinary way, and I perfectly remember on <u>one occasion</u> in the course of the summer paying for <u>additional reporting services</u> no less a sum than £13.13.0 entirely on account of Mr A.P. Vivian not one shilling of which would have been incurred in the ordinary way.

I very much regret that this explanation is necessary as I thought it had been understood all the way through that we were to have done our best for him even as we would for one of ourselves.

Trusting that this explanation will prove satisfactory and thanking you for the courtesy we have always met at your hands.

[P.S.] I think it only right to mention that this application is the first of the kind I have received during this Election or any one previous.

PV 36/22/2

S.T.G. DOWNING TO EDWARD HEARD

Redruth, 3 February 1869

Dear Sir,

<u>W. C. E.</u>

I really wish you could see your way clear to make some reduction from the Supplements as well as from the advertisements.

I quite agree with you that the attendance of the reporters at the meetings was quite necessary, but as Mr Grylls puts it, your paper is in the habit of sending its reporter to attend political and other meetings without charging their fees to the promoters of the meeting; for instance, at the Stannary Meeting on Monday the Reporters for your paper and the *Cornwall Gazette* were present for many hours but of course no charge will be made on that account to the Stannary Committee.

Be assured I quite appreciate the services of the *West Briton* but the total amount of its charges for these supplements and the advertisements runs to so large a sum that with a view to prevent dissatisfaction on the part of any of the persons concerned I should be very glad if you could reconsider the scale and let me have an amended account within a post or two

PV 36/24/1–3

S.T.G. Downing to A.P. Vivian

Redruth, 4 February 1869

My dear Sir

The enclosed are copies of two letters that reached me by this post from Heard—The Rebate of 5/ an advertisement if applied to all the papers would save us about £10.

The saving on the *West Briton* would be 2.15.0 only.

Mr Williams was here yesterday and as he seemed anxious about the matter I have sent him copies of the letters and have also—of course—shown them to Mr Hy Grylls.

The question now is—what will you do?—There are 5 supplements charged for in Heard's bill (of which I send you a copy as you may want to refer to it).

1st	Camborne Meeting (ie the Great County Meeting on the 16th June)	15. 7. 0
2nd	June 19. Redruth & Falmouth	16. 7. 0
3rd	23 & 24 Camborne Truro etc	13.18. 0
4th	25 & 27 Penzance & Helston	7. 9. 0
5th	Nov 26. Reporter with St Aubyn (November report)	7. 7. 0

The 1st item I recollect was incurred at the request of Mr Grylls and others, we thinking it very desirable that the County should know the liberal party had fixed upon you as the Candidate as soon as possible

Item 2—The Redruth meeting contained your first speech and also Mr John Michael Williams' statement of his intention to support you thoroughly, and then I recollect all the party thought ought to be at once made known to the County

Item 3 & 4, about these I have no certain recollection but Mr Grylls tells me as to item 4 he thinks some order was given about it as it was thought important to get the speech of Mr T.S.B. distributed thro' the West.

As to item 5 Cornish on behalf of St Aubyn said he thought there should be a supplement and told Heard so in my presence and as I did not object it may be said that I assented thereto. So that probably item 3 is the only item with reference to which we can say there was no express order, and as to that item if the account were at all reasonable I should not have liked to have raised the issue, of order or no order. But the sums charged don't seem reasonable and we must now decide what is to be done.

Mr Grylls tells me he has been informed that Mr Hooper leads Heard, but I must say I have never seen Hooper (who is a very nice person but quiet) take any such position, and the policy of our carrying the matter further all depends on whether Heard is (or is ever likely to be) independent of Mr Budd, for if so we should commit a great blunder in making Heard (as he will be if we press the matter) a bitter enemy: in fact the course to be now adopted depends entirely on Mr Budd's position in the *West Briton*, both present and in the future, and perhaps the better way would be to ask him the question frankly.

PV 36/25

S.T.G. Downing to A.P. Vivian

Redruth, 4 February 1869

My dear Sir

I return the *Cambrian* letter—you will observe the twenty nine thousand only applies to the Stamped circulation. I should think the *Cambrian* unstamped circulation must be much more for I find the *West Briton* stamped and unstamped circulation amounts to 3.500 a week, and that its stamped circulation is 1600 a week or 3 times that of the *Cambrian*. The *West Briton* is certainly an important paper. You did quite right to answer Mr Wright in the way you did. I told Cornish to pay him what was reasonable and fair.

PV 36/26

Henry Grylls to A.P. Vivian

Redruth, 4 February 1869

My dear Sir

I am in receipt of your favor of yesterday's date and have seen your communication to Mr Downing and Mr Heard's letter to him and find the latter offers to take off the paltry sum of 55^{s}/ on his entire charge.

Mr Downing will send you Heard's letter—I have casually been informed that Mr Hooper the Editor of the *West Briton* is the principal man connected with that newspaper. If so, and you wish it, I will see him, and make another effort to obtain more moderate charges. But it will be necessary to be assured that Mr Hooper is the proper party to whom to apply, or the seeing him will rather be an injury than benefit. I regret exceedingly you have been put to so great expense especially without a contest. The Bills would have been frightful if a contest had taken place which happily was prevented, and on any future election previous arrangements, I hope, will prevent the recurrence of such charges. Mr Basset, who was to have been you opponent, is, I fear, hopelessly ill.

PV 36/27/1

S.T.G. Downing to A.P. Vivian

Redruth, 9 February 1869

My dear Sir

I am favoured with your letter of the 8th. There is no question about the understanding as to the 10.10.0 retainers—but unfortunately with the exception of the item in some of the bills for 'attending the nomination', there is not a single charge that could be called an Election charge. The extra charges are made up

1st of the Registration Charges to which of course we should be told the £10.10.0 retainers did not apply.

2nd The services rendered by Messrs Roscorla, Rogers, Daniell and one or two others with reference to the preliminary meetings and which are Charges against you personally and are not covered by the joint retainer of Mr St Aubyn and yourself: this is shown by reference to the list for you will find that Messrs Genn (Falmouth)

Trevenna [sic] (Redruth) and one or two others who did not interfere with the registration only claim their 10.10.0. I have sent cheques for your moiety of the joint charges to the different parties and shall hope to send you a complete return within a post or two.

[P.S.] The Stannary Meeting was very well attended today. Lord Falmo: St Aubyn, Sir W Williams, Bolitho etc etc. Mr Bolitho read your letter and I took care quietly to move round the table in the course of the day and say something civil to everybody about your absence and it was well received.[1]

Poor Basset died this morning[2]

1. Beginning in 1869 and continuing until 1885, A.P.V. was far more often absent from Cornwall than his fellow county member St Aubyn. The problem partly resulted from the former's principal residence being in Wales.
2. John Basset (1831–69) was briefly succeeded by his brother Arthur (1833–70). Upon his death the Tehidy estates passed to another brother, Gustavus (1834–80).

PV 36/28

Henry Grylls to A.P. Vivian

Moreton House, Redruth, 11 February 1869

My dear Sir

Being from home yesty I was not able to acknowledge by return your favor of the 8th Instant. I had seen your views to Mr Downing, and concur in opinion that you have come to a wise decision to pay—all circumstances considered—all the demands made on you for election expenses. At the same time there can scarcely be two opinions of the exorbitant charges in some of the Bills.[16] You have been exceedingly welcome to the little services of my son and self and rejoice that, in co-operation with others they were so successful.

I was not able to attend the Stannaries Committee on Tuesday at Truro, but hear the result was favorable after some content. There is to be a final meeting on the 22nd Inst at Redruth—Whether of Sufficient importance to call you from so far I cannot venture an opinion. Mr Bolitho is evidently desirous of a full meeting and I am told Lord Falmouth will be present.

1. See PV 36/2 Claims presented by Downing.

PV 36/29

A.P. Vivian Esq MP

Sir

In drawing your attention to the enclosed documents relative to the Abolition of Light dues I have to inform you that I have a letter from the secty of the Falmouth Chamber in which he informs me that they have passed a resolution strongly in favour of the proposed and that he has little doubt that if convenient you will attend the deputation.

PV 36/31/1–2

S.T.G. Downing to A.P. Vivian

Redruth, 25 February 1869

My dear Sir

I have now, I believe, paid every single claim on you with reference to the West Cornwall Election except of course my own fees.

I send you in parcel marked no 1 all the vouchers for the payments on the joint account.

You will see that I have carried into this account every bill in which there were any items for which Mr St Aubyn was liable the result being that I have paid for you £ 577.7.7 whilst Mr St Aubyn's payments are £ 443.11.1. You will see that the registration work done here was more than that done at Penzance, but Mr St Aubyn does not complain because the suggestion that the charges should be carried in to the joint account came from his own Solicitor. He loses however 15 £ 00^{d} by the arrangement. In parcel no 2 you will find the receipt for the payments made by me on your separate account they amount to £ 456.19.1. You will find some little differences between the payments and the bills (for instance Mr Danniell receives in the joint account £10 more than in the original statement. This arose from an error in the addition of his payments) but on the whole the account is substantially the same as that originally submitted to you with the addition of the registration accounts of Mr Cornish and myself.

If then you will send me a cheque for balance due from you on

joint a/c 577. 7.7
separate 456.19.1
1034. 6.8

you will have paid everything connected with your candidature except my fees (or respecting the registration fees) a note of which I will send you in a post or two and in preparing which I shall of course consider the payment made by you of a moiety of the registration account.

I don't know that there is anything further to remark except to say that I think you were a little in error in supposing that no services were rendered by the professional men for the £5.5.0 retainer you have paid them.

For this sum we have had all their influence with their respective clients, they have spoken to their neighbours and friends and in fact secured the support of their respective districts for you. On this point therefore I think there is nothing to find fault with, but I shall always consider that some of the registration charges and printers bills were large and now that you are firmly in the seat would not again be submitted to and in fact will never again be charged because there will be no occasion to again put the Register right or advertise so extensively.

[P.S.] Please return me all the Vouchers as I have to lodge them with the Sheriff—and we ought not to delay this any longer. St Aubyn's will be lodged in a day or two.

PV 36/5

West Cornwall Election

List of Amounts paid on account of Arthur Pendarves Vivian Esqre MP and Sir John St Aubyn Esqre MP

Name	Residence	Nature of Claim	Solely A.P. Vivian Esq			Solely J. St Aubyn Es		
1. Thomas Tabb	Redruth	Carriage hire	25	5	-			
2. J.N. Earle	Do	Printer	2	12	6			
3. Wm Warne	Falmouth	Agency						
4. J.S. Doidge	Redruth	Printer	2	-	-			
5. Wm Angwin	St Just		1	17	6			
6. Joseph Newton	St Agnes	Agency						
7. Samuel Richards	Redruth	Carriage hire		14	-			
8. T.N. Roberts	London	Printer						
9. Christopher Ellis	Hayle							
10. W.P. Metchim & Son	London	Printers						
11. Hodge Hockin & Marrack	Truro	Solicitors						
12. W.R. Pender	Falmouth	Do						
13. J.G. Plomer	Helston	Do						
14. G.A. Jenkins	Penryn	Do	11	6	6			
15. Wm Trevenen	Helston	Do						
16. John Roscorla	Penzance	Do	28	5	4			
17. Henry Rogers	Helston	Do	24	-	11	8	1	1[illegible]
18. Pearse Jenkin	Redruth							
19. John Dale	Helston	Solicitor	7	4	-			
20. Matthew Courtenay	Truro							
21. Edmund Michell	Gwennap							
22. J.T. Trevena	Redruth	Solicitor						
23. Henry Thomas	Penzance	Do						
24. W.J. Genn	Falmouth	Do						
25. F. Hearle Cock	Truro	Do						
26. W. Hoskins Richards	Penzance							
27. Thos Leggo	Ludgvan							

Joint			Total A.P. Vivian Esq			Total J. St Aubyn Esq			Total			Remarks
3	10	-	27	-	-	1	15	-	28	15	-	
	7	-	2	16	-		3	6	2	19	6	
			9	17	9	19	17	9	19	15	6	
2	5	-	3	2	6	1	2	6	4	5	-	
7	14	9	5	14	11	3	17	4	9	12	3	
35	-	-	17	10	-	17	10	-	35	-	-	
-	10	-	-	19	-	-	5	-	1	4	-	
-	19	9	-	9	11	-	9	10	-	19	9	
1	3	11	-	11	11	-	12	-	1	3	11	
4	-	6	2	-	3	2	-	3	4	-	6	
49	7	4	24	13	8	24	13	8	49	7	4	
15	15	-	7	17	6	7	17	6	15	15	-	
21	10	2	10	15	1	10	15	1	21	10	2	
20	2	10	21	7	11	10	1	5	31	9	4	
13	13	0	6	16	6	6	16	6	13	13	-	
16	9	1	36	9	10	8	4	7	44	14	5	
173	18	6	111	-	2	95	1	1	206	1	3	
15	8	-	7	14	-	7	14	-	15	8	-	
31	10	-	22	19	-	15	15	-	38	14	-	
2	2	-	1	1	-	1	1	-	2	2	-	
2	2	-	1	1	-	1	1	-	2	2	-	
10	10	-	5	5	-	5	5	-	10	10	-	
10	10	-	5	5	-	5	5	-	10	10	-	
10	10	-	5	5	-	5	5	-	10	10	-	
26	5	-	13	2	6	13	2	6	26	5	-	
17	17	6	8	18	9	8	18	9	17	17	6	
3	3	-	1	11	6	1	11	6	3	3	-	
arried over			£361	5	8	266	1	9	627	7	5	

Name	Residence	Nature of Claim	Solely A.P. Vivian Esq			Solely J. St Aubyn Es		
28. H.M. Praed	Marazion							
29. Christopher Hichens	Morvah							
30. Saml Harvey	St Buryan							
31. Charles Ellis Junr	St Levan							
32. James Jenkin	Redruth	Printer	8	10	6			
33. W.M. Grylls	Do		5	19	3			
34. Thos Nicholls	St Columb	Solicitor						
35. W.T. Tresidder	St Ives	Do						
36. N.T. Trengrouse	Helston							
37. J.R. Daniell	Camborne	Solicitor	20	14	2			
38. Heard & Son	Truro							
39. H.S. Stokes	Bodmin							
40. R.T. Hall	Devoran							
41. James Tregaskis	Redruth	Printer	3	8	6			
42. Thos H. Edwards	Helston							
43. H.S. Stokes	Bodmin (2nd Bill)							
44. E. Rowe	Penzance							
45. Beare & Son	Do							
46. W. Cornish	Do							
47. T.N. Roberts	London (2nd Bill)							
48. J.N. Earle	Redruth (2nd Bill)							
49. Sundry Payments								
50. Mr Cornish's Bill of Coasts—Registration								
51. Mr Downings Do								

Joint			Total A.P. Vivian Esq			Total J. St Aubyn Esq			Total			Remarks
Brought Over			£361	5	8	266	1	9	627	7	5	
5	5	-	2	12	6	2	12	6	5	5	-	
2	2	-	1	1	-	1	1	-	2	2	-	
2	2	-	1	1	-	1	1	-	2	2	-	
2	2	-	1	1	-	1	1	-	2	2	-	
1	3	-	9	2	-	-	11	6	9	13	6	
11	15	2	11	16	10	5	17	7	17	14	5	
21	-	-	10	10	-	10	10	-	21	-	-	
26	5	-	13	2	6	13	2	6	26	5	-	
5	5	0	2	12	6	2	12	6	5	5	-	
70	19	7	56	4	-	35	9	9	91	13	9	
-	6	9	-	3	4	-	3	5	-	6	9	
1	7	3	-	13	8	-	13	7	1	7	3	
-	5	-	-	2	6	-	2	6	-	5	-	
7	1	3	6	19	2	3	10	7	10	9	9	
10	10	-	5	5	-	5	5	-	10	10	-	
-	16	-	-	8	-	-	8	-	-	16	-	These sums have been paid by Mr Cornish who has the receipts
1	18	6	-	19	3	-	19	3	1	18	6	
2	11	9	1	5	10	1	5	11	2	11	9	
1	10	11	-	15	6	-	15	5	1	10	11	
-	12	4	-	6	2	-	6	2	-	12	4	
-	7	-	-	3	6	-	3	6	-	7	-	
10	17	8	5	8	10	5	8	10	10	17	8	
			492	19	9	359	3	3	852	3	-	
			34	9	5	34	9	5	68	18	10	
			49	18	5	48	18	5	99	16	10	
			£577	7	7	443	11	1	1020	18	8	

PV 36/30

Harry Tilly to A.P. Vivian

Falmouth, 27 February 1869

Dear Sir,

I confess I was not a little surprised that I had not received any reply from you to my note, but your letter today has quite explained how it arose.

I am the more sorry at the accident in as much as if you are successful in your application the berth will have been given to a Tory, to the further serious damage of our cause here.

PV 36/32/1–2

S.T.G. Downing to A.P. Vivian

Redruth, 27 February 1869

My dear Sir

The £ 577.7.7 your proportion of the joint expenses may be divided between Election and Registration expenses as shown in the enclosed statement: namely registration £ 356.14.5 election £ 220.13.2.

With reference to the question how much of the expenses may be assumed to have been incurred in consequence of your being a stranger I should say <u>all</u> the separate expenses amounting to 456.19.1 were so incurred except, say Sheriff 39.1.6 and a further sum of 20 £ which would more than cover your printing and advertising in case you were to offer yourself for re-election. As I think I told you Mr Davey's re-election did not cost him more than 10 £ above the Sheriff's fees.

With reference to my own Election fees, I send you a note showing what was done <u>in addition</u> to the work the charges for which are included in the registration account as against Mr St Aubyn and yourself.

I have not filled in any charges for my Election fees as I should much prefer your reading through the bill and then filling in at the end such sum as you may think right. In fixing on the sum to be so filled in you will kindly remember that I shall be satisfied with whatever amount you may decide on, and that I much regret that the exceptional circumstances of the Election arising from your being a stranger should have rendered it necessary that so much time and labour should have been expended.

PV 36/23/1

ANALYSIS OF DOWNING'S ELECTION A/C 1868

1

		£	s	d
May 28	Short conference	1	1	0
" 29	Whole day - -	3	3	0
" 30	" "	3	3	0
" 31	Sunday short conference	1	1	0
June 1st	Important letter -		5	0
" 2	Short conference - -	1	1	0
" 3	Whole day - -	3	3	0
" 4	" "	3	3	0
" 5	" "	3	3	0
" 6	1/2 day - -	2	2	0
" 7	Sunday - short conference (at home)	1	1	0
" 8	1/2 day - -	2	2	0
" 9	Whole day - -	3	3	0
" 10	1/2 day	2	2	0
" 11	Whole day - -	3	3	0
" 12	" "	3	3	0
" 13	" "	3	3	0
" 14	Sunday (3 letters @ 3/6)		10	6
" 15	1/2 day -	2	2	0
" 16	Whole Day	3	3	0
	Carried forward	44	17	6

2

		£	s	d
	Brght forward	44	17	6
June 17	7 letters (4 @ 3/6, 3 @ 5/-)	1	10	0
" 18	1/2 day	2	2	0
" 19	Whole day	3	3	0
" 20	" "	3	3	0
" 21	Sunday	3	3	0
" 22	Whole day - -	3	3	0

" 23	" "	3	3	0
" 24	" "	3	3	0
" 25	" "	3	3	0
" 26	" "	3	3	0
" 27	" "	3	3	0
" 30	2 letters @ 3/6 - -		7	0
July 1st	Downings clerk - Whole day	2	2	0
" 2	Do Do - - - o	3	3	0
" 6	Do Do 1/2 day	1	1	-
" 13	Nine unimportant letters found @ 3/6	1	11	6
" 14	One letter @ 5/0		5	0
" 15	" " "		5	0
	carried forward	85	11	0

3

		£	s	d
	Brght forward -	85	11	0
July 17	3 letters @ 3/6		10	6
" 18	1 letter @ 5/-		5	0
" 20	2 letters @ 5/-, @ 3/6		8	6
" 25	" @ 3/6 to self		3	6
" 28	" " " "		3	6
Aug 4	" " " "		3	6
" 8	" " " "		3	6
" 13	" " " "		3	6
" 15	Whole day -	3	3	0
" 19	Conference letter -	1	1	0
" 24	1 letter to self -		3	6
" 25	" " " "		3	6
" 26	" " " "		3	6
" 29	" " " "		3	6
" 31	" " " "		3	6
Sept 14	" " " "		3	6
" 19	" " " "		3	6
" 22	Short conference	1	1	0
" 23	Letter to Self -		3	6
" 29	Short conference	1	1	0

Oct 6	Long letter to Self		5	0
" 16	Letter to self -		3	6
	carried forward £	95	15	0

4

		£	s	d
	Brght forward -	95	15	0
Oct 17	Half day conference -	2	2	0
" 19	Long letter to Self -		5	0
" 20	1 unimportant letter		3	6
" 23	Long letter to self -		5	0
Nov 5	2 unimportant letters @ 3/6		7	0
Nov 7	1 letter to Self @ 3/6		3	6
" 9	2 letters @ 3/6 - -		7	0
" 10	1 " @ 5/ - - -		5	0
" 11	5 " @ 3/6		17	6
" 15	Sunday conference - -	1	1	0
" 17	Whole day - -	3	3	0
" 19	" " - - - -	3	3	0
" 20	Conference - - - - -	1	1	0
" 21	Half Day - - - -	2	2	0
" 24	5 letters @ 3/6 - - -		17	6
" 25	few hours - - - -	1	1	0
" 30	1 letter @ 5/-		5	0
Dec 3	1 " @ 3/6		3	6
" 5	Conference - - - -	1	1	0
" 8	1 letter to self @ 3/6		3	6
" 15	3 " " " @ 3/6		10	6
" 16	1 " " " @ 3/6		3	6
	carried forward	115	6	0

PV 36/23/2

5

		£	s	d
	Brght forward -	115	6	0
Dec 18	1 letter to Self - -		3	6
" 23	1 letter @ 5/- attendance 10/6		15	6

Date		Item	£	s	d
"	24	1 letter to Self - -		3	6
"	28	" " " "		3	6
"	30	" " " "		5	0
"	31	" " " "		5	0
1869					
Jan[y]	4	1 letter to Self - - - -		3	6
"	5	1 " " "		3	6
"	6	1 " " "		5	0
"	8	2 " " "		7	0
"	11	1 " " "		3	6
"	23	2 letters @ 3/6, 1 @ 5/-		12	0
"	25	Conference	1	1	0
"	26	2 letters @ 3/6 - - -		7	0
"	28	1 " @ 3/6		3	6
"	29	1 " " 3/6		3	6
Feb[ry]	1	Conference	1	1	0
"	4	Attendance & letters - -	1	1	0
"	13	1 letter @ 5/-		5	0
"	15	1 " @ 3/6		3	6
"	16	1 " @ 3/6		3	6
"	18	2 Whole days @ 3/3/0	6	6	0
		Total £	129	11	6

PV 36/33/2

S.T.G. Downing to A.P. Vivian

Redruth, 14 March 1869

My dear Sir

I was very glad to find from your note that the Stannary bill has been read a second time and have no doubt you did right to reserve yourself until after Easter when you will have the bill in Committee.

I am glad you will be able to return me the vouchers etc with reference to the Election tomorrow for Wm Coode the Under sheriff writes under date the 12th 'I have today received instructions to make a return of Election expenses || to the House of Commons, how am I to forward these for West Cornwall!'

I have written to him to keep back the return for a day or two for of course it would not do for us to be reported to the House as defaulters

PV 36/34

S.T.G. Downing to A.P. Vivian

Redruth, 16 March 1869

My dear Sir

Election a/c

I am obliged for your favour of yesterday's date covering cheque for £1034.6.8, the amount of the payments made on your account as per vouchers bundles 1 & 2

I am sorry you have been troubled by my having sent my own account in blank and trust you will still kindly consent to fix the amount of the fee yourself and I beg again to assure you I shall readily concur in your decision whatever it may be. If you would name the amount you decide on by telegram before one o'clock tomorrow I should be able to include it in the return to the Sheriff which I have arranged to send by tomorrow's post.

[PV 38/39 omitted—fragments not related to election expenses]

PV 53

[This is a small book in which Pendarves Vivian set down his thoughts on the election of 1868, 1874, 1880, 1885 as well as listing all expenses etc.

He begins the 1868 entry: 'Analysis of Expenses of Registration and Election for myself alone in West Cornwall—1868.']

[See PV 36/1 for the accounts referred to below.]

Many of the foregoing charges are exorbitant in the extreme (as testified to by HHV Jany 23rd 1869. J.M. Williams Feb^{ry} 2nd 1869. Mrs Williams 3rd Feb^{ry} 1869. H Grylls Jany 28 or Feb^{ry} 11$^{th.}$ In many of Downing's own letters) Perhaps the most decidedly excessive charge is that for <u>advertising and printing</u>. (£407.2.1) Downing ought to have watched and checked this, first by settling a rate at which my address was to be entered, and then by not putting it in oftener than was necessary which I believe has been [segment missing]. Mr Heard's bill for the *West Briton* services was <u>very</u> excessive £124.9.6) the rate 56/-

for each insertion was enormous. It is quite true that my address was a long one, but at the 'Cambrian' rate as charged HHV (per words) it should have been 52^{s}/3^{d} (see H Grylls' letter Jany 30) hence next time my address should be as short as possible and in as few papers— then again Special Editions should never be ordered without special orders, or great urgency. The four special Editions this time cost £53 I might have applied to E. Budd to reduce *West Briton* Bill, but I don't think it would have been of any avail as he told me afterwards that he trusted implicitly to Mr Heard as regards financial working of the paper and that he would sooner relinquish his share of it, than interfere; himself and J.P. Budd hold 11/32^{d} each of the paper, and Mr Heard 10/32, so they have a majority in the management, and he assured that I need not trouble myself about employing Mr Heard as its columns should never be used against me as long as he had anything to say to it but that he could not interfere in any of the financial matters which he left entirely in Mr Heard's hands. Mr Hooper was the paid Editor and solely conducted the matter of the paper under E. Budd's supervision and approval. There is no doubt whatever that the Advertising and Printing on this occasion was very far and excess of what it should have been, had proper care and supervision been exercised. The only excuse is that I was a complete stranger to nearly everybody and that the Introduction cost a great deal. This is of course the case but not in any way to account for this excessive expenditure. The advertising and printing for Sir J Trelawny and Brydges Williams [sic] together in East Cornwall and that notwithstanding a contest of two months or more was only £369.7.6 some £ 37.14.7 less than mine alone. Mr Heard only consented to take off 5/- from each advertisement of address which could have amounted to £ 12.15.0 on his Bill and £10 on all the papers. (See Downing's letter Feb^{ry} 4th/69) and this I refused.

There is no doubt too that Mr D. ought to have done far more as regards making arranging and tying down paid agents that their charges should not have been run up in the way they were. The understanding was that half retaining fees (10 guineas) should be issued by St Aubyn and myself to certain solicitors etc agreed on and both HHV and self understand that their services for Registration were to be secured by this—but D denied this and the consequence was shameful Bills (such as Rogers of Helston, Daniell of Camborne, Newton of St Agnes etc) which never ought to have been allowed and which D ought to have insisted on being reduced before handing to me—but this he was very slack about and very adverse to as see his letters—it was thought however better to meet these bills untouched as D was himself so slack which I did—otherwise it might have established ill feeling both in D himself who has great influence with J.M.W and others and other solicitors etc on this my first coming forward but another time it will no doubt to arrange distinctly beforehand on fixed sums and fees which are not on any pretext to be exceeded. & no charge of time or service to be allowed in fact all other charges but fees to be abolished. HHV made my arrangements this time but somehow or other they were not made distinct and decided enough and every advantage was taken of this—. Downing says in his letter of the 23rd Janry that tho expenses were incurred owing to my being a complete stranger to the 'middle classes' that 'we shall never again want to retain the lawyers' and he puts the expenses down at '£400 in excess of what they ought to have done'—but that he doesn't think by taxing the accounts we could reduce them more than £150 which he does not advise. In his letter of the 27th Febry in reply to a question of mine how much of the foregoing expenses may be assumed to have been incurred on account of my being a stranger? he replies 'I should say all the separate expenses amounting to 456-19-1 except the Sheriffs [sic] fee £39-1-6 and a further sum of £20 which would more than cover your printing and advertising, in case you were to offer yourself for re-election. As I think I told you Mr Davey's re-election did not cost him £10 above the Sheriff's fee' In his letter of 28th Jany 1869 he says 'I find Mr R Davey's first election cost him with[in] £250 of the claims on you and we must remember Mr D only came forward 8 days before the nomination day so that his advertising expenses were almost nil' and no daily papers then 'Mr Tremayne retired before the Nomination so that what we call the "contest" really did not last a week and in that time Mr M Williams spent £800 and Mr Davey £700' 'no subsequent Election of Mr D. cost more than £30 but I cannot disguise from myself the fact the £100 he saved by cutting some of the Bills would have seriously affected his chance of re-election if there had been a subsequent contest'. In letter of Febry 25 D says 'that some of the Registration charges are large and now that you are firmly in the seat would not again be submitted to.' If then we take out Downing's estimate of expenses incurred on account of my being a stranger as above £456.19.1 and Registration fees etc £361.2.11 and D's own fee of £165 reckoned on time and charges from being introduced so long before the public, it would amount up to £983, leaving only £217. If I had been going to be re-elected only—say add £50 as Downing's fee (the amount St Aubyn gave Cornish this time) and we get £267 Election fees £361 Registration £20 advertising (D's estimate as in foregoing) together £648.0.0 not far in excess of the amount actually published as St Aubyn's expenses this time viz. £633.9.9

It was stated in the H of C on the 30th April 1869 that a county Election Vote should not cost more 15/- to 30/- on every vote polled: this was not contradicted.

In paying Downing I had some little difficulty to know what to give him, as he sent me in a list of services and charges with no money carried out, requesting me to do so. Under these circumstances acting on HHV's advice I took the Bill to Coulthurst[?] And he recommended me as a basis to put down the whole days in which he was acting for me at 3 guineas, half days at 2 gs, important conferences at 1 guinea, and important letters at 5/- each, unimportant etc at $3^s/6^d$. this I carried out and it amounted in all, to £129-11-6. There was no fee in this and Coulthurst said it ought not to be expected but in order to be liberal with D and make him satisfied I sent him first of all a cheque for the amount £1034.6.8 (from V and S or Robartes & Co) and then another cheque for himself of £165.13.4. making a total of £1200 as my Election expenses. (out of this cheque of £165.13.4. D had afterwards pay some small accounts to £4.8.6 which reduced his own nett payments from myself alone to £161-4.10 besides which he had received from St Aubyn and self jointly the amount of £99.10.10 for Registration Services so that in nett Receipt on the Election was £260.15.8. Of course these Registration services will not occur again but it will be very desirable if at all practicable to get D's services secured at a certain fee which it was not to exceed. He charged for Sundays in his a/c which Coulthurst much objected to.)

Hussey means to employ a clerk at each of the principal towns in Glamorganshire Cardiff, Swansea and Merthyr at a salary and pay proper attention to employ their whole time in keeping the Register, Canvassing books etc, so that in the event of a contest these books could at the first warning be issued out to working committees. (and no professional men except [?] at say £50 fee). T Collins (MP for Boston) in his speech on the General Election April 30th 1869, estimated the cost of each vote polled at a County election contested at from 15/- to 30/- everything included. (this was advanced as an argument against the purity of the General Election which cost about £40 per vote.)

Nov 21st 1871. Had a talk with J. St Aubyn, Downing and Shilson—on the strength of the Wesleyans in our Division. The latter (a remarkably good judge) regards them of great strength. They would all oppose anybody who they considered in any way irreligious either politically or privately. Shilson does not think they would all combine to oppose in any minor Education question such as the 25th clause of the 1870 Education Bill.

PV 53

[Also in the Notebook (at the back)]

[Inside cover]

Downing in Novr 1868 stated to me that in his opinion £100 to £120 a year ought to cover my subscription donations etc. J. St Aubyn afterwards said that £50 his [?]

CORNISH SUBSCRIPTIONS & DONATIONS 1868

Description	Through whom	date	Subscription	Donation	Remarks
Royal Cornwall Infirmary	Dr Barham	Decr 9th/68	£5.5.0		important
Polytechnic Society (Falmouth)	Lloyd Fox Esq	Sept / 68	2.2.0		” ”
Geological Society (Penzance)	Seymour Tremeneheere	March / 69	2.2.0		” ”
Marazion Regatta	J Blight	July / 68		£1-1-0	” ”
Truro Organ Fund	E.T. Carlyon	July / 68		£2-2-0	
Penzance Regatta & Swimming Club	J. Roscorla	Aug / 68		2-2-0	
Truro Swimming Club	R. John	Aug / 68		1-1-0	
Helston Wrestling Club	P.G. Hill	” ”		1-1-0	
Penzance Fire Works	H.C. Cornish	” ”		2-2-0	
Falmouth Regatta	H. Tilly	” 26th / 68		3-3-0	
Wesleyan (missing)	F. John	” 31st / 68		1-0-0	
Falmouth Gymastic [sic]	Ph Buckett	Septr 6th / 68		1-1-0	
Wesleyan Chapel Redruth	H. Grylls	” 10th / 68		5-0-0	
Royal Institution of Cornwall	T.W. Newcombe	Dec 10th / 68		1-1-0	
Redruth Town Mission	Revd G.W. Hawksley	” ”		2-2-0	
Cup to Volunteers	Captn Carew	Sept / 68		12-12-0	
			[£9.9.0]	[£37.8.0]	
			£46 . 17 . 0		

Cornish Subscriptions & Donations 1869

Description	Through whom	date	Subscription	Donation	Remarks
Royal Cornwall Agricultural Association	H. Tresawna	Jany 12	£5-5-0		
St Ives Branch Lifeboat Association	Grenfell		1-1-0		
Falmouth Branch Lifeboat Association	T. Webber	Feb^{ry} 24	1-1-0		
Probus Ploughing Match	L.F. Kendall	" 13	1-1-0		
Kenwyn Ploughing Match			1-1-0		
Wesleyan Body	N.B. Downing	Feb^{ry} 25		£50 - -	STG thinks this might do for 5 yrs
Falmouth Chamber of Commerce	J. Hullamore	March 31	1-1-0		
West Cornwall Mining Convalescant Hospital	G. Lightly	" "	2-2-0		
Falmouth Liberal Association	Howard Fox	April 5	1-1-0	2-2-0	
Miners' Association of Cornwall & Devon	J.H. Collins	" 10	1-1-0		
Penwith Agricultural Association (Penzance)	J. Roscorla	" 28		1-1-0	
Falmouth Shipwrecked Sailors & Fishermen	R. Williams	May 6		1-1-0	On a/c of late severe winter

F.B. Hounds (cheque)	Robins Foster	May 14		10-10-0	Lady Falmouth's recommendation on a/c of g'father
ornwall Chamber of Agriculture	Martin Magor	" 26	1-1-0		Paid by self at Penzance
Penzance Swimming Association	T. Cock	June 24		1-1-0	Tickets to this amount
R. Polytechnic Art Union	Howard Fox Falmouth	" 28		1-0-0	last year 3-3-0 but J.S. & A
R. Cornwall Regatta (Falmouth)	James Tilly	" 29		2-2-0	gives 2-2-0
Porthoustock Lifeboat	E.P. Roskruge St Keverne Helston	Aug 9		1-1-0	(Manacles Rocks)
Grampound Rd Hotel Co	Wm Trethewy	Aug 16		25-0-0	5 shares of £5 each
Marazion & St Michaels Mt Royal Regatta	John Blight	Aug 21		1-1-0	
Mounts Bay Regatta	C Mathew	" "		1-1-0	
Ticket in Art Union— Polytechnic Society	R. Broad Falmouth	Aug 31		-10-0	At Dolcoath Mine
Mechanics' Institute— St Just (repairs)	R. Boyns?			2-2-0	
St Just Horticultural Society	Wm Chenalls	Nov 3		1-1-0	
Royal Cornwall Geological Society	W. Bolitho Jnr	" 10	£1-1-0		
R. Cornwall Polytechnic Soc	W. Dymond	" "	£2-2-0		
S. Pascoe, Truro County Library	S Pascoe (in person)	Decr 8		1-0-0	Fund for removing to new buildings
	Total for the year—	1869—	£19-14-0	£98-10- 0	together = £118-4-0

	1870	Donations	46- 5-0	
		Subscriptions	27-15-0	
			£74- 0-0	
	1871	Donations	33- 7-0	
		Subscriptions	39-10-3	
			£72-17-3	
	1872	Donations	£19-13-0	
		Subscriptions	£50- 8-6	
			£70- 1-6	
	1873	Donation	35-19-0	
		Subscription	46- 6-0	
			£82- 5-0	
Election	1874	Donation	53- 4-0	
		Subscription	55-14-6	
			£108-18-6	Election year
Election	1880	Donations	82-15-0	(12 +)
		Subs	66- 8-6	(30 +)
			£149- 3-6	
Last full year	1884	Donations	£317- 8-7	
		Subs	60-14-6	
			£378- 3-1	

By 1884 APV was including West Cornwall Registration (moiety) payable thro W. Grylls of £194-5-5 and Electioneering Expenses of £51-10-2.

1882 W Cornwall Registr £250
1883 W Cornwall Registr £125

PV 36/35/1–2

S.T.G. Downing to A.P. Vivian

Redruth, 19 March 1869

My dear Sir

I am obliged for your letters of the 17th and for your cheque for 165.13.4. therein enclosed.

That sum is an amply sufficient fee in fact it is somewhat more than the ordinary charges would amount to and it will thus enable me to meet a little difficulty that has arisen in the West.

It appears that Cornish since we prepared the accounts thinks that Mr Wright (your noisy supporter at the Penzance meeting) should be paid 2-12-6 by Mr St Aubyn and a like sum by yourself, and I am afraid there are some other little trifles in the Penzance district that were not included in the accounts furnished us by Cornish: the £165 however is such an ample fee that I shall be enabled to discharge thereout these little Western claims so as to keep the total of your expenses at the £1200 and still leave the fair fees for myself.

I have written to Cornish insisting on the account being settled at once and he will probably come up tomorrow for that purpose. After I have seen him you shall have the corrected a/c which you would probably like to keep.

In the meantime allow me again to thank you for your cheque. I will write on County matters tomorrow

PV 36/36/1–2

S.T.G. Downing to A.P. Vivian

Redruth, 20 March 1869

My dear Sir.

I have had the little Western claims submitted to me by Cornish and have paid your surety c/-

Wright	5. 5. 0
Polkinghorne (for Sancreed Committee)	2. 2. 0
Glasson	10. 6
Giles	19. 6
	8.17. -

Your surety is therefore only £4. 8. 6

Should anything else of the same kind be sent me by Cornish I will discharge it for as I told you yesterday the fee you have sent me is amply sufficient to enable me to do this. All the accounts have been duly lodged with the undersheriff. St Aubyn's expenses are as follow

Professional agents	400. 5. 3
Non professional agents	75. 3. 3
Printing & advertising	109. 4. 8
Undersheriff	39.11. 3
General expenditure	13. 2. 6
	637. 6.11

You will see that our advertising and printing costs 3^{00}£ more than St Aubyns! The difference is the other items between your expenses and his are just what under the circumstances we might assume they would have been.

However the matter is all over and it will never be again necessary that you should advertise more extensively than your colleague. I think you have done yourself no harm by <u>not</u> voting on the Revenue Officers Bill—some people would have preferred the majority being the other way.

I don't think any one here cares about the Sea Birds bill, on such a question you will be pretty safe if you go into the same lobby with St Aubyn.

PV 36/4

West Cornwall Election 1868

Bills paid on separate Account of A. Pendarves Vivian Esq. M.P.

		£	s.	d.
1	*West Briton*	124	9	6
2	*Cornwall Gazette*	32	8	6
3	*Western Morning News*	57	9	-
4	*Western Daily Mercury*	57	9	8
5	W. Kernick	3	10	-
6	James Gripe	2	5	-
7	James Snow	1	1	-
8	Thomas Angove	6	11	6
9	Gill & Son	10	14	-
10	R. C. Richards	1	11	-
11	Fred H. Earle	13	10	-
12	*Cornish Telegraph*	24	11	6
13	Heard & Son	33	9	-
14	W. Philp	-	15	-
15	Henry Grylls	5	18	3
16	Undersheriff	39	1	6
17	William Tregaskis	1	1	-
18	Banfield Brothers	3	4	-
19	*"One and, all" Newspaper*	12	12	-
20	Polytechnic Society	2	13	6
21	Sundry payments	21	9	2
		£456	19	1

PV 35/122

Dear Sir,

Allow me to tender to you and the other members of the Liberal Committee my warmest thanks for the kindness with which you received my candidature, and for the very valuable assistance you have rendered the Liberal Cause by your cordial support of Mr. St. Aubyn and myself.

I fear I shall be obliged to leave the County in a few days, but trust, on some not very distant occasion, to have the opportunity of personally thanking you.

I am, Dear Sir,

Yours very faithfully,

A. Pendarves Vivian

Truro,

November 24th, 1868.

PV 35/109

EAST CORNWALL ELECTION.

CENTRAL COMMITTEE ROOM,

LISKEARD,

21st October, 1868.

Sir,

On behalf of the Central Committee for conducting the Election of the Liberal Candidates, SIR JOHN SALUSBURY TRELAWNY, BART., and EDWARD BRYDGES WILLYAMS, Esq., I beg to solicit your vote and interest for these Gentlemen ; and as it is important that the views of those friendly to their return should be ascertained with the least possible delay, a Form is enclosed, which the Committee hope you will fill up and return at your earliest convenience.

I am, Sir,

Your obedient Servant,

FRANCIS HOWELL,

CHAIRMAN.

Your Polling place is ....

PV 35/110

EAST CORNWALL ELECTION.

No..........

Sir,

It is* .... my intention to Vote for

....

and ....

at the present Election for EAST CORNWALL.

YOURS, &C.,

Signed ....

Place of Abode ....

* *Or "not" if you should decline.*

To

PV 35/67

Moreton House, Redruth, 22 July 1868

Dear Sir,

All parties are desirous of knowing the result of the efforts made by the Liberal Committees in reference to the Registration. Will you kindly fill in the figures in the annexed schedule, as correctly as you have the means, and forward it to me, as Chairman of the General Committee ?

Yours very truly,
HENRY GRYLLS.

The Number of NEW Claimants, including Freeholders, Leaseholders, and Occupiers .... }

What proportion of such New Claimants are probably Liberal .... }

PV 35/77

The Western Daily Mercury, 27 July 1868

THE REPRESENTATION OF ST. IVES.

The two political parties of St. Ives have now commenced what promises to be an unusually severe battle. The Tories especially are working with extraordinary ardour and energy, and they will continue so to work until the time arrives that will convince them that their labour has been in vain. They know that they are now left to their own resources, having been almost entirely deprived of the power which they have so long possessed, of applying the screw upon the dependent voters, and at th... time there seems to be no doubt whatever that Paull will have to go to the wall. He has for many years enjoyed the high honour of misrepresenting in Parliament the proper political feeling of the borough, although at the last general election a gallant attempt was made to oust him, but without effect. It is now pretty well known that Mr Edward Vivian, of Torquay, fought the battle of the Liberal party at that time, and it was that election which sealed the doom of the Tories, inasmuch as it brought to light the fact that the screw had been used in the most unprecedented manner. Mrs Davies Gilbert is a large landowner in the neighbourhood, and it was ascertained that through the instrumentality of her agents her tenants voted for Mr Paull. Other Tory landowners gave their tenants to understand that they were to vote in the same direction, and hence it was that Mr Paull was returned by a majority of sixty-six over Mr Vivian. Since that, however, circumstances have strangely altered, and that alteration will most assuredly lead to the defeat of Mr. Henry Paull at the coming election. The late owner of Tregenna was so decided a Tory that he compelled his tenants to follow him, but his brother, Mr John Augustus Stevens, who has just come into possession of the property, has declared himself to be a staunch Liberal, and he has in an excellent letter which he has recently addressed to Mr Vivian Stevens, chairman of the Liberal Committee in St. Ives, expressed in strong terms the pleasure he feels that a gentleman of the position and ability of Mr Henry Riversdale Grenfell should have been invited to contest the next election. In addition to this we are also given to understand that he has insisted upon his tennants being allowed to vote as they please, and he has intimated to his agents, who are Penzance lawyers, and who, according to rumour, have accepted a retainer from Mr Paull, that they are not in any way to interfere during the forthcoming contest. Mrs Gilbert has promised Mr Grenfell her most cordial support, and therefore there is no doubt that Mr Paull is quite right when he says—as he has said—that the Tory party are thrown almost entirely upon their own resources. Mr Grenfell commenced to address the electors of the borough on Tuesday evening last, when he delivered a lengthy and very able address, and he at once enlisted the sympathies of a large number of the electors of the borough. The electors of Lelant, Towednack, and other places included in the political borough, have also had the advantage of hearing him, and at public meetings they have pledged themselves to use every exertion to secure his election [in] a legitimate manner. Mr Paull has thought it necessary to follow closely upon his footsteps, & he has in various places been giving an account of his stewardship, but while he has been speaking Mr Grenfell and his friends have been prosecuting a most active and successful canvass, and he has been everywhere received with the utmost cordiality. On all sides there seems to be a feeling of gladness on the part of the electors that they will at length be able to give practical expression to their views without any fear of the consequences, and although, no doubt, the contest will be a severe one, yet it is certain to result in favour of the Liberal candidate, and Mr Paull will please accept from us the assurance that as M.P. for St. Ives his days are numbered. The Liberal electors of the borough have now only to be united, and the day of their redemption is at hand.

Mr Grenfell having to attend a meeting at the Bank of England today, was compelled to leave St. Ives on Saturday afternoon, but he will return again on Saturday next, and will be the guest of Mr T.S. Bolitho. Already the Tories have commenced their trickery by the publication of squibs, in which they endeavour to turn the minds of the electors from the real point at issue by representing to them that Mr Vivian has been shabbily turned aside in favour of Mr Grenfell. It is, however, well known that Mr Vivian had no desire to go to Parliament, and that he was himself extremely anxious to give way in favour of any gentleman who could make a certainty of that of which he had only sanguine expectations. He sacrificed personal considerations for the good of the Liberal party, and Mr Vivian will, we are sure, be the first to say that he retired voluntarily, and that he has not been in the least degree slighted by the Liberal party of the borough. But the Tories feel that they are about to suffer a defeat, and they seem to entertain the hope that the new electors of St. Ives are to be duped by false representations, and consequently to be drawn into their meshes. The hope is a forlorn one, for St. Ives will at the next general election follow the footsteps of the other Cornish boroughs, and send to Parliament men who will give a hearty support to the policy of Mr Gladstone.

Index

Acland, T.D., 42, 46
Angove, Thomas, 96, 134
Angwin, William, 89, 96, 114
Atkinson, H.J., xlix

Backhouse, Edmund, 71
Bain, David, 58
Banfield Brothers 96, 134
Barham, Dr, 128
Barrett, Sergeant, 74
Basset, Francis, (1st Baron De Dunstanville) xix, xxi, xxiii, xxxiv, xlii
Basset, John Francis xxvii, xxviii, xlii, 10–11, 27, 42, 64, 72, 110, 111
Bawden, Charles, 74
Beare & son 90, 96, 116
Bennetts, Mr, (of Falmouth) 9, 40
Berryman, Mr, 32
Bevan, Mr, 54
Blamey, William, 94
Blee, Robert, 30, 48
Bligh, J.M., xxi
Blight, John, 128, 130
Boase, Francis, 78
Bodmin xix, xxii, xxiv, 66, 98, 116
Bolitho, Thomas S., xlvii, li, 6, 8, 17, 29, 30, 34, 54, 57, 100, 109, 111, 140
Bolitho, William, 31, 39, 44
Bolitho, William Jr, 78, 130
Bossiney xviii
Botallack 73
Bottral, Mr, 32
Boulton, Matthew, xxxiii
Boyns, R., 130
Bridgend 65
Brighton 76
Broad, Robert, 30, 78, 130
Brogden, Alexander, 64
Brompton 39
Bruce, H.A., 26, 42
Bryant, Mr, 32
Bucket, Ph, 128
Budd, Edward, 9, 55, 58, 124
Budd, Henry, 101, 105, 109
Budd, J.P., 124
Buller, J.H., 57, 61, 72

Callington 76
Camarthen, Marquess of, (George Godolphin) 25
Camborne xiii, xlix, 1, 6–7, 12–13, 15, 21, 24, 29–30, 32, 37, 42, 46, 53, 55, 67–8, 96, 98, 108, 116, 124
Cambrian 101–4, 109, 124
Cardiff 126
Carew, Captain Robert H., 69, 74, 128
Carlyon, E.T., 128
Carne, William, 32, 72
Chamberlain, Joseph, xlix
Chenalls, William, 130
Chiverton 13, 30, 66, 93
Churston, Lord, xxvii, xlv
Clyma, George, xv, 10, 24
Cock, Francis Hearle, 43, 48–53, 55–6, 89, 98, 114
Cock, T., 130
Coleridge, Mr, 22
Collins, J.H., 129
Collins, T., 126

Conservative (Tory) xiii, xiv, xvii, xix–xx, xxi–xxviii, xxx, xxxv–xxxvi, xxxix, xl–xlvi, xlvii–xlviii, xlix, l, liii, 13, 23, 25, 27, 39, 42, 50–3, 56–9, 64, 66, 68–9, 73, 83, 84, 118
Constantine & Mawnan 67
Conybeare, Charles, xiii, xvi, xlix
Coode, Edward, 75, 77, 101
Coode, William, 78, 79, 122
Cornish Telegraph 96, 134
Cornish, Coulson, (H.C.) 63, 128
Cornish, Thomas, xlviii, 10, 13, 15, 23, 29, 30, 32, 35–8, 41, 44, 45, 50, 51, 53, 56, 57, 63, 65, 78, 80, 90, 94, 105, 109, 112, 117, 125, 132, 133
Cornish, W., 90, 116
Cornwall 6, 8, 10, 11, 15, 17, 18, 19, 22, 25, 30, 32, 40, 54, 55, 57, 60, 66, 69, 79, 82, 86, 87, 92, 102, 108, 109, 141
Cornwall Advertiser 14
Coulthurst, Mr, 126
county reformers xx, xxi, xxxi
Courtenay, Matthew, 32, 48, 89, 98, 114
Cowley, Lord, 40
Crantock 42
Craufurd, Mr and Mrs, 57, 61
Creed 67

Dale, John, 89, 98, 114
Daniell, J.R., 90, 98, 110, 116, 112, 124
Davey, Richard, xiii, xvi, xxii, xxiv, xxv, xxvi, xxx, xxxi, xxxiii, l, lii, 3, 7, 9, 11–12, 21, 30, 54, 74–5, 78, 86, 102, 118, 125
Davey, Stephen, 30
Davey, Sydney, 30
Davey, William Horton, xxxi
Devon 61
Devoran 45, 47, 49, 87, 98, 116
Disraeli, Benjamin, (Dizzy) 27
Dissent (ers) xliv, xlv, 15–16
Doidge, J.S., 89, 96, 114
Downing, N.B., 129
Downing, Theophilus, (S.T.G.) xvii, xxix, xxxvi, xxxix, xl, xliii, xlvi, li–liii, 3, 9, 14, 23–4, 30–3, 35–8, 42–8, 50, 52–3, 55–7, 60, 63–6, 68–70, 72, 74, 76–80, 87–8, 90, 92–6, 100–12, 116, 118–20, 122–7, 132
Drake, Reverend, 44
Dymond, W.V., 71, 96, 130

Earle, Fred H., 96, 134
Earle, J.N., 89, 96, 114, 116
East Cornwall (parliamentary division) xiv, xx–xxii, xxv, xxvi, xxxix, xl, xli, lii, 10, 34, 43, 54, 56–7, 63–4, 66, 75–7, 124, 136, 137
East Devon 45
Edwards, Thomas Hyne, 35, 90, 98, 116
election issues,
  agriculture 23, 24
  education 18, 22, 26, 86
  financial questions 18, 22, 85
  Irish Church Dissestablishment xvi, 16, 18, 21, 84, 85
  local taxation 22, 24
electors—*see* voters
Eliot, Charles, 25
Eliot, Henry, 25
Eliot, Lord, xxxvi
Ellis, Charles Jr, 90, 116
Ellis, Christopher, 89, 98, 114
Enys, John Samuel, 6, 28, 30, 31, 60, 72
Enys, Mrs, 6, 60
Exeter 57, 80, 81

Falmouth (Port) 9, 10, 24, 30, 40, 41, 46, 72, 96, 98, 114, 108, 110, 130
Falmouth
  Branch Lifeboat Association 129
  Chamber of Commerce 129
  Gymnastic 128
  Liberal Association 129
  Regatta 128
  Shipwrecked Sailors and Fishermen 129

Falmouth, Fifth Viscount, (Lord Boscawen Rose) xxiii, xxiv, xli, xlii
Falmouth, Sixth Viscount, xxiii, xxviii, xxix, xlii, li, 4, 5, 6, 10, 16, 17, 32, 35, 36, 47, 48, 51, 72, 111
Falmouth, Lady Mary Frances Elizabeth, 8, 54
Feock 49, 67, 91
First Reform Act (1832) xviii, xx, xxii, xxiii, xxv, xxxviii, xliv
Folkestown 28
Fortescue, George Matthew, 34, 43
Foster, Richard, 34
Fox, A. Lloyd, 71, 128
Fox, Charles, lii, 30, 70, 71, 74, 78
Fox, Howard, 129, 130
Fox, R.W., 72
Freiberg (Germany) 18

Genn, W.J., 89, 98, 110, 114
Geological Society (Penzance) 128
Gibson, Mr, 103
Gilbert, Carew Davies, xlix, 6, 15, 45, 60, 139
Giles, Mr, 132
Gill & Son 96, 134
Gladstone, W.E., xlvii, 7, 16, 18, 21–2, 27, 84, 85, 141
Glamorganshire 126
Glasson, Mr, 132
Graham, Sir James, xxxviii
Grampound 30, 31, 37
Gregor, Clanville, 28
Gregor, Francis, xx
Gregor, Gordon, xxv, xxvi
Grenfell, H.R., 30, 51, 57, 98, 129, 139
Grylls & Hill (Helston) 33, 40
Grylls, H.M., (Henry) xxix, xxxvi, xl, xli, xlvi, li, 3, 7, 12–14, 16–17, 19, 20, 23, 30–1, 34–5, 37–8, 41–3, 50–2, 63, 65, 68, 73, 87, 98, 101–5, 107–11, 123–4, 128, 134, 138
Grylls, Henry Jr, 38
Grylls, Major S.M., xxviii
Grylls, Reverend, xliv
Grylls, William, 14, 35, 37, 46, 69, 90, 98, 116, 131
Gwennap 47, 67, 68, 98, 114
Gwinear 32, 42, 67

Hall, R.T., 90, 98, 116
Harvey, Samuel, 90, 116
Harvey, William, 41, 42
Hawkins, Sir Christopher, xix, 13
Hawksley, Reverend, G.W., 128
Hay, Captain, 30
Hayle 32, 41–2, 96, 98, 114
Hayter, Reginald, xxxiii
Haze, John, 69
Heard and Sons 9, 12, 90, 96, 106, 116, 134
Heard, Edward, 14, 24, 40, 52, 101–5, 107–10, 123–4
Helston xviii, xix, xxiii, xxvii, xli, xliii, xliv, xlv, xlvii, xlix, 9, 24, 29, 33, 35–8, 42–3, 46, 55, 64–6, 98, 101–2, 108, 114, 116, 124, 130
  Wrestling Club 128
Hext, Reverend G., 66
Hichens, Christopher, 90, 116
Hill, Frederick, 33
Hill, P.G., 128
Hodge Hockin & Marrack 89, 98, 114
Hooper, W.F., 24, 124
Howell, Francis, 136
Hullamore, J., 129
Huthnance, Mr, 32

Illogan 42, 47, 67, 68
influence (electoral) xiv, xix, xxi–xxii, xli, 10, 25, 29, 45, 47, 53–4, 57–8
interest (of property owners) xxvi, xxxv, 36, 47, 56, 58
Ireland 84, 85
Isle of Wight 26

James, J.H., 73
Jenkin, Alfred, 30, 58
Jenkin, James, 90, 96, 116
Jenkin, Pearse, 89, 98, 114

Jenkins, David James, 31, 46
Jenkins, G.A., 89, 98, 114
John, F., 128
John, R., 128
Jolliffe, Sir William, xxvi, xxx
Jones, Mr, 103

Kea 67
Kendall, John, 65, 66
Kendall, L.F., 129
Kendall, Nicholas, xxi, xxv, xxvii, xl, xli, 34, 43, 54, 63–4, 80
Kenwyn 32, 67
  Ploughing Match 129
Kernick, W., 96, 134
Kimberley, Earl of, li, 10, 13, 21, 40
King, Edward, 9, 40

Launceston xxii, 98
Loggo, Thomas, 89, 114
Lelant 140
Lemon, Sir Charles, xx, xxiii–xxv, xxvii, xxxiii, xlii
Lemon, Sir William, xx
Leveson-Gower, E.F., 25
Liberal (Whig) xiii, xvi, xvii, xxi–xxviii, xxx–xxxi, xxxiii, xxxv, xxxvi, xxxix, xl, xlii–xliv, xlvi, xlviii, xlix, l–liii, 3, 5–11, 13, 15, 19, 21, 25, 28, 30–1, 34, 39, 42, 54, 48, 50, 52–4, 56, 59, 63–6, 68–9, 73, 83–4, 86, 91, 108, 135–6, 138–9
Lightly, G., 129
Liskeard xix, xxii, 34, 136
London 9, 12, 14, 19, 27–9, 32, 46, 59, 62, 98, 114, 116
Lostwithiel 34
Ludgvan 67, 114
Lyth, Dr, 47

Magniac, Charles, 66
Magor, John, 91, 92
Magor, Martin, 130
Manchester 103
Marazion 6, 30, 67, 116
  Regatta 128
Marrack, Richard, 35–6, 38, 48, 50–1
Marriott, Edmund, 58
Martin, Mr, 73
Mathew, C., 130
Merthyr-Tydvil 126
Metchim, W.P., & Son 89, 98, 114
Methodists (Wesleyans) xliv, xlv, xlvi, xlvii, 16, 29, 46–7, 66, 73, 126, 129
Michell, Edmund, 30, 89, 98, 114
Middleton, Mr, 35, 38
Miners' Association of Cornwall 129
Mitchell xviii, xxiii
Mitchell, R.R., 6, 30
Morcom, Mr, 58
Morvah 72, 116
Mt Edgecumbe, Earl of, 72

Namier, Sir Lewis, xviii
Newcombe, T.W., 128
Newlyn East 42
Newton, Joseph, 89, 96, 114, 124
Newton, Mr, 30
Nicholls, Thomas, 90, 98, 116
Noakes, G., 9, 40
North Devon 42
Northey, William Henry, 64
Northumberland, Duke of, xxii

One & All 96, 134

Pascoe, S., 130
Paul 67
Paul, R.M., 2
Paull, Henry, 45, 51, 59, 60, 139
Paynter, Reginald, 39, 53
Pendarves, Edward, xx, xxiv, xxv, xxxv, 14
Pendarves, Tryphena, 27, 33, 35, 61
Pender, W.R.T., 89, 98, 114
Penrose 36
Penryn 30–2, 41, 58, 67, 96, 98, 114
  & Falmouth xxii, xxiv
Penwith Agricultural Association (Penzance) 129

Penzance 6, 10, 13, 15, 24, 29–30, 37, 41–2, 46, 53, 63, 67, 69, 70–1, 96, 98, 103, 106, 108, 112, 114, 116, 132, 139
Fire Works 128
Regatta and Swimming Club 128
Perran 67
Perranaworthal 80
Perranzabuloe 67, 68
Peter, John Thomas, 13, 30, 34, 37, 41, 52, 66, 93
Peter, William, xx
Peters, J. Penhallow, xxi
Phillips, John, xix
Philp, W., 98, 134
Plomer, John Gilbert, 35, 89, 98, 114
Plymouth 96, 105
Pole Carew, William, xxv, xxvi, xlii
Polkinghorne, Mr, 132
Polytechnic Society (Falmouth) 128
Port Eliot 25
Praed family 58
Praed, H.M., 90, 116
Probus 93
Ploughing Match 129
Pursey, Dr, 66

Rashleigh, John Colman xx
Rashleigh, Jonathan, xlviii
Rashleigh, William, 36, 58
Read, James B., 30
Redruth xxix, xlv, xlix, 6, 7, 9, 14, 17, 24, 30, 35, 37, 40, 46, 47, 53, 54, 59, 67, 68, 96, 98, 104, 108, 111, 114, 116
Cornwall Infirmary 128
register of voters—*see* registration
Registration associations—*see* registration
registration xxvii, xxviii, xxxvi–xxxix, xli, xliii–xlv, xlvii, xlix, li–liii, 24, 32–3, 35–9, 41, 43, 46–9, 51–2, 55, 58, 67, 88–90, 110, 113, 118, 123–6, 131, 138
Reynolds, Mr, 48, 50, 51
Richards, R.C., 96, 134
Richards, Samuel, 89, 96, 114
Richards, W.H., 89, 114
Richmond 71
Robartes, Thomas J.A., xxviii, xxix, xl, li, 4, 5, 6, 8–11, 13, 32, 43, 46–7, 58, 74–81, 86, 126
Roberts, Joseph, 33
Roberts, T.N., 89, 90, 98, 114, 116
Robins Foster (solicitors) 130
Rodd & Cornish (Penzance) 45, 60
Rodd, Mr, 15
Rogers, Henry, xlvii, 89, 98, 101, 110, 114
Rogers, John Jope, xxviii, xlviii, 36, 54, 64
Rogers, Thomas, 35, 102, 124
Roscorla, John, 51, 89, 98, 114, 102, 110, 128, 129
Roskruge, E.P., 130
Rowe, E., 90, 116
Rowe, John, xxxiii, 96
Royal Cornwall Agricultural Association 129
Royal Cornwall Gazette xx, xxvi, 10, 17, 36, 61, 63, 96, 107, 134
Royal Cornwall Infirmary 128
Royal Institution of Cornwall 128

Saltash 86
Sampson, Mrs R.M., 91
Sampson, R.M., 11, 49, 87, 91, 93
Saunders, Mr, 15
Scotland 85
Second Reform Act (1867) xxviii, xxxvi, xxxviii, xxxix, 83, 84
Sennen 67
Shilson, Henry 58, 126–7
Shilson, William, 13, 58
Smith & Roberts (Truro) 33, 40
Smith, Augustus, 11, 29, 48–9, 72
Smith, Dr, 6
Smith, Jervoise, 72
Smith, Major Bickford, 6, 30, 46, 78
Smith, P.P., 10, 29, 59
Snow, James, 96, 134
'South Country' 46–7, 54

South Wales xvi, 45, 78, 81
Spencer, Edward, 70
St Agnes 30–2, 47, 53, 67–8, 96, 114, 124
St Allen 67
St Aubyn, Lady Elizabeth, 76
St Aubyn, Sir Ed, 72
St Aubyn, Sir John, xvii, xxiv, xxvii, xxx, xli, xlvii–xlix, l, lii, liii, 10, 13, 17, 19, 23, 27–8, 36, 38, 44–7, 50–1, 56–7, 59–60, 62–3, 65, 69–72, 75, 78–80, 83, 91, 93–4, 97, 99, 104–5, 108–15, 117–18, 124–7, 132–3, 135
St Austell 58, 87, 92
St Buryan 116
St Clements 67
St Columb 64, 98, 116
St Erth 67
St Gluvias 67
St Hilary 67
St Ives Branch Lifeboat Association 129
St Ives xxii, xxiii, xxvii, xli, xlv, xlix, 15, 30, 31, 40, 44, 51, 57, 59, 60, 66, 96, 98, 116, 139, 141
St Just 29, 30, 52, 67, 96, 114
St Keverne 130
St Levan 116
St Mary's (Truro) 67
St Mawes 35
Stephens, John Augustus 57–9, 61–2, 139
Stephens, Vivian, 139
Stokes, H.S. 16, 24, 29, 41, 81, 90, 98, 116
Stithians 47, 67
Swansea xv, xxix, xxiv, xxxv, 10, 126
Switzerland 55

Tabb, Thomas, 89, 96, 114
Talbot, C.R.M., 1
Taylor, Messrs, 9, 40
Taylor, Richard, 72
Tehidy 29
Thomas, Henry, 89, 98, 114
Thomas, P.W., 9, 40
Tilly, Henry, 91, 118, 128
Tilly, James, 130
Tooke, William, xlv
Topham, C.F., 30
Torquay 139
Totnes 35
Towednack 140
Travers, Edward Charles, 91
Tregaskis, James, 90, 96, 116
Tregaskis, William, 96, 134
Tregony xviii, xix, 67
Trelawny, Sir John, xl, 43, 64, 124, 136
Tremayne, Colonel Arthur, xvii, xxvii, xxviii, xlii, xlvii, 27, 72, 91, 106
Tremayne, John Jr, xvii, xxiv, xxv–xxviii, xlii, 1, 54, 72, 102, 125
Tremayne, John Sen., xx, xxiv, xliii
Trembath, Mr, 30
Tremeneheere, Seymour, 128
Trengrouse, N.T., 90, 116
Tresawna, H., 129
Tresidder, W.T., 90, 98, 116
Trethewy, H., 24, 30, 35, 92
Trethewy, William, 130
Trevena, J.T., 89, 98, 110, 114
Trevenen, William, 89, 98, 114
Triscott, Samuel, xxx, xxxi
Truro xv, xix, xxiii, xxvii, xxx, xxxiii–xxxv, xli, xlii, xlv, xlviii, 3, 9, 11–12, 14, 16, 24, 29, 30, 32–3, 35–6, 38–9, 41, 44, 46, 48–51, 55, 60, 63–4, 73–4, 79–80, 91–3, 103, 105, 108, 111, 114, 116, 135
Truro-Helston (parliamentary division) xlix, 1
Truro Organ Fund 128
Truro Swimming Club 128
Tyacke, Richard, xliv, xlv
Tyringham, Mr, 15, 45, 58

Veryan 67, 94
Vivian & Sons 45
Vivian family xii
(family tree) xv, xvi, xxxiv, xxxv, li

Vivian, Arthur Pendarves, (references to) xiii–xviii, xx, xxii, xxiv, xxviii, xxix, xxxi, xxxiii, xxxv–xxxvi, xxxix, xl, xli, xliii, xlvi–liii, 3, 8, 23, 27, 45, 61, 70, 72, 77, 101, 106–7, 112, 114, 115, 117, 123, 131, 134–5
Vivian, Captain John C.W., xxxiv, xxxv, xxxix, 9, 12, 16, 19, 28, 29, 41, 83
Vivian, Charles C., xxxiv
Vivian, Edward, 15, 24, 44, 139
Vivian, Henry Hussey, xv, xxiv, xxxv, xxxix, xlvii, li, liii, 3, 8, 10, 13, 19, 26–9, 49, 81, 101–2, 123–6
Vivian, John, (Truro) xv, xxxiii, xxxiv
Vivian, John Henry, xv, xxxiv
Vivian, Lady Augusta, xv, 6, 7, 54, 59, 60, 61, 80, 106
Vivian, Lady Jane, xv
Vivian, Richard, xv, 45, 49
Vivian, Richard Hussey, xxxiv
Vivian, William Graham, xv, 3, 45
Volunteers, Cup to, 128
voters xiv, xix, xxvii, xxviii, xxxv–xxxix, xli, xliii, xliv, xlvii, xlix, li, liii, 6, 7, 9, 12, 16, 17, 21, 32, 37–8, 42, 45, 47, 52, 65, 68, 76, 82, 139, 140
Vyvyan, Sir Richard, xx–xxvii, xxx, xl, xliii, xlv, 43, 49, 54, 64

Wales xiii, 47, 64
Warn, William, 89, 96, 114
Webber, T., 129
Wendron 47
Wesley, John and Charles, xliv
Wesleyan Chapel Redruth 128
West Briton xvii, xx, xlii, li, lii, 12, 14, 15, 17, 24, 29, 40, 52, 58, 93, 96, 101–2, 104–5, 108–10, 123–4, 134
West Cornwall (parliamentary division) xiii–xvii, xx–xxiv, xxvi–xxviii, xxx, xxxi, xxxiii, xxxv, xxxvi, xxxvii, xxxix, xl, xli, xlii, xliv, xlvi–li, liii, 4–9, 11, 14–15, 17, 19, 21, 34–5, 37–8, 41–3, 56, 59–60, 62–6, 69, 73, 75–8, 81–2, 86, 88, 95–6, 105–6, 109, 112, 114, 122, 131–2, 134
West Cornwall Mining Convalescent Hospital 129
Western Daily Mercury 17, 58, 87, 96, 105, 134, 139
Western Morning News 15, 17, 24, 66, 70, 96, 106, 134
Westmoreland 71
Williams family xxxii
(family tree) xxix–xxxi, xxxiii, xxxv, xliii
Williams, Catherine Ann, 60
Williams, Charlotte, xxx, xxxi
Williams, Elizabeth Maria, xxviii, xxix, xxx, xxxi, xxxiii, xli, li, lii, liii, 4, 5, 6, 7, 38, 53, 56–7, 59–62, 72, 80–2, 105, 123
Williams, Frederick, xxvii, xxx, xliii
Williams, George, xxx, xxxi, xxxiii, xliii, 59
Williams, Henry, 30, 87, 106
Williams, John, xxix
Williams, John, (Anglesey) xxxiv
Williams, John Michael, xvi, xvii, xxvi, xxviii, xxix, xxx, xxxi, xxxiii, xxxv, xl, xli, xliii, xlvii, xlix, li–liii, 3, 5, 6–9, 11, 13, 19–20, 30, 33–5, 37, 42, 47, 54–6, 59, 61, 64–5, 72, 75, 77–8, 80–1, 92, 103–5, 108, 123, 125
Williams, Michael Henry, xxii, xxiv, xxv, xxvi, xxix, xxx, 53, 55, 58–60, 102, 125
Williams, R., 129
Williams, Sir William, xxvii, xxviii, xxix, xxxi, xxxiii, xliii, 24, 59, 111
Willyams, E.W. Brydges, xl, 3, 4, 8–11, 17, 28, 30, 43, 50, 56–7, 60, 64, 124, 136
Willyams, Humphrey, xl, l, 3, 11
Wright, Mr, 109, 132

Yewens, W., 98
Yorkshire 71

Zennor 67

THE DEVON AND CORNWALL RECORD SOCIETY

(Founded 1904)

The Devon and Cornwall Record Society (founded 1904) promotes the study of history in the South West of England through publishing and transcribing original records. In return for the annual subscription members receive the volumes as published (normally annually) and the use of the Society's library, housed in the Westcountry Studies Library, Exeter. The library includes transcripts of parish registers relating to Devon and Cornwall as well as useful genealogical works.

Applications to join the Society or to purchase volumes should be sent to the Assistant Secretary, Devon and Cornwall Record Society, c/o Devon and Exeter Institution, 7 Cathedral Close, Exeter EX1 1EZ. New series volumes 7, 10, 13, 16, and 18, however, should normally be obtained from the Treasurer of the Canterbury and York Society, St Anthony's Hall, York, YO1 2PW.

PUBLISHED VOLUMES, NEW SERIES

(Volumes starred are no longer available)

*1. *Devon Monastic Lands: Calendar of Particulars for Grants, 1536–1558*, edited by Joyce Youings (1955).

2. *Exeter in the Seventeenth Century: Tax and Rate Assessments, 1602–1699*, edited by W. G. Hoskins (1957, reprinted in 1973).

*3. *The Diocese of Exeter in 1821: Bishop Carey's Replies to Queries before Visitation*, edited by Michael Cook, Volume I, Cornwall (1958).
4. *The Diocese of Exeter in 1821: Bishop Carey's Replies to Queries before Visitation*, edited by Michael Cook, Volume II, Devon (1960).
*5. *Cartulary of St. Michael's Mount, Cornwall*, edited by P. L. Hull (1962).
6. *The Exeter Assembly: The Minutes of the Assemblies of the United Brethren of Devon and Cornwall, 1691–1717, as Transcribed by the Reverend Isaac Gilling*, edited by Allan Brockett (1963).
7. *The Register of Edmund Lacy, Bishop of Exeter, 1420–1455: Registrum Commune*, Volume I, edited by G. R. Dunstan (1963).
*8. *The Cartulary of Canonsleigh Abbey*, calendared and edited by Vera C. M. London (1965).
*9. *Benjamin Donn's Map of Devon, 1765*, with an introduction by W. L. D. Ravenhill (1965).
10. *The Register of Edmund Lacy, Bishop of Exeter, 1420–1455: Registrum Commune*, Volume II, edited by G. R. Dunstan (1966).
*11. *Devon Inventories of the Sixteenth and Seventeenth Centuries*, edited by Margaret Cash (1966).
12. *Plymouth Building Accounts of the Sixteenth and Seventeenth Centuries*, edited by Edwin Welch (1967).
13. *The Register of Edmund Lacy, Bishop of Exeter, 1420–1455: Registrum Commune*, Volume III, edited by G. R. Dunstan (1968).
14. *The Devonshire Lay Subsidy of 1332*, edited by Audrey M. Erskine (1969).
15. *Churchwardens' Accounts of Ashburton, 1479–1580*, edited by Alison Hanham (1970).
16. *The Register of Edmund Lacy, Bishop of Exeter, 1420–1455: Registrum Commune*, Volume IV, edited by G.R. Dunstan (1971).
17. *The Caption of Seisin of the Duchy of Cornwall (1337)*, edited by P. L. Hull (1971).
18. *The Register of Edmund Lacy, Bishop of Exeter, 1420–1455: Registrum Commune*, Volume V, edited by G. R. Dunstan (1972).
19. *Cornish Glebe Terriers, 1673–1735, a calendar*, edited by Richard Potts (1974).
20. *John Lydford's Book*, edited by Dorothy M. Owen (1975).
21. *A Calendar of Early Chancery Proceedings Relating to West Country Shipping, 1388–1493*, edited by Dorothy A. Gardiner (1976).
22. *Tudor Exeter: Tax Assessments 1489–1595, including the Military Survey, 1522*, edited by Margery M. Rowe (1977).
23. *The Devon Cloth Industry in the Eighteenth Century: Sun Fire Office Inventories, 1726–1770*, edited by Stanley D. Chapman (1978).

24. *The Accounts of the Fabric of Exeter Cathedral, 1279–1353. Part I: 1279–1326*, edited by Audrey M. Erskine (1981).
25. *The Parliamentary Survey of the Duchy of Cornwall, Part I: (Austell Prior–Saltash)*, edited by Norman J. G. Pounds (1982).
26. *The Accounts of the Fabric of Exeter Cathedral, 1279–1363, Part II: 1328–53*, edited by Audrey M. Erskine (1983).
27. *The Parliamentary Survey of the Duchy of Cornwall, Part II: (Isles of Scilly–West Antony and Manors in Devon)*, edited by Norman J. G. Pounds (1984).
28. *Crown Pleas of the Devon Eyre of 1238*, edited by Henry Summerson (1985).
29. *Georgian Tiverton: the Political Memoranda of Beavis Wood, 1768–98*, edited by John Bourne (1986).
30. *The Cartulary of Launceston Priory*, edited by P. L. Hull (1987).
31. *Shipbuilding on the Exe: the Memoranda Book of Daniel Bishop Davy (1799–1874)*, edited by Clive N. Ponsford (1988).
32. *The Receivers' Accounts of the City of Exeter, 1304–53*, edited by Margery M. Rowe and John M. Draisey (1989).
33. *Early-Stuart Mariners and Shipping: the Maritime Surveys of Devon and Cornwall 1619–1635*, edited by Todd Gray (1990).
34. *Joel Gascoyne's Map of Cornwall, 1699*, with an introduction by W. L. D. Ravenhill and Oliver Padel (1991).
35. *Nicholas Roscarrock's Lives of the Saints: Cornwall and Devon*, edited by Nicholas Orme (1992).
36. *The Local Customs Accounts of the Port of Exeter, 1266–1321*, edited by Maryanne Kowaleski (1993).
37. *Charters of the Redvers Family and the Earldom of Devon, 1090–1217*, edited by Robert Bearman (1994).
38. *Devon Household Accounts, 1627–1659, Part I*, edited by Todd Gray (1995).
39. *Devon Household Accounts, 1627–1659, Part II*, edited by Todd Gray (1996).
40. *The Uffculme Wills and Inventories, 16th to 18th Centuries*, edited by Peter Wyatt, with an introduction by Robin Stanes (1997).
41. *The Cornish Lands of the Arundells of Lanherne, Fourteenth to Sixteenth Centuries*, edited by H.S.A. Fox and O.J. Padel (2000, for 1998).

FORTHCOMING VOLUMES

43. John Hooker's *Synopsis Chorographicall of the County of Devon* (for 2000).
44. Maryanne Kowaleski, *Havener's Accounts of the Duchy of Cornwall* (for 2001).
45. Richard Carew, *The Survey of Cornwall* (for 2002).

EXTRA SERIES

I. *Exeter Freemen, 1266–1967*, edited by Margery M. Rowe and Andrew M. Jackson (1973).

II. *Guide to the Parish and Non-Parochial Registers of Devon and Cornwall, 1538–1837*, compiled by Hugh Peskett (1979): a new edition, including Somerset, is in preparation.